SISTERS IN ARMS

Monographs in German History

The complexities and peculiarities of German history present challenges on various levels, not least on that of historiography. This series offers a platform for historians who, in response to the challenges, produce important and stimulating contributions to the various debates that take place within the discipline.

For full volume listing, please see pages 165 and 166

SISTERS IN ARMS

Militant Feminisms in the Federal Republic of Germany since 1968

Katharina Karcher

First published in 2017 by
Berghahn Books
www.berghahnbooks.com

© 2017, 2020 Katharina Karcher
First paperback edition published in 2020

All rights reserved. Except for the quotation of short passages for the purposes of criticism and review, no part of this book may be reproduced in any form or by any means, electronic or mechanical, including photocopying, recording, or any information storage and retrieval system now known or to be invented, without written permission of the publisher.

Library of Congress Cataloging-in-Publication Data
A C.I.P. cataloging record is available from the Library of Congress

British Library Cataloguing in Publication Data
A catalogue record for this book is available from the British Library

ISBN 978-1-78533-534-1 hardback
ISBN 978-1-78920-508-4 paperback
ISBN 978-1-78533-535-8 ebook

To Sarah, who made this and so much more possible

Contents

Acknowledgements	viii
Note on Translations	x
List of Figures	xi
List of Abbreviations	xii
Introduction	1
1 The New Women's Movement in West Germany	21
2 Terrorism, Feminism and the Politics of Representation	45
3 Militant Feminist Protest against the Abortion Ban	71
4 Women Fighting Back: Feminist Responses to Violence against Women	90
5 Sisters in Arms? Militant Feminist Protest and Transnational Solidarity	114
Conclusion	136
Bibliography	143
Index	159

ACKNOWLEDGEMENTS

This book is the product of more than seven years of research, and it would not have been possible to complete it without the guidance and support of numerous individuals and institutions. I would like to thank the Modern Humanities Research Association, which supported this book with a postdoctoral research fellowship at the University of Warwick, and the Schröder Fund, whose generous support allowed me to complete the research for this book as a postdoctoral researcher at the University of Cambridge.

I want to thank my interviewees and the many political activists and archivists who helped me collect data for this study. Without their input, patience and active support, it would not have been possible to realize this project. In particular, Adrienne Gerhäuser's passion and ideas were of vital importance to this study. Staff and volunteers at the Federal Archives in Koblenz, the Papiertiger archive, the *konkret* archive, the *Emma* archive, the Hamburg Institute for Social Research, the International Institute of Social, the FFBIZ archive, the Umbruch archive, the Stasi archive and the Frauenmediaturm archive have done more to help me than I could have expected. I am especially grateful to Barbara Klemm, Hermann Bach, Wolfgang Schneider, Reinhart Schwarz, Roman Klarfeld, Dagmar Nöldge and Jasmin Schenk.

I am deeply indebted to my family, colleagues and friends, who were patient and supportive throughout the writing process. I am immensely grateful to my PhD supervisors Christine Achinger and Miranda Alison, colleagues at Warwick and Cambridge, fellow 'violent women' experts Patricia Melzer and Clare Bielby, and my wonderful mentors Rosi Braidotti and Sarah Colvin. I would also like to thank the lovely people at the Coventry Peace House, and Marga, Anna, Rita, Bernd, Guy, Virginia, Cary, James, Emanuela, May, Naomi and Rosana for their support and encouragement. Special thanks are due to Dariush, who has read numerous drafts of this book, and whose critical yet affirmative feedback was pivotal to this project.

Parts of the discussion about the Red Zora and feminist 'counter-violence' were included in the article 'How (not) to "Hollaback": Towards a transnational debate on the "Red Zora" and militant tactics in the feminist struggle against gender-based violence', which was published online in *Feminist Media Studies* in October 2015, and in the article 'From Student Riots to Feminist Firebombs: Debates about "Counter-violence" in the West German Student Movement and Women's Movement' in the *Women in German Yearbook*, volume 32 (2016).

Note on Translations

Unless stated otherwise, all translations from German to English were done by the author. Translations of single words or short phrases include the original text. In the case of longer quotations, the original text can be found in the endnotes.

FIGURES

Figure 1.1	Flyer by a women's group in the SDS, November 1968	24
Figure 3.1	First claim of responsibility by the Red Zora	82
Figure 3.2	Flyer for the first Walpurgisnight protest in Berlin	84
Figure 4.1	Walpurgisnight demonstration in Frankfurt, 1978	97
Figure 4.2	'Kidnapping' of Nicolas Becker by the 'Movement of 12 June'	100
Figure 4.3	*konkret* cover, April 1977	105
Figure 4.4	Brick wall with feminist graffiti. From *konkret*, May 1977, 4	106
Figure 4.5	Die Rote Zora: 'Clandestine Joy'. From *Emma*, no. 3, 1978, 49	108

ABBREVIATIONS

APO	Außerparlamentarische Opposition (Extraparliamentary Opposition)
BAK	Bundesarchiv Koblenz (The Federal Archives, Koblenz)
CDU	Christdemokratische Union Deutschlands (Christian Democratic Union of Germany)
DM	Deutschmark
FFBIZ	Frauenforschungs-, -bildungs- und -informationszentrum e.V. (Women's Research and Education Centre)
FMT	Frauenmediaturm (Women's media tower)
FRG	Federal Republic of Germany
GDR	German Democratic Republic
HIS	Hamburger Institut für Sozialgeschichte (Hamburg Institute for Social Research)
IISH	International Institute of Social History
MJ2	Movement of June 2nd (Bewegung 2. Juni)
NGO	Non-governmental organization
OPEC	Organization of the Petroleum Exporting Countries
PFLP	Popular Front for the Liberation of Palestine
RAF	Red Army Faction (Rote Armee Fraktion)
RC	Revolutionary Cells (Revolutionäre Zellen)
RK	Revolutionärer Kampf (Revolutionary Struggle)
RZ	Red Zora (Rote Zora)
SDS	Sozialistischer Studentenbund (Socialist German Student League)
SM	Sadomasochism
SPD	Sozialdemokratische Partei Deutschlands (Social Democratic Party of Germany)
taz	Die tageszeitung
TdF	Terre des Femmes
TW	Tupamaros Westberlin
WoRC	Women of the Revolutionary Cell
WWII	The Second World War

Introduction

The feminist movement in the Federal Republic of Germany (FRG) is well known for its provocative and media-effective protest campaigns. In her seminal study *Women in German History*, Ute Frevert highlights how West German feminists 'disrupted beauty contests, bricked up sex-shops, sat in at churches and doctors' conventions' and organized tribunals on abortion, violence against women and other central themes in the women's movement.[1] While it is widely acknowledged that feminist groups in West Germany have engaged in creative and provocative protest activities, there is little awareness of the fact that some groups have used confrontational or violent methods to advance the cause of women. This book is the first to investigate the fascinating and controversial role of such tactics in feminist campaigns in the decades following the Second World War (WWII). The aim is not to assess whether feminist activism in the 1960s and 1970s was more or less militant than today. Rather it seeks to show that there was a complex interplay between old and new, conventional and innovative, constitutional and unlawful, and peaceful and violent protest tactics, which led to different results in different feminist campaigns.

The women's movement that started to emerge in West Germany in the late 1960s became one of the broadest, most diverse and dynamic social movements in the history of the FRG. Gisela Notz identifies three different strands of feminism that shaped the development of the women's movement in the 1970s. The first is the 'liberal and "moderate" feminists' who demanded that women should be granted the same rights and entitlements as men.[2] Second is the 'radical autonomous feminists who considered patriarchal oppression to be

---

Notes for this section begin on page 16.

the fundamental structural category of modern societies, and whose prime aim was therefore the abolition of patriarchy'.[3] The third strand is the 'socialist or leftist feminists' who sought to achieve 'a fundamental transformation of capitalist and patriarchal structures'.[4] In the most detailed and comprehensive study of feminist activism in the FRG to date, Ilse Lenz shows that there were a number of other strands that were less visible but equally important, including the lesbian movement, mothers' organizations, Afro-German feminism and the struggles of migrant women.[5]

Second-wave feminism in the United States played an important role in the formation of the women's movement in West Germany.[6] The language of German feminists, however, was different from that of their American contemporaries. The differentiation between a biologically determined *sex* and a socially constructed *gender* was developed in the 1950s in the United States in the context of medical research. In the following decades it has been adopted by Anglo-American feminists and scholars from various other fields. In Germany, the term did not gain popularity until the 1990s, when a new generation of feminist activists and academics discovered the work of Judith Butler, Joan Scott and other poststructuralist feminist thinkers. Following Scott and other gender historians, I consider gender a useful category of historical analysis, although the term was not used by feminist activists in West Germany. Of course, gender is just one of a number of factors that have to be considered. In her study of German gender politics, Myra Marx Ferree has rightly pointed out that gender intersects with a range of other social factors, including ethnicity, nationality, age, sexuality and class in particular local manifestations.[7]

The women's movement in the FRG developed structures and a political agenda that differed considerably from those of feminist movements in the late nineteenth and early twentieth centuries.[8] 'In contrast to the historical women's movement', highlights Ute Gerhard, 'the new one founded no associations or organizations, and had no leaders, but was rather composed of a loose network of groups and broader networks, projects and organized meetings which informed the public about specific issues.'[9] To underline the variety of topics, political views and forms of organization in feminist circles, some feminist scholars do not refer to *the* German women's movement but to women's movements in the plural.[10] Although I agree that it is important to highlight the diversity of feminist theory and activism, previous research on other political movements in the FRG and in other countries shows that one does not have to use the plural form to highlight the heterogeneous and diverse nature of these movements.

There are different terms to describe the women's movement in the FRG. Some authors refer to it as the 'autonomous women's movement' (*autonome Frauenbewegung*), because many of the women involved sought to achieve 'self-determination for the individual as well as institutional freedom from established forms of politics'.[11] However, this name can be misleading, because not all feminists in the FRG aspired to be autonomous, and because '*Autonomie*' became the primary aim and distinguishing feature of a different political movement.

In line with other scholars therefore, I refer to the feminist movement in the FRG in this study as the 'New Women's Movement' (*neue Frauenbewegung*). On the one hand, this name emphasizes that the movement developed a new political agenda and new organizational structures. On the other, it highlights that this movement was inspired by the theoretical framework, political spirit and protest activities of the New Left. Many founding members of the New Women's Movement had played an active role in student protests, and they identified with the aims and principles of the New Left: they were fundamentally opposed to the existing political structures and aimed to create a society based on anti-authoritarian, anti-fascist, anti-imperialist and anti-capitalist principles. Since the New Left provided important theoretical and political reference points for militant feminists in the FRG, I want to discuss it here in some more detail.

The New Left in West Germany

The 1960s, in a range of Western countries including the FRG, saw a number of groups emerge 'at the Left of the Old Left' and go on to make up what became known as the 'New Left'.[12] While there were significant political and ideological differences among them, all shared, as Donatella Della Porta notes, 'a concern for a [more] participatory democracy'.[13] 'In its rejection of orthodox Marxism and anti-Communism and its dissatisfaction with the Cold War, materialism, and apathy in society', the New Left in West Germany, write Martin Klimke and Joachim Scharloth, 'found a connecting point to similar movements in France, Great Britain, the United States and elsewhere.'[14] However, due to Germany's fascist history and its geopolitical position in the Cold War, the social context in which the New Left developed in the FRG had a distinctive character. In the 1950s, not only the majority of military officers and judges but also many politicians and other public figures had actively supported or sympathized with the Nazi regime.[15] The student and protest movement in West Germany was, among other things, a rebellion by a postwar generation that refused the authority of this ruling elite. Karin de Ahna and Dieter Claessens highlight that due to the long-lasting ideological and social effects of its National Socialist past, the Federal Republic of Germany 'has never had a traditional relationship to social phenomena such as anarchism, deviance and so on. . . . The willingness to see the dissenter as an enemy of the state or of the people remained, at least until the late 1950s, unchanged.'[16]

The republic's first government under Chancellor Konrad Adenauer adopted politically and economically a pro-Western and anti-communist course.[17] All forms of political opposition and extra-parliamentary campaigns in this period were 'from the outset seriously handicapped by the relative ease with which Adenauer was able to tar them with the brush of communism'.[18] Soon, communists and socialists 'found themselves outside the spectrum of legitimate politics'.[19] In 1956, the communist party was banned in West Germany. With the Godesberg programme of 1959, the Social Democratic Party (SPD) distanced itself once and for all from its socialist heritage.[20] In 1966, the SPD formed a grand coalition with the conservative Christian Democratic Union (CDU).[21] Since it had the necessary majority in parliament, the grand coalition could pass fundamental reforms such as the 1968 emergency laws[22] without noticeable resistance.[23] Facing a lack of active political participation, a number of leftist groups in West Germany united to form a protest movement that became known as the extra-parliamentary opposition (Außerparlamentarische Opposition, or APO).[24] Left-wing student activists and other members of the political opposition used the APO as a platform for debate and protest outside of party politics.

The student movement in West Germany had originated in the mid-1960s in Berlin and spread quickly throughout the country.[25] The Socialist German Student League (SDS)[26] played a central role in the theory, development and coordination of the emerging student movement.[27] As 'the main representative of the New Left, it built on the organizational and personal networks of the Easter March campaign, a movement for peace and nuclear disarmament supported by the German trade unions, which had gathered momentum at the beginning of the 1960s'.[28] In the course of the 1960s, the number of female students at West German universities grew significantly. In 1965, they still accounted for only 28 per cent of the student population, but in 1970 they made up 37.9 per cent.[29] Women played an active role in the student movement, although only a few publications focus on their contributions.[30]

Central themes in the student movement of the 1960s included university reforms, German rearmament plans, the Vietnam War, fascism, imperialism and internationalism. The 'reconstruction of the repressed traditions of Marxism and psychoanalysis through the theoreticians of the Frankfurt school' constituted the theoretical point of departure for many students.[31] In the late 1960s, Rudi Dutschke and other leading thinkers of the movement promoted a globalization of revolutionary forces based on the 'foco theories' of Che Guevara, Fidel Castro and Régis Debray and on Frantz Fanon's liberation concepts.[32] 'At the 1967 national convention, Rudi Dutschke and Hans-Jürgen Krahl, the leading theoretician of the Frankfurt SDS, jointly demanded that West German students should move toward a "propaganda of action" in the metropolis, complementing the "propaganda of bullets" in the Third World.'[33]

Activists from the so-called Third World played an active role in student protests in West Germany, and they had a marked influence on discussions about protest tactics in the student movement.[34] By 1962, the number of foreign students in the FRG had risen to about 12,000.[35] Some of the first events that illustrated their important role in student protests were the demonstrations against the visit of the Congolese politician Moïse Tshombe in December 1964. The Tshombe protest was organized by the African Student League, members of the SDS and other student organizations, and by Rudi Dutschke and other members of the small radical leftist group Subversive Aktion. According to Timothy Scott Brown, 150 of the 800 participants in an anti-Tshombe demonstration in West Berlin on 18 December 1964 were foreign students. Brown highlights that the protest was a key experience for Dutschke and other anti-authoritarian student activists, because the African students 'helped turn what had originally been planned as "a silent demonstration" . . . into an assault on public order involving catcalls, thrown tomatoes, and scuffles with the police'.[36]

Inspired by demonstrations in the United States, political struggles in the Third World and by the collaborations with foreign students in the FRG, activists in the West German student movement drew on innovative and creative forms of protest such as sit-ins, teach-ins and civil disobedience. According to Della Porta, the dominant position in the SDS in the 1960s involved 'the limited violation of rules (*begrenzte Regelverletzung*), that is, a conscious, nonviolent use of lawbreaking as a disruptive form of action'.[37] But what does 'nonviolent' mean in this context? The German term *Gewalt* is characterized by an ambiguity that was of critical importance to discussions about the scope and limits of political protest in the FRG. Going back to the Indo-Germanic word *giwaltan*, *Gewalt* can imply both violence (*violentia*) and power (*potestas*). It can be used to refer to empowering and limiting, positive and negative, abstract and concrete social interactions and structures.[38] In the late 1960s, many student activists distinguished between two different forms of violent actions: damage to or destruction of property and violence against people.[39] While they were opposed to behaviour that could harm or kill people, an increasing number of those in the radical Left considered property destruction a tolerable or even necessary form of political activism.

Two events in the late 1960s fuelled discussions about violence and violent resistance in the student movement. The first was the killing of a student, Benno Ohnesorg, by a police officer during a demonstration on 2 June 1967.[40] 'A photograph of the dying Ohnesorg lying on the street, with his head bleeding and a helpless woman in an elegant fur coat leaning over him', highlights Martin Klimke, 'was to become one of the most iconic images of the German student movement and the 1960s in West Germany.'[41] Many felt that the bullets that killed Ohnesorg were directed against the entire student and protest movement. Some were convinced that only violence could prevent further attacks. The fact that the founding members of one of the armed leftist groups in the FRG decided to call themselves the 'Movement of June 2nd' indicates the importance that they attributed to the Ohnesorg killing. Initially charged with manslaughter, the officer that shot Ohnesorg was acquitted of all charges a few months later.[42] For the first time, West German student activists 'saw themselves in a position of vulnerability comparable with their Third World colleagues'.[43] The fact that a member of the police force could get away with killing a peaceful demonstrator shocked and enraged them. Their anger was also directed at the tabloid *Bild* and other newspapers that blamed the protesters for Ohnesorg's death and other acts of violence during the demonstration.

In light of the Ohnesorg killing and other attacks against protesters, many student activists began to discuss the limits of nonviolent protest. A few weeks after the attack against Ohnesorg, the newsmagazine *Der Spiegel* published an interview with student leader Dutschke, in which he declared: 'Violence is a key constituent of power and thus requires demonstrative and provocative counter-violence on our part. What form it [the counter-violence] takes, depends on the form of the confrontation.'[44] The issue of counter-violence (*Gegengewalt*) had been discussed in the West German student movement at least since the publication of Herbert Marcuse's essay 'Repressive Toleranz' (Repressive Tolerance) in 1965. Like Marcuse, Rudi Dutschke and other leading thinkers in the movement considered the use of violence legitimate, if it was a response to a greater form of violence, if it was limited to situations in which other means of protest were futile and if it took the form of a symbolic provocation rather than being an end in itself.

A second dramatic and agitational event followed just months after the Ohnesorg killing: the attempted assassination of Rudi Dutschke on 11 April 1968.[45] On the night after the attack, a mixed crowd of students and groups associated with the Berlin Underground scene[46] tried to stop the delivery of *Bild* and other newspapers published by the Axel Springer group, which had crudely misrepresented the Ohnesorg killing and repeatedly stirred resentment towards Dutschke, the student movement and the New Left. In November 1968, leftist lawyer and political activists Horst Mahler stood trial for playing a leading role in this protest. Outside the court, a group of about one thousand protesters clashed with police forces. In what became known as 'the Battle of Tegeler Weg' (*Schlacht am Tegeler Weg*), the conflict between members of youth subcultures in Berlin and the police reached a new intensity: dozens of protesters and hundreds of police officers were injured, some of them seriously.[47]

While the student movement in West Germany experienced an increasing fragmentation and polarization in the late 1960s, a new feminist movement gathered momentum. There is no official founding moment for the New Women's Movement, but one incident during the twenty-third conference of the SDS in Frankfurt on 12 September 1968 played a significant role in its formation.[48] On that day, the feminist filmmaker Helke Sander, spokeswoman of the Action Council for the Liberation of Women (*Aktionsrat zur Befreiung der Frauen*) gave a speech in which she criticized patriarchal structures in the SDS and called for a joint effort to tackle the oppression of women.[49] When it appeared that the SDS board members wanted to move on to other issues without commenting on Sander's speech, SDS member Sigrid Rüger threw tomatoes at them. Although their position was not without controversy, Sander's speech and Rüger's protest mobilized many women in the New Left. Although it is widely acknowledged that the tomato throwing marked the beginning of a wave of provocative, and at times very confrontational, feminist protest in West Germany, this is the first study to explore and analyse the critical role of militancy in this protest.

Why Militancy Matters

One of the reasons why militancy is rarely used as an analytical category in research on feminism in the FRG is that the term is strongly associated with violent protest tactics in the radical Left, and in the Autonomen movement in particular. Since debates about militancy in the Autonomen movement offer critical insights into political militancy and feminist politics in the FRG, they provide a good starting point for a conceptualization of feminist militancy.

In the 1980s, autonomist groups became a driving force in the increasingly violent conflict between police forces and squatters in West Berlin and other West German cities, and participated in a range of other movements including the anti-nuclear movement, the peace movement, the environmental movement and the New Women's Movement. Like many leftist and feminist groups in the FRG, the Autonomen movement sought and seeks 'to create and institutionalize "dominance-free" forms of political, economic, and social interaction'.[50] What distinguishes Autonomists from most groups in the New Women's Movement is that militancy formed an integral part of their self-image and public perception. Loosely inspired by neo-Marxist and neo-anarchist beliefs, the movement brought together a range of radical leftist groups who rejected what the sociologist Max Weber famously described as the state's 'monopoly of legitimate physical violence'.[51]

Militancy is central to the self-conception and public image of the Autonomen and features prominently in internal movement documents. While there was a clear tendency in parts of the Autonomen movement to romanticize and glorify militancy, controversial debates in internal movement publications show that there was no consensus about the scope and limits of militant protest.[52] Although the 'legitimacy of militant conflict – as counterviolence that also offered protection from police violence – was not questioned', opinions differed when it came to the question of where it was necessary and appropriate.[53] According to historian Freia Anders, it is precisely the vagueness of the term 'militancy' that made it so appealing to the Autonomen. Activists in the movement refused to distinguish between legal and illegal and peaceful and violent protest because they held the view that these categories were defined by the state and served the interests of the state.[54] It would be wrong to reduce the meaning of militancy in the Autonomen movement to confrontational or violent forms of protest, although both played an important role in the theory and practice of the movement. In this context, militancy also 'signifies a refusal to be co-opted or to let one's decisions and behavior be dictated by the laws and norms of the dominant society'.[55]

In the 1980s, militancy in the Autonomen movement came under scrutiny from a gender perspective. A growing number of autonomous women's groups and 'pro-feminist' men's groups denounced sexual violence within the movement, and criticized dominating behaviour in group discussions and macho militancy.[56] Despite all criticism within and outside the movement, the Autonomen have remained committed to militancy. Patricia Melzer has offered one of the first scholarly discussions of militant feminism in the Autonomen movement. Based on an analysis of the writings of the Hamburg-based group Women against Imperialist War (*Frauen gegen Imperialistischen Krieg*), Melzer's insightful study shows that feminists in the Autonomen movement had an important role to play in Germany's Left: they established theoretical and political links between the militant Left and the New Women's Movement.[57]

In this context, the theory and practice of the militant feminist group Rote Zora (RZ) deserve particular attention. Although the RZ, whose ideology and activities will be discussed in more detail in the following chapter, formed in a different political context, the group developed a notion of feminist militancy that resonated strongly with women in the Autonomen movement. The brochure 'Mili's Tanz auf dem Eis' from December 1993 offers the most detailed discussion of militancy in the history of the Red Zora. Literally, the title of the book can be translated as 'Mili's dance on the ice'. This translation, however, does not retain the play on words in the German original: 'Mili's Tanz' resembles 'Militanz', meaning militancy. As the title suggests, the RZ saw militancy as a political balancing act. While criticizing a tendency in the radical Left to glorify and practise 'macho militancy', the authors took the stance that tactics that the state defined as illegal and violent could play a vital role in political protest. The RZ insisted that it 'did not see a hierarchy in different forms of actions. Handing out flyers, squatting, spraying graffiti, gluing locks, throwing stones, planting bombs and setting fire – all was right, if it was coordinated well.'[58] While highlighting the need for a diversity of tactics, the Red Zora clearly placed particular emphasis on militant and violent tactics.

In their first position paper, the Red Zora insisted that it could be liberating and empowering for women to use violent means to fight against male perpetrators of violence and authorities who abused their power. The group stated: 'Personally, we found it tremendously liberating to break with the feminine peaceableness that was imposed on us and to take a conscious decision for violent means in our politics. We experienced that with our actions, we could break through fear, powerlessness and resignation, and we wanted to pass this on to other women/lesbians.'[59] By trying to develop a theory and practice of feminist 'counter-violence',[60] the Red Zora and other militant feminist groups in West Germany challenged the idea that feminism is inherently and necessarily peaceful and tried to convince other women of the worth of militant tactics. These efforts had remarkably little success: with the exception of feminist groups in the Autonomen movement and in the radical fringes of the New Women's Movement, most feminists in West Germany did not want to be associated with militant tactics.[61] Since many feminist historians in the FRG share this view, they have shown little interest in militant and violent protest with a feminist agenda.

Other historical examples show that one does not have to agree with the political views or tactics of militant feminist groups to see their activities as a part of the long and varied history of feminist movements. Undoubtedly, one of the best-researched episodes of militancy in the history of European women's movements is militant protest in the British movement for female suffrage at the turn of the twentieth century, and the activities of the Women's Social and Political Union (WSPU) in particular.[62] Laura Mayhall notes: 'The WSPU introduced the use of militancy, first interrupting Liberal Party meetings and heckling political speakers, then moving to the use of street theatre, such as large-scale demonstrations, and ultimately the destruction of government and private property, including smashing windows, slashing paintings in public galleries and setting fire to buildings and pillar-boxes.'[63] While some of these activities involved spectacular performances and attacks against property, Mayhall rightly insists that it would be wrong to reduce suffragette militancy to such highly visible acts. According to her, suffragettes practised militancy along a continuum that needs to be understood within the broader context of 'radicalism and women's political activism in the late-Victorian and Edwardian eras'.[64]

The context of women's political activism in Germany was very different from that in Britain. Since the 1840s, German women had fought – primarily but not exclusively with nonviolent means – against patriarchal structures and discriminatory laws. Feminist historians trace the German Women's Movement back to the period of the 'pre-March' (*Vormärz*) that led to the March revolution in 1848. During the revolution, thousands of women organized in democratic groups to support fighters and their families.[65] A few women, however, 'did not want to leave it at listening, supporting and petitioning. They helped to build barricades and fought alongside the democratic insurgents against the military.'[66] Between the 1840s and the 1940s, the different living conditions of proletarian and bourgeois women, fundamental political changes, and not least the two world wars had a crucial impact on the feminist movement in Germany. 'Recognizing the interconnections between militarized masculinity and violence', women anti-militarists in the Weimar Republic and in post-WWII Germany called for a new spirit of peacefulness.[67]

The development of the German Women's Movement was, as Ute Gerhard highlights, no 'continuous process', but 'a history of repeated setbacks, stagnation and of many new beginnings under constantly changing social and political circumstances'.[68] The term 'New Women's Movement' indicates that the feminist groups and networks that emerged in the late 1960s in the context of the anti-authoritarian student movement marked such a new beginning. Radicalized by the attacks against Ohnesorg and Dutschke, repeated clashes with police and polemical attacks against the New Left in the media, a few former student activists took up arms. As the discussion in chapter 2 shows, the violent confrontation between these left-wing militants and the West German state, which peaked in the 'German Autumn'[69] in 1977 but continued into the 1990s, has strengthened pacifism and anti-militarism in the German women's movement.

Until today, all but a few feminist activists and scholars in the FRG have taken the view that militant tactics are irreconcilable with feminist principles. Against this background, it is hardly surprising that the activities of the Red Zora and other militant feminist groups have received little attention in the history of the German women's movement. If they mention the Red Zora at all, feminist historians tend to reinforce the assumption that its attacks were not feminist, even if the actors involved protested otherwise. Vojin Saša Vukadinović, for instance, argues that the 'feminist-inspired militancy' (*frauenbewegte Militanz*) of the Red Zora should not be mistaken for feminism.[70] The aim of this book is not to challenge this widely shared view. What I do want to challenge, however, is the fact that alternative perspectives have been marginalized and silenced. Consciously or unconsciously, historians of German feminism have created a narrative about 'good' feminism and 'bad' militancy, which is based on a limited understanding of both terms.

According to the Oxford Dictionary, the adjective 'militant' means 'favouring confrontational or violent methods in support of a political or social cause', and the German dictionary Duden offers a very similar definition.[71] Derived from the Latin word '*miles*', for soldier, the adjective has been used in a range of political contexts including but not limited to violent conflicts. Charity Scribner highlights that the term has a long tradition in theology, where *ecclesia militans* (militant church) refers to the struggle of devout Christians against earthly sins.[72] In the late nineteenth century, the German adjective '*militant*' was primarily used to refer to the valiant and fearless defence of a political view.[73] Unlike in France and in Italy, where the term is now often used synonymously with the term 'political activist', militancy is now strongly associated with confrontational and violent tactics in Germany.

According to Heidrun Kämper and Elisabeth Link, the meaning of the term changed in the mid-twentieth century, when militancy became increasingly associated with aggression, physical violence and armed conflict.[74] In the 1950s, legal authorities in the newly formed Federal Republic banned communist parties and other political groups that they considered to be a militant threat to German democracy. By taking a tough stance on left-wing political extremists, the West German state tried to establish itself as a 'militant democracy' (*wehrhafte Demokratie*). Karrin Hanshew's insightful study of terrorism and democracy in the FRG shows how 'almost overnight, democracy's defense went from a point of academic debate to a cornerstone of West Germany's liberal order, evident in the constitutional designation of the state as a *wehrhafte Demokratie* – literally, a democracy well-fortified to defend itself'.[75] Against this background, it is interesting to note that militancy featured prominently in the writings of leftist groups who promoted a confrontational, and at least in some cases violent, approach to social change in the FRG.

Despite the negative connotations of the term, members of the Red Zora and women's groups in the Autonomen movement were not the only political activists in West Germany who tried to adopt and redefine militancy in the context of feminist activism. Feminist campaigner and journalist Alice Schwarzer, for instance, argues that militancy, in the form of 'hatred' against male oppressors, was a driving force in the formation of the New Women's Movement, and provided a much needed break with the political opportunism and passivity that have shaped German history: 'But what would a liberation movement be without hatred? Without the question: Are we really going far enough? Are we really not cowards? Are we really not deceiving ourselves? Can we show solidarity also with those who are not, or no longer, acting with 'prudence' when trying to tackle this blatant injustice? Courage to militancy was never a German strength. Nevertheless, it took hold of women in this period [i.e. the post-1968 years].'[76] Schwarzer is one of the best-known and most-criticized feminists in the FRG. While acknowledging that she has played an important role in the New Women's Movement, the historian Miriam Gebhardt and other feminist critics claim that Schwarzer simplifies and misrepresents the history of feminist struggles in West Germany to present herself in a good light.[77] Regardless of what one may think of Schwarzer, it is worth noting that she is one of the few feminist authors to draw attention to militant and violent feminist protest.

Drawing on a range of archival sources, autobiographical accounts, interview data and previous studies of feminist protest in the FRG, this book offers the first comprehensive study of militant feminisms in West Germany. Following the feminist theorist bell hooks, I understand feminism as a joint 'struggle to end sexist oppression' – a definition that emphasizes the diversity of feminist theory and practice, and which allows me to explore and analyse a range of protest forms within and outside the New Women's Movement.[78] Feminist militancy, as understood in this context, refers to historically and politically specific sets of ideas and practices that aim to overcome sexist oppression and are based on the assumption that this objective can only be reached with a confrontational attitude. This broad definition allows me to analyse the complex interplay of different protest tactics in feminist campaigns without reinforcing ahistorical notions of feminism and nonviolence.

Rather than assuming that there is a clear-cut difference between violent and peaceful or militant and nonmilitant feminist activism, I argue, following Laura Mayhall, that feminist activists in post-WWII Germany practised militancy along a constantly evolving continuum of feminist militancy. On one side of the spectrum there were constitutional forms of protest involving little or no confrontation, e.g. petitions. At the other extreme, there were highly visible attacks against property, e.g. bombings and arson attacks with a feminist agenda. In between, there was a whole range of colourful, creative and provocative protest, which involved varying degrees of confrontation. Whether feminist protest actions were perceived as confrontational and/or violent was not determined by the protesters alone. Patricia Melzer rightly emphasizes that property destruction and other less peaceful forms of protest in post-WWII Germany were quickly associated with terrorism and even explicitly peaceful forms of protest in West Germany were often 'perceived as violent by mainstream society'.[79]

The peaceful/violent dichotomy that underlies much feminist activism and research is fraught with problems. A first problem is that a binary distinction makes it difficult if not impossible to account for important nuances, developments and contradictions within feminist protest movements. Another problem is that the categories 'violent' and 'peaceful' are ideologically charged. One of the first major campaigns in the New Women's Movement was the struggle against violence against women. Melzer has shown that in the context of this campaign, women were often categorically positioned as victims of violence, while violence was seen as inherently masculine or male. At times, this approach to violence was very popular in the New Women's Movement.[80] Yet it is problematic, because it ignores the many open and hidden ways in which feminists who endorse nonviolent tactics can benefit from violent structures (e.g. because they belong to a privileged class or ethnic group). Another problem with this approach to violence is that it suggests that nonviolence is the only legitimate and effective form of feminist protest, which categorically excludes the possibility that women can draw on confrontational or violent tactics to fight against sexist oppression.

The legendary tomato throwing at the twenty-third SDS conference in Frankfurt in 1968 and other spectacular protest actions discussed in this book illustrate that the use of confrontational and violent tactics in the struggle against sexist oppression in the FRG was sometimes extremely effective. However, this study also shows that a high degree of confrontation is by no means a recipe for success. Some of the most confrontational feminist protest actions in the FRG had little, if any, impact. Others, by contrast, seem to have contributed to the success of protest campaigns but were met with harsh criticism by feminist activists (e.g. because of a lack of communication with fellow activists). When analysing feminist protest in Germany and other parts of the world, we must therefore ask not just one but several questions: How confrontational was the approach taken by the actors involved? What effects, if any, did their actions have? Were the actions considered violent? And, finally, how did feminist activists respond to them? The picture that emerges from an analysis based on these questions is fascinating, complex and at times contradictory.

About the Book

One of my key assumptions is that expressions of feminist militancy and feminist debates about the use of militant and violent tactics have to be analysed both in the context of concrete feminist struggles and in the light of broader political developments; the structure of this book reflects this approach. The first two chapters introduce two political movements that were critical for the formation of militant feminisms in the FRG: the New Women's Movement and left-wing terrorism in West Germany (as mentioned above, armed leftist groups in the FRG did not identify with the label of 'terrorism' and saw themselves as part of the 'militant Left', or used other terminology). Chapter 1 gives a brief overview of the formation and development of the New Women's Movement with particular focus on themes, campaigns and networks that have been important for the development of militant feminisms in West Germany. It shows that militancy played an important role in the New Women's Movement and manifested itself in a range of ways, including provocative protest activities, civil disobedience and, at least occasionally, arson attacks and bombings.

On 14 May 1970, a group of women and one man liberated the prisoner Andreas Baader at gunpoint from the German Central Institute for Social Issues in Berlin. One of them was the leftist journalist Ulrike Meinhof. Less than two years after writing an article in which she stressed the importance of the tomato throwing and the politics of everyday life, Meinhof and other founding members of the Red Army Faction (RAF) turned to violence to overthrow the West German state. In January 1972, a group of militants in Berlin followed their example and founded the Movement of June 2nd (MJ2). Like the RAF, the MJ2 considered violent attacks against state authorities and institutions not only legitimate but imperative to overcome a political order that they understood as a form of illegitimate violence. Women constituted a significant part of the membership of both groups, and their involvement in leftist political violence was repeatedly presented as an 'excess of women's liberation'. Chapter 2 shows that although a heated public debate on feminism and political violence took place in the 1970s, little attention was paid to actual militant feminist activities. In contrast to most women in the RAF and MJ2, the Red Zora and a part of the militant leftist network Revolutionary Cells (RC) showed an active interest in themes and debates in the New Women's Movement. Trying to combine the politics of the militant Left and the New Women's Movement, the Red Zora developed a distinctively feminist notion of counter-violence.

Chapters 3 to 5 analyse the activities of the Red Zora and other militant protest in the context of three major feminist campaigns: the movement for a decriminalization of abortion, the struggle to end violence against women and a transnational feminist solidarity campaign. This selection does not aim to give a complete picture of militant feminisms in West Germany, and could not possibly do so. Rather, the campaigns discussed have been chosen for two reasons. First, they were initiated and/or decisively shaped by feminist groups, and involved a range of feminist practices including actions that were seen as militant and violent. Second, although previous research has contributed greatly to a better understanding of social and political dynamics in these campaigns, it has paid little attention to the role of militancy. The existing body of literature on the Autonomen movement, the squatting scene, the anti-nuclear movement and other political campaigns and subcultures in the FRG, by contrast, has critically examined the role of militant ideas and practices in these movements, and some studies discuss militant groups with feminist aims and principles.[81]

The feminist struggle for free and safe abortions, which is discussed in chapter 3, played an important role in the formation of the New Women's Movement. Following the example of a range of other countries, the West German government passed legislation that exempted abortions within the first three months of pregnancies from punishment in 1974, but the Federal Court of Justice overruled this decision a few months later. While church representatives, conservative politicians and the German Medical Association welcomed the judgement, it was met with disappointment and anger among the many groups who had campaigned for a reform of the existing abortion legislation. Focusing on the years from 1970 to 1977, this chapter gives an overview of a particularly eventful period in the feminist mobilization against the abortion ban. Although the overwhelming majority of feminist activists were committed to nonviolent tactics, some protest activities were seen as violent, and a few caused substantial property damage. In March 1975, a group of women in the militant leftist network 'Revolutionary Cells' planted a bomb at the Federal Court of Justice to protest the court's decision on the abortion ban. A second bombing with a feminist agenda followed in April 1977, when members of the Red Zora carried out an attack on the headquarters of the German Medical Association in Cologne.

Violence against women was a second central topic in feminist activism in West Germany in the 1970s. Although many girls and women in the Federal Republic of Germany experienced sexual abuse and domestic violence on a daily basis, there was little awareness of this problem. In fact, some forms of violence against women were legitimized by tradition or law (e.g. spousal rape). In a joint effort with women from other parts of the world, feminists in West Germany tried to create awareness of and mobilize against gender-based violence. As highlighted earlier, the term 'gender' was not used in the New Women's Movement. What is now commonly known as gender-based violence was referred to as 'violence against women' (*Gewalt gegen Frauen*). A key difference between the two terms is that the former explicitly acknowledges that people of different genders and sexual orientations face discrimination and violence, while the latter focuses primarily or exclusively on people of the female sex. The focus on biologically defined women was both a mobilizing force and a weak spot of the New Women's Movement.

The question of how broadly violence against women had to be defined to tackle visible and invisible forms of abuse was the subject of vivid debate among feminists in the FRG. Even more controversial was the question of what forms of action were necessary and legitimate in the fight against gender-based violence. Focusing on feminist responses to rape and sexual objectification, this chapter analyses and compares different definitions of gender-based violence and gives an overview of feminist initiatives to tackle this issue, ranging from women's shelters to self-defence courses, street protests and attacks against sex shops. Although violent protest played a marginal role in the feminist movement against gender-based violence, it met with more sympathy than in the campaign against the abortion ban.

Global inequalities and transnational solidarity were central topics for the radical Left and the New Women's Movement and played a prominent role in feminist activism in the 1980s. Focusing on a transnational solidarity campaign for women workers in South Korea from 1986 until 1987, this chapter explores the complex interplay of violent and nonviolent tactics, local and global struggles and different notions of feminist solidarity. In May 1986, the Korean Women's Group in West Berlin received a call for 'sisterly help' from women workers in South Korea. It included a report in which trade unionists described the poor working conditions in a garment factory in a Free Trade Zone in South Korea. The factory produced clothes that the German company Adler sold at cheap prices to customers in West Germany and other European countries. The plea for help from South Korea sparked a thriving solidarity campaign in West Germany that involved groups across the political spectrum. For the most part, protests against Adler in West Germany proceeded peacefully. However, there were some exceptions. In 1987, radical women's groups carried out a series of arson attacks against Adler stores in Germany to support the Korean workers in their struggle. Chapter 5 shows that that there is no universal answer to the question of which forms of protest are considered legitimate and effective from a feminist perspective – feminist responses to the attacks against Adler ranged from celebratory enthusiasm to grave concern. Although militant feminist activity in the FRG quieted down after 1987, a recent example discussed in the book's conclusion illustrates that feminist militancy has lost none of its urgency and explosiveness.

Above, I have proposed that we understand feminist militancy in very broad terms as ideas and practices that aim to overcome sexist oppression and are based on the assumption that this objective can only be reached with a confrontational attitude. According to this definition, expressions of feminist militancy can but do not have to involve violent tactics. As the campaigns discussed in the following chapters show, feminist militancy in West Germany occasionally manifested itself in bombings, arson attacks and other highly confrontational protest actions. However, far more often it took the form of small acts of provocation and resistance in everyday life. Although feminist protest with a high degree of confrontation accounts for a small part of feminist protest in the FRG, it deserves our attention. The protest activities and campaigns discussed in this study show that the scope and limits of feminist protest have developed and changed as a result of discussions within and between feminist groups, and in response to broader social and political developments.

The questions identified above can help us to develop a richer understanding of feminist protest in the FRG and of the role of feminist militancy in it. My analysis reveals that feminist protest cultures in post-WWII Germany were more dynamic and diverse than previous research suggests. I discuss activities that were perceived as nonviolent alongside others that were understood as violent, and analyse the interplay and effects of both. I anticipate that many readers will consider at least some of the events and campaigns discussed incompatible with feminist ethics. This, however, should not stop us from critically examining the causes, forms and consequences of militant and violent tactics in the context of feminist activism in the FRG. Precisely because they had the potential to provoke such reactions, the expressions of feminist militancy discussed in this study have triggered important discussions about the ethics and politics of feminist protest.

Notes

1. U. Frevert (1997), *Women in German History: From Bourgeois Emancipation to Sexual Liberation*, translated by Stuart McKinnon-Evans, Oxford and New York: Berg, 296.
2. G. Notz (2004), 'Die autonomen Frauenbewegungen der Siebzigerjahre: Entstehungsgeschichte, Organisationsformen, politische Konzepte', *Archiv für Zeitgeschichte*, 123–48, 133.
3. 'radikal autonome Feministinnen, die die patriarchale Geschlechterunterdrückung als grundlegende Strukturkategorie moderner Gesellschaften ansahen, und daher die Abschaffung des Patriarchats als oberstes Ziel verfolgten'; ibid.
4. 'sozialistische oder linke Feministinnen, die eine grundlegende Transformation der kapitalistischen *und* patriarchalen Verhältnisse anstrebten'; ibid.
5. I. Lenz (2010), *Die Neue Frauenbewegung in Deutschland: Abschied vom kleinen Unterschied: Eine Quellensammlung*, 2nd rev. edn, Wiesbaden: VS-Verlag, 25.
6. The Action Council for the Liberation of Women discussed in chapter 1 and other groups in the emerging feminist movement in West Germany showed an active interest in radical feminist texts from the United States.
7. M. Marx Ferree (2012), *Varieties of Feminism: German Gender Politics in Global Perspective*, Stanford, CA: Stanford University Press, 9.
8. E.M. Silies (2011), 'Ein, zwei, viele Bewegungen?' in C. Baumann, S. Gehrig and N. Büchse (eds), *Linksalternatives Milieu und Neue Soziale Bewegungen in den 1970er Jahren*, Heidelberg: Universitätsverlag Winter, 87–106, 94.
9. U. Gerhard (2002), 'The Women's Movement in West Germany', in G. Griffin and R. Braidotti (eds), *Thinking Differently*, London: Zed Books, 321–31, here 328–29.
10. See e.g. G. Notz (2006), *Warum flog die Tomate? Die autonomen Frauenbewegungen der Siebzigerjahre: Entstehungsgeschichte, Organisationsformen, politische Konzepte*, Neu-Ulm: AG-SPAK-Bücher.
11. Gerhard, 'The Women's Movement in West Germany', 329.
12. D. Della Porta (1995), *Social Movements, Political Violence, and the State: A Comparative Analysis of Italy and Germany*, Cambridge: Cambridge University Press, 24.
13. Ibid., 24.
14. M. Klimke and J. Scharloth (2008), *1968 in Europe: A History of Protest and Activism, 1956–1977*, Basingstoke: Palgrave Macmillan, 100.
15. J. Varon (2004), *Bringing the War Home: The Weather Underground, the Red Army Faction, and Revolutionary Violence in the Sixties and Seventies*, Berkeley: University of California Press, 33.
16. 'nie ein traditionelles Verhältnis zu Erscheinungen wie Anarchismus, Abweichung usw. gehabt. ... Die Bereitschaft, den Abweichler als Staats- oder Volksfeind zu sehen, ist geblieben, – mindestens war sie bis Ende der 50er Jahre unverändert'; D. Claessens and K. de Ahna (1982), 'Das Milieu der Westberliner "Scene" und die "Bewegung 2. Juni"', in W. von Baeyer-Katte (ed.), *Gruppenprozesse*, Opladen: Westdeutscher Verlag, 20–181, 23.
17. W.D. Narr (2008), 'Der CDU- Staat (1949–1966)', in R. Roth and D. Rucht (eds), *Die Sozialen Bewegungen in Deutschland Seit 1945: Ein Handbuch*, Frankfurt and New York: Campus, 51–70.
18. R. Burns and W. van der Will (1988), *Protest and Democracy in West Germany: Extra-Parliamentary Opposition and the Democratic Agenda*, Basingstoke: Macmillan Press, 9.
19. S. Scheerer (1988), 'Die Ausgebürgerte Linke', in H. Hess et al. (eds), *Angriff auf das Herz des Staates. Soziale Entwicklung und Terrorismus*, Frankfurt: Suhrkamp, 193–429, 221.
20. Klimke and Scharloth, *1968 in Europe*, 98.
21. W. Lindner (1996), *Jugendprotest seit den fünfziger Jahren: Dissens und kultureller Eigensinn*, Opladen: Leske und Budrich, 93.
22. The emergency legislation that the Grand Coalition passed in 1968 was met with fierce resistance from other political parties, from the extra-parliamentary opposition and a range of other

groups, because it 'threatened to expand the powers of the executive branch at the expense of constitutional rights in the event of an internal or external state emergency'; Klimke and Scharloth, *1968 in Europe*, 98.
23. For a more detailed discussion, see S. Reichardt (2008), 'Große und Sozialliberale Koalition (1966–1974)', in R. Roth and D. Rucht (eds), *Die Sozialen Bewegungen in Deutschland seit 1945: Ein Handbuch*, Frankfurt and New York: Campus, 71–91.
24. See S. von Dirke (1997), *All Power to the Imagination! The West German Counterculture from the Student Movement to the Greens*, Lincoln: University of Nebraska Press, 34.
25. Della Porta, *Social Movements*, 37.
26. SDS (Sozialistischer Deutscher Studentenbund), not to be confused with the US movement of the same period, Students for a Democratic Society. Jeremy Varon's comparative study *Bringing the War Home: The Weather Underground, the Red Army Faction, and the Revolutionary Violence in the Sixties and Seventies* offers a detailed discussion of the two student organizations and their roles in the development of militant politics in West Germany and the United States.
27. For a detailed discussion of the development of the SDS and the APO, see T. Fichter and S. Lönnedonker (1976), *Kleine Geschichte des SDS*, Berlin: Rotbuch Verlag; P. Richter (1998), 'Die Außerparlamentarische Opposition in der Bundesrepublik Deutschland 1966 bis 1968', in I. Gilcher-Holtey (ed.), *1968, Vom Ereignis zum Gegenstand der Geschichtswissenschaft*, Göttingen: Vandenhoeck und Ruprecht, 35–55.
28. Klimke and Scharloth, *1968 in Europe*, 98–99.
29. G. Diewald-Kerkmann (2009), *Frauen, Terrorismus und Justiz: Prozesse gegen weibliche Mitglieder der RAF und der Bewegung 2. Juni*, Düsseldorf: Droste, 51.
30. See e.g. Heinrich-Böll-Stiftung and Feministisches Institut (eds) (1999), *Wie weit flog die Tomate? Eine 68erinnen-Gala der Reflexion*, Berlin: Heinrich-Böll-Stiftung; U. Kätzel (2002), *Die 68erinnen: Porträt einer rebellischen Frauengeneration*, Berlin: Rowohlt.
31. Von Dirke, *All Power*, 33.
32. I. Gilcher-Holtey (2008), 'Kritische Theorie und Neue Linke', in I. Gilcher-Holtey (ed.), *1968 – Vom Ereignis zum Mythos*, Frankfurt: Suhrkamp, 223–47, 244.
33. Klimke and Scharloth, *1968 in Europe*, 101.
34. The term '"Third World"' was coined during the Cold War, and referred to countries in Africa, Asia, Latin America and Oceania, and has remained in use since, although it has been the subject of much criticism. Quinn Slobodian has shown that in the eyes of many foreign student activists in West Germany, this category '"did not denote comparative backwardness or inferiority"'; Q. Slobodian (2012), *Foreign Front: Third World Politics in Sixties West Germany*, Durham, NC: Duke University Press, 5. Rather, they saw it as a tool for their empowerment.
35. Slobodian, *Foreign Front*, 17.
36. T.S. Brown (2015), *West Germany and the Global Sixties: The Antiauthoritarian Revolt, 1962–1978*, Cambridge: Cambridge University Press, 39.
37. Della Porta, *Social Movements*, 37.
38. T. Lindenberger and A. Lüdtke (eds) (1995), *Physische Gewalt: Studien zur Geschichte der Neuzeit*, 2nd edn, Frankfurt: Suhrkamp, 7.
39. U. Kätzel (2005), 'Geschlecht, Gewalt und Pazifismus. 1968 und die Anti-Vietnamskriegsbewegung in der Bundesrepublik Deutschland', in J.A. Davy, K. Hagemann and U. Kätzel (eds), *Frieden, Gewalt, Geschlecht: Friedens- und Konfliktforschung als Geschlechterforschung*, Essen: Klartext, 222–43, 233.
40. K. Fahlenbrach (2002), *Protest-Inszenierungen: Visuelle Kommunikation und kollektive Identitäten in Protestbewegungen*, Wiesbaden: Westdeutscher Verlag, 166; Diewald-Kerkmann, *Frauen, Terrorismus und Justiz*, 31.
41. Klimke and Scharloth, *1968 in Europe*, 97. While Klimke is right to point out that the Ohnesorg killing was a central moment in the West German protest movement, his description of the photograph here reinforces the gendered stereotype that women were more interested in fashion than in politics and played a largely passive role in the 1968 movement.

42. 'Urteil im Zwielicht', *Der Spiegel*, 27 November 1967, 74.
43. Slobodian, *Foreign Front*, 132.
44. 'Gewalt ist constituens der Herrschaft und damit auch von unserer Seite mit demonstrativer und provokatorischer Gegengewalt zu beantworten. Die Form bestimmt sich durch die Form der Auseinandersetzung'; 'Wir fordern die Enteignung Axel Springers', *Der Spiegel*, 10 July 1967, 29–33, 32.
45. Della Porta, *Social Movements*, 37.
46. The 'Berlin Underground' is a name given to the alternative intellectual and youth subcultural scene in Berlin during the 1960s and 70s.
47. W. Kraushaar (2006), 'Die Tupamaros West-Berlin', in W. Kraushaar (ed.), *Die RAF und der linke Terrorismus*, Hamburg: Hamburger Edition, 512–30, 527.
48. See e.g. H. Schlaeger and N. Vedder-Shults (1978), 'The West German Women's Movement', *New German Critique*, 59–68; E.H. Altbach (1984), 'The New German Women's Movement', *Signs* 9, 454–69; Heinrich-Böll-Stiftung and Feministisches Institut, *Wie weit flog die Tomate?*; K. Schulz (2002), *Der Lange Atem der Provokation: Die Frauenbewegung in der Bundesrepublik und in Frankreich, 1968–1976*, Frankfurt and New York: Campus; G. Notz (2006), *Warum flog die Tomate? Die autonomen Frauenbewegungen der Siebzigerjahre: Entstehungsgeschichte, Organisationsformen, politische Konzepte*, Neu-Ulm: AG-SPAK-Bücher; S. Hertrampf (2008), 'Ein Tomatenwurf und seine Folgen. Eine neue Welle des Frauenprotests in der BRD', in *bpb dossier*. Retrieved 1 March 2012 from http://www.bpb.de/gesellschaft/gender/frauenbewegung/35287/neue-welle-im-westen?p=0; Gerhard, 'Frauenbewegung'; I. Lenz (2010), *Die Neue Frauenbewegung in Deutschland: Abschied vom kleinen Unterschied: Eine Quellensammlung*, 2nd rev. edn, Wiesbaden: VS-Verlag.
49. H. Sander (1999), 'Rede des Aktionsrates zur Befreiung der Frauen', in A. Conrad and K. Michalik (eds), *Quellen zur Geschichte der Frauen*, Stuttgart: Reclam, 358–68.
50. D.K. Leach (2009), 'An Elusive "We": Antidogmatism, Democratic Practice, and the Contradictory Identity of the German Autonomen', *American Behavioral Scientist* 52, 1042–68, 1044.
51. Although Weber's notion of the 'Gewaltmonopol des Staates' can also be translated as 'the monopoly of the use of legitimate force', the translation as 'monopoly of legitimate physical violence', as suggested by Rodney Livingstone and others, is better suited for my analysis; M. Weber et al. (2004), *The Vocation Lectures*, Indianapolis, IN: Hackett Pub, 33.
52. For a detailed analysis of debates on militancy in internal movement publications, see S. Haunss (2004), *Identität in Bewegung: Prozesse kollektiver Identität bei den Autonomen und in der Schwulenbewegung*, Wiesbaden: VS Verlag für Sozialwissenschaften, 169–89.
53. F. Anders and A. Sedlmaier (2013), 'The Limits of the Legitimate: The Quarrel over "Violence" between Autonomist Groups and the German Authorities', in W. Steinmetz, H.G. Haupt and I. Gilcher-Holtey (eds), *Writing Political History Today*, Frankfurt: Campus, 291–316, 296–97.
54. F. Anders (2006), 'Die Zeitschrift radikal und das Strafrecht', in F. Anders and I. Gilcher-Holtey (eds), *Herausforderungen des staatlichen Gewaltmonopols. Recht und politisch motivierte Gewalt am Ende des 20. Jahrhunderts*, Frankfurt: Campus, 221–59, 231.
55. Leach, 'An Elusive "We"', 1050.
56. Haunss, *Identität in Bewegung*, 160–69.
57. P. Melzer (2012), '"Frauen gegen Imperialismus und Patriarchat zerschlagen den Herrschaftsapparat": autonome Frauen, linksradikaler feministischer Protest und Gewalt in Westdeutschland', in H. Balz and J.H. Friedrichs (eds), *'All we ever wanted . . .' eine Kulturgeschichte europäischer Protestbewegungen der 1980er Jahre*, Berlin: Dietz, 157–77, 175.
58. 'Wir sahen keine Hierarchie in verschiedenen Aktionsformen. Flugblatt verteilen, Besetzungen, Sprühaktionen, Schlösser verkleben, Steine schmeißen, Spreng- und Brandsätze legen – alles war wichtig, wenn es zusammengriff'; Die Rote Zora (1993), 'Mili's Tanz auf dem Eis. Von Pirouetten, Schleifen, Einbrüchen, doppelten Saltos und dem Versuch, Boden unter die Füße zu kriegen'. Retrieved 3 December 2015 from http://www.freilassung.de/div/texte/rz/milis/milis1.htm.

59. 'Wir selbst empfanden das Verlassen der uns zudiktierten weiblichen Friedfertigkeit bzw. die bewußte Entscheidung für gewalttätige Mittel in unserer Politik als ungeheuer befreiend. Wir erlebten, daß wir mit unseren Aktionen Angst, Ohnmacht und Resignation durchbrechen konnten, und wollten dies anderen FrauenLesben weiter vermitteln'; ibid. With the term 'women/lesbians', the Red Zora used an expression that was common in women's groups in West Germany. It was used to draw attention to the fact that the position of women and lesbians was related yet not always identical.
60. Chapter 2 offers a more detailed discussion of the RZ's notion of counter-violence.
61. For a more detailed analysis of feminist responses to the Red Zora, see K. Karcher (2015), 'How (not) to "Hollaback": Towards a transnational debate on the "Red Zora" and militant tactics in the feminist struggle against gender-based violence', *Feminist Media Studies*, DOI: 10.1080/14680777.2015.1093099.
62. Important studies of militancy in the British suffrage movement include M. Joannou and J. Purvis (1998), *The Women's Suffrage Movement: New Feminist Perspectives*, Manchester: Manchester University Press; Mayhall (2000), (2003); E.P. Ziarek (2008), 'Right to Vote or Right to Revolt? Arendt and the British Suffrage Militancy', *differences* 3(19), 1–27; J. Purvis (2013), 'Gendering the Historiography of the Suffragette Movement in Edwardian Britain: Some Reflections', *Women's History Review* 4(22), 576–90; L.N. Mayhall (2003), *The Militant Suffrage Movement: Citizenship and Resistance in Britain, 1860–1930*, Oxford: Oxford University Press.
63. L.N. Mayhall (2000), 'Defining Militancy: Radical Protest, the Constitutional Idiom, and Women's Suffrage in Britain, 1908–1909', *Journal of British Studies* 39, 340–71, 341.
64. Mayhall, *The Militant Suffrage Movement*, 8.
65. U. Frevert (1986), *Frauen-Geschichte: Zwischen bürgerlicher Verbesserung und neuer Weiblichkeit*, Frankfurt: Suhrkamp, 74.
66. 'Einige wenige Frauen gaben sich mit Zuhören, Unterstützen und Petitionieren nicht zufrieden, sondern halfen beim Barrikadenbau und kämpften auf der Seite der demokratischen Freischaren gegen das Militär'; ibid.
67. J.A. Davy (2005), '"Manly" and "Feminine" Antimilitarism', in J.A. Davy, K. Hagemann and U. Kätzel (eds), *Frieden, Gewalt, Geschlecht: Friedens- und Konfliktforschung als Geschlechterforschung*, Essen: Klartext, 144–63, 160.
68. 'eine Geschichte wiederholter Rückschläge, Stillstände und vieler mühsamer Neuanfänge unter immer wieder veränderten gesellschaftlichen und politischen Bedingungen'; U. Gerhard (2008), 'Frauenbewegung', in R. Roth and D. Rucht (eds), *Die Sozialen Bewegungen in Deutschland seit 1945*, Frankfurt and New York: Campus, 188–217, 191.
69. According to Tobias Wunschik, the core of the group consisted in autumn 1977 of exactly twenty members; T. Wunschik (2006), 'Die Bewegung 2. Juni', in W. Kraushaar (ed.), *Die RAF und der linke Terrorismus*, Hamburg: Hamburger Edition, 531–61, 472.
70. S.V. Vukadinović (2013), 'Spätreflex. Eine Fallstudie zu den Revolutionären Zellen, der Roten Zora und zur verlängerten Feminismus-Obsession bundesdeutscher Terrorismusfahnder', in I. Bandhauer-Schöffmann and D. van der Laak (eds), *Der Linksterrorismus der 1970er-Jahre und die Ordnung der Geschlechter*, Trier: Wissenschaftlicher Verlag, 140–61, 147ff.
71. Retrieved 21 November 2015 from http://www.oxforddictionaries.com/definition/english/militant. According to the Duden definition, 'militant' means 'mit bewusst kämpferischem Anstrich für eine Überzeugung eintretend'. Retrieved 21 November 2015 from http://www.duden.de/rechtschreibung/militant.
72. C. Scribner (2015), *After the Red Army Faction: Gender, Culture, and Militancy*, New York: Columbia University Press, 13.
73. H. Kämper and E. Link (2013), *Wörterbuch zum Demokratiediskurs 1967/68*, Berlin: Akademie Verlag, 679–80. Retrieved 4 November 2015 from http://alltitles.ebrary.com/Doc?id=10861362.
74. Ibid., 680.

75. K. Hanshew (2012), *Terror and Democracy in West Germany*, New York: Cambridge University Press, 35.
76. 'Das ist es wohl, was den Frauen, wie allen unterdrückten und gedemütigten Gruppen, am meisten ausgetrieben worden ist: der Mut zum Hass! Was wäre eine Freiheitsbewegung ohne Hass? Ohne die Frage: Gehen wir wirklich weit genug? Sind wir wirklich nicht feige? Machen wir uns wirklich nichts vor? Reicht unsere Solidarität auch für die, die nicht, nicht mehr, die Nerven haben, dieses ganze himmelschreiende Unrecht immer nur in "Besonnenheit" lösen zu wollen? Mut zur Militanz war noch nie eine deutsche Spezialität. Dennoch ergriff er in dieser Zeit auch deutsche Frauen'; A. Schwarzer (1981), *So fing es an! 10 Jahre Frauenbewegung*, Cologne: Emma-Frauenverlag, 24.
77. M. Gebhardt (2012), *Alice im Niemandsland – Wie die deutsche Frauenbewegung die Frauen verlor*, Munich: DVA. For a similarly critical account, see B. Mika (1998), *Alice Schwarzer. Eine kritische Biographie*, Reinbek: Rowohlt.
78. B. hooks (2000), *Feminist Theory: From Margin to Center*, Cambridge, MA: South End Press, 28.
79. P. Melzer (2015), *Death in the Shape of a Young Girl: Women's Political Violence in the Red Army Faction*, New York: New York University Press, 29.
80. Ibid., 69.
81. See e.g. Geronimo (1990), *Feuer und Flamme*, Berlin: Edition ID Archiv; Haunss, *Identität in Bewegung*; Anders, 'Die Zeitschrift radikal und das Strafrecht'; Melzer, 'Frauen gegen Imperialismus und Patriarchat'.

Chapter 1

THE NEW WOMEN'S MOVEMENT IN WEST GERMANY

*I*t is widely acknowledged that the provocative protests by women in the New Left in the late 1960s and early 1970s played a significant role in the formation of the New Women's Movement.[1] I want to discuss protest activities in this period here in more detail, because they illustrate that feminist militancy was a driving force in the development of the feminist movement in West Germany. The aim of this chapter is not to give a complete overview of the history of the New Women's Movement, as there is already excellent work on this subject. Rather, I want to introduce and contextualize some of the themes, campaigns and networks that have been important for the development of militant feminisms in West Germany. The first event that deserves attention in this context is the legendary tomato throwing in 1968.

On 12 September 1968, the film-maker Helke Sander addressed the conference delegates at the twenty-third conference of the SDS in Frankfurt. Sander spoke as an active member of the anti-authoritarian Left in West Germany, but she spoke also as the mother of a nine-year-old son and as a representative of the Berlin-based women's group Action Council for the Liberation of Women (*Aktionsrat zur Befreiung der Frauen*).[2] Since January 1968, Sander and other women in West Berlin had held regular meetings to develop ideas on how to translate the politics of the New Left into their daily lives. There was a very pragmatic reason for their interest in the politics of everyday life: many of them still carried the sole responsibility for housework and childcare. In an attempt to tackle the isolation and oppression of women in the private sphere, the Action Council set up a number of revolutionary kindergartens in West Berlin. To

---

Notes for this section begin on page 39.

develop this project further, the group wanted to collaborate with the SDS if – and only if – its members were willing to confront sexism in their own ranks. If they failed to do so, declared Sander to the conference delegates in Frankfurt, the SDS would be no more than a 'bloated counterrevolutionary yeast-dough'.[3] She concluded with a warning: if men in the anti-authoritarian Left would continue to ignore critical contributions by female comrades, women would 'draw the necessary consequences'.[4]

When it appeared that the SDS board members wanted to move on to other issues without commenting on Sander's speech, the pregnant SDS activist Sigrid Rüger drew her own conclusions: she stood up from her chair and pelted them with tomatoes. Rüger and Sander knew each other only from sight and had not coordinated their protest in advance. Thirty years later, Sander still vividly remembered Rüger 'standing there in her green dress, with her red hair and her big belly, looking gorgeous. And then, she threw two pounds of tomatoes, at first into a complete silence, then in a great tumult.'[5] Sander was amazed by Rüger's expressive protest, which she understood not primarily as an act of aggression against the SDS board members but as an expression of solidarity among women.

According to Damm-Rüger (née Rüger), the lecture theatre turned into a 'bubbling cauldron' with reactions ranging from spontaneous enthusiasm to bewilderment and indignation.[6] In this turmoil, Ines Lehmann, a student of politics, jumped to the defence of the SDS board members. She was one of several conference participants who openly criticized the 'secessionist aspirations' of the Action Council for the Liberation of Women.[7] Lehmann felt that the protest was directed against the wrong people (because the SDS was one of the few political organizations where men and women worked together towards radical political change), and that the scandal could not have come at a worse time: in the months leading up to the conference in Frankfurt, the SDS had experienced a number of setbacks and factional disputes, which resulted in its disintegration in the second half of the year.[8]

Many women in the anti-authoritarian Left, however, shared Sander's frustration and felt inspired by Rüger's unusual protest. A few weeks after the SDS conference in Frankfurt, journalist Ulrike Meinhof stressed the importance of the tomato throwing in an article in the leftist magazine *konkret*.[9] She argued that, unlike similar protest activities in the past (e.g. the throwing of tomatoes and eggs during a demonstration against a visit from the Iranian Shah in 1967), Sander and Rüger's rebellion was more than a symbolic gesture: two women on the Left had made very clear that they would no longer accept that their views and experiences were simply ignored. 'The lesson to be learned from Frankfurt', concluded Meinhof, 'can only be that women think more about their problems, get organized, and learn to work through their issues and to articulate them. Initially, they should demand only that their men leave them alone and wash their tomato-stained shirts themselves.'[10] Like Sander, Meinhof knew only too well how difficult it could be for women on the anti-authoritarian Left to combine work, political activism and parenting responsibilities. After divorcing the leftist publisher Klaus Röhl in spring 1968, she moved to West Berlin with her two six-year-old daughters. Her article 'Women in the SDS: Acting on Their Own Behalf' became a foundational text of the New Women's Movement in West Germany.[11]

Inspired by the provocative protest in Frankfurt, SDS women formed Crones' Councils (*Weiberräte*) in several West German university cities.[12] According to Morvarid Dehnavi, male comrades had mockingly referred to the first socialist women's groups in Frankfurt as 'crones' councils', so the participants then appropriated this terminology.[13] Two months after the tomato throwing, members of the newly formed Frankfurt Crones' Council caused a scandal at the twenty-fourth SDS conference, which took place in Hannover in November 1968. They distributed a flyer with a short statement and an image depicting a naked woman wearing a witch's hat and holding an axe (see figure 1.1). Behind her, six 'trophies' – severed penises that were linked to the names of leading SDS members – were hanging on the wall. According to a former member, the group had included the image from a Dutch Provo pamphlet to remind the 'heroes' of the student revolution in a humorous way that they should 'keep their feet on the ground'.[14] In the short statement with the ironic title 'Statement of Accounts', the Frankfurt Crones' Council listed dozens of stereotypes and forms of sexist behaviour that they faced in the anti-authoritarian Left and asserted: 'women are d i f f e r e n t'.[15] The short declaration ended with the explicit slogan: 'Liberate the socialist eminences from their bourgeois cocks.'[16] While the depicted men and a number of other SDS members found the flyer 'despicable', others considered it a humorous and necessary provocation.[17]

Although they disrupted SDS conferences and employed confrontational tactics to criticize sexism in the SDS, most members of the Action Council and the Crones' Councils were firm believers in the principles and politics of the anti-authoritarian Left. They saw their struggle against the oppression of women not as a break with the revolutionary politics of the SDS but as a concrete realization and consistent development of leftist ideas and principles.[18] Drawing on the language and theoretical foundations of the New Left, the Berlin Action Council criticized the SDS for reinforcing a 'bourgeois distinction' between private life and public affairs and ignoring the political and economic relevance of the oppression of women in the private sphere.[19] Initially, women in the SDS tried to convince their comrades that the liberation of women was an important step towards the liberation of all humans, and that it had to begin with practical solutions to everyday problems. However, faced with a lack of engagement in the SDS, they began to organize independently.

As the conflicts at the twenty-third and twenty-fourth SDS conferences illustrate, there was no discursive space that women in the anti-authoritarian Left could have occupied to discuss their problems as political issues. The late 1960s and early 1970s were an explorative phase in which women on the Left began to organize, think and mobilize independently from their male comrades to work towards new forms of political subjectivity. Although this feminist

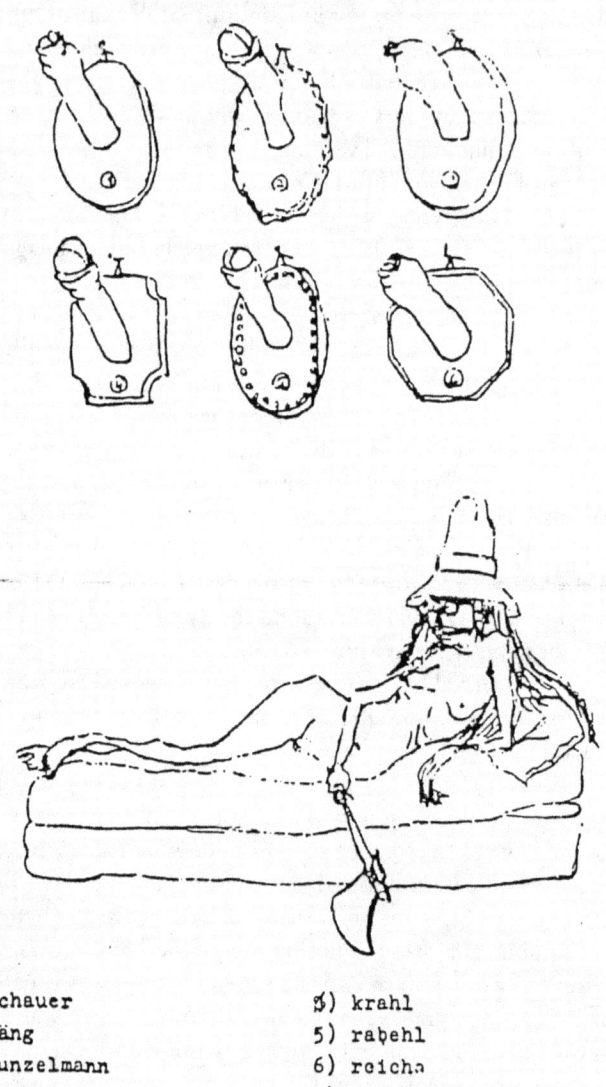

Figure 1.1 Flyer by a women's group in the SDS, November 1968. Courtesy FrauenMediaTurm, Cologne (FB.04.188a).

mobilization was not limited to West Germany, it took different, less visible forms in the GDR. Against the background of state repression, the women's groups and lesbian networks that formed in East Germany after 1968 remained small and informal. The work of Irmtraud Morgner, Christa Wolf, Maxi Wander and other authors has focused on women's experiences and problems in real existing socialism.[20] In particular, Morgner's work is often associated with protest movements in the 1960s and 1970s because it 'addresses a variety of relevant themes, among them the Cold War, the Vietnam War, feminism and the Civil Rights movement'.[21]

The Long 1960s

The Berlin Action Council

One of the first women's groups that formed in the context of the radical Left in West Germany in the late 1960s was the Berlin Action Council. It is no coincidence that the history of the Action Council for the Liberation of Women began in December 1967 in a communal kitchen in West Berlin. Most members of the group were political activists and/or partners of men in the SDS who were fed up with the gender dynamics of the anti-authoritarian Left.[22] Childcare was a particularly important topic for the Action Council, not least because many members had children and struggled to combine parental responsibilities with political activism. In January 1968, the Action Council organized a first public debate on childcare. According to the organizers, this event alone attracted eighty women, and successive gatherings attracted even more interest.[23] At the peak of popularity, the Action Council had, according to Helke Sander, five hundred members.[24] Due to the great interest in this topic, the group began to hold weekly meetings in the anti-authoritarian 'Republican Club' in West-Berlin. One of the first political projects of the Action Council was to create 'storefront day-care centres' (*Kinderläden*),[25] where political activists tried to raise their children collectively and in an anti-authoritarian manner.[26] In her speech to the SDS in September 1968, Sander noted that five storefront day-care centres in Berlin were already up and running and that more were planned.

The Berlin Action Council tried to combine the work on concrete political projects with a theoretical and political analysis of the problems that women faced in industrialized capitalist societies. A newsletter from June 1968 listed no fewer than twelve working groups, ranging from children's books to women's economic dependency and sexual health.[27] Minutes from group meetings and other internal documents indicate that the Action Council discussed texts by Sigmund Freud and other psychoanalysts as well as socialist classics such as August Bebel's *Woman and Socialism*, Friedrich Engels's *The Origin of the Family, Private Property and the State* and Clara Zetkin's *On the History of the Proletarian Women's Movement in Germany*.[28] Yet, the group also read more recent publications such as the previously mentioned article and other works by Ulrike Meinhof, as well as Robin Morgan's anthology *Sisterhood is Powerful* and other radical feminist texts from the United States.[29] In addition to these texts, the women read and discussed campaign-specific literature. When planning the first storefront day-care centres, for instance, they found inspiration in the work of Russian psychoanalyst Vera Fedorowna Schmidt, Scottish educator Alexander Sutherland Neill and German psychologist Klaus Horn as well as communal childcare projects in Dutch Provo collectives and in the Israeli kibbutz-movement.[30]

Although the members of the Berlin Action Council shared an interest in the problems that women faced in the family, at the workplace and in society, they set different priorities. Some group members wanted to focus on the analysis of socialist classics, while others prioritized the work on the storefront day-care centres and other concrete projects. Unable to resolve this tension, the Action Council dissolved in 1970. Then, sociologist Frigga Haug and other group members with an interest in Marxist thought and socialist theory formed the 'Socialist Women's Union West Berlin', which remained active until 1980. In 1971, Helke Sander and a few other women set up the group 'Bread & Roses' (*Brot und Rosen*) and provided counselling and advice on abortion, contraception and sexual health. In 1972, Bread & Roses published the 'Women's Handbook' (*Frauenhandbuch*), which became one of the most popular books in the New Women's Movement with two editions and more than 100,000 copies sold.[31] While Sander and other group members became important voices in the New Women's Movement, other women gave up political activism in the early 1970s or joined leftist splinter parties. Marianne Herzog, who was a founding member of the Berlin Action Council, and Ulrike Meinhof, who had attended a few of the group's meetings, joined the militant leftist group 'Red Army Faction'.

The fact that Herzog, Meinhof and other women in the RAF had showed an active interest in feminist politics before they decided to take up arms led to wild speculations about the dangers of feminism. In the 1970s, state and police authorities, journalists and other authors repeatedly imputed feminist motives to the RAF.[32] As the following chapter illustrates, the RAF did not have a feminist agenda, but female involvement in left-wing violence was repeatedly presented as an 'excess' of women's liberation.[33] In an attempt to challenge this misrepresentation and to distance the New Women's Movement from the militant Left in West Germany, feminist activists and scholars placed great emphasis on the peaceful nature of feminist protest in West Germany. Testimonies by former members of the Berlin Action Council, however, highlight the critical importance of militancy played in the formative years of the New Women's Movement.

In 1988, former member Ingrid Schmidt-Harzbach explained in an interview with the newspaper *die tageszeitung*: 'We in the Action Council thought of ourselves as very militant, also when we were out on the streets to demonstrate. This was our way of participating in the small frenzy of power. When we were blocking the crossroads in front of the "Kranzler"[34] in our flamboyant clothes, we felt as if the streets belonged to us.'[35] Since the Action Council served as a platform for women with different political priorities and personal interests, Schmidt-Harzbach's view on street militancy is by no means representative. Yet, it is likely that many, if not all, members of the Action Council had first-hand experience of student protest and violent clashes with the police. Another former member of the Berlin Action Council, Margit Eschenbach, recalls that she contemplated cutting her long hair, because the police kept on pulling it during demonstrations.[36] Years after the twenty-third SDS conference, Sigrid Damm-Rüger explained that her tomato throwing was inspired by a demonstration at the Amerika Haus in West Berlin in 1966, during which students had pelted the building with eggs.[37]

Radical Women's Groups in Frankfurt

While the activities of the Berlin Action Council are well documented, there is no comparable data on leftist women's groups in Frankfurt in the late 1960s. Like West Berlin, Frankfurt am Main had been a hotbed of student protest and became an early centre of the New Women's Movement, but it was also a key logistical hub for rail and air traffic (both civil and military air transport) and a centre of migration and industrial activity. Student activists and women's groups in Frankfurt tried to reach out and work with migrant communities, factory workers and other local groups in the city. Previous research suggests that there were two attempts to set up Crones' Councils in Frankfurt. The first formed in autumn 1968 and had an estimated membership of fifty to one hundred women.[38] After a few months, the group dissolved due to internal tensions.

In 1970, student activists made a second attempt at forming a Crones' Council. The reading list of this group was as diverse and international in scope as that of the Action Council in Berlin. In an interview, a former member of the group described their ideas as a 'very strange cocktail: a bit of Marx, Lenin, Bakunin, Mao. But also Rosa Luxemburg. And then of course different theories of emancipation, Wilhelm Reich and the Sex-Pol movement and feminism obviously.'[39] Initially, the second Crones' Council faced similar problems to the first one, but in 1971 the group was united by one common goal: together with many other women in West Germany, they began to campaign for a decriminalization of abortion.[40]

Rather than organizing separately from their male comrades, many women on the radical Left in Frankfurt tried to promote feminist ideas and politics in existing political campaigns and networks. As early as 1967, student activist Monika Seifert set up the first anti-authoritarian kindergarten in the Federal Republic: a collectively run children's school (*Kinderschule*) in Frankfurt.[41] Seifert viewed some of the social experiments in the Kinderladen movement in West Berlin with great scepticism, and it seems that there was little or no discussion between her and feminist activists in Berlin.[42] In 1970, a group of student activists co-founded the radical leftist publishing house Red Star (*Roter Stern*). Red Star publications from the early 1970s included, among a range of magazines and books, feminist texts such as Clara Zetkin's *On the History of the Proletarian Women's*

Movement in Germany, a translation of Pamela Allen's *Free Space: A Perspective on the Small Group in Women's Liberation* and the first edition of the radical feminist Women's Yearbook (*Frauenjahrbuch*).[43]

The dissemination of the scandalous 'penis flyer' at the twenty-fourth SDS conference in November 1968 was not the only provocative protest by women on the radical Left in Frankfurt in the late 1960s. Forty years before members of the Ukrainian women's group FEMEN staged their first topless protest, members of the Frankfurt Crones' Council exposed their breasts to provoke public authorities.[44] On 12 December 1968, a group of women disrupted the court proceedings against student activist Ursula Seppel, who was charged with aggravated trespass, with a topless performance freely adapted from Berthold Brecht.[45] In April 1969, three women staged a similar protest during a lecture by Theodor W. Adorno, whose critical theory was of great importance for the West German student movement. According to one of the actors involved, they regretted the protest when they realized how horrified Adorno was by the attack. The media, however, was fascinated by the unusual protest and reported extensively about the 'breast attack' (*Busenattentat*) against Adorno.[46]

In the early 1970s, Frankfurt became the centre of the West German Spontimovement. Like the Italian *autonomia*, the Spontis 'wanted to organize a total, anti-Capitalist – and militant – struggle, against the complete domination of capital over the sphere of production and reproduction. Their political mobilizations outside the factory, including rent strikes and house squattings, expressed their rejection of the domination of capitalism well beyond the sphere of production as well.'[47] From the very beginning, women have played an active role in the Sponti-movement. The group 'Revolutionary Struggle' (*Revolutionärer Kampf*, or RK) was one of the best-known groups in Frankfurt's militant Sponti-scene.[48] In the early 1970s, a group of women in the RK began to study the history of the proletarian women's movement and tried to mobilize female workers in Frankfurt.

In 1973, members of the 'women's group in the revolutionary struggle' (*Frauengruppe im Revolutionärer Kampf*) published some of their thoughts and experiences in a pamphlet. Although the texts in the pamphlet were characterized by the same revolutionary rhetoric and Leninist terminology as other flyers by the RK, the authors adopted a militant feminist stance. The brochure featured a number of explicit cartoons and slogans including, 'The reign of cocks has its limits – Women together are strong', and 'Whether in the office, at the assembly line, or in the department store, women embrace militancy more and more'.[49] In spring 1973, members of the 'women's group in the revolutionary struggle' disrupted a beauty contest in a discothèque in Frankfurt. Apparently, the intruders handed out flyers, chanted 'Now, let's survey the penises of the jury' and other slogans, stormed the dance floor and threw pigs' tails and pork knuckles at the jury to protest what they considered a sexist 'meat inspection'.[50] In the April issue of the Sponti-magazine *Wir Wollen Alles* (We Want Everything), the group published a sarcastic report about their unusual protest. According to the authors, the men in the jury, who did not want to accept that a group of women could ruin their event, attacked the intruders. The intruders fought back, and the beauty contest ended in a brawl.[51] A feminist 'go-in' at a conference of the German Medical Association in the same year led to similar turmoil. When women activists interrupted the annual general assembly of the association to show their protest against its anti-abortion position, medics told them to go home and to abort with an iron poker.[52] One participant recalls that the assembled members physically attacked the protesters.[53]

According to Alice Schwarzer, Frankfurt was one of the places where militancy and activism came together, and she claims that the provocative protest there helped women across the country to develop and express rage against patriarchal structures and against the men who exploited and oppressed them.[54] Many members of women's groups on the radical Left in the late 1960s, however, were socialist feminists who rejected Schwarzer's radical feminist stance. In a statement from 1969, the members of the Action Council in Berlin emphasized, 'We are not claiming that man is the class enemy. However, we cannot but use as much force as necessary to make him realize that simply by keeping us from doing the work that needs to be done to create a socialist society he acts in many ways as an agent of the class enemy.'[55] Monika Steffen, a founding member of the Frankfurt Crones' Council, insists that the Crones' Councils 'never intended to use the anger of women in the SDS to convert them to feminism'.[56] She argues that the organization, aims and tactics of women's groups on the Left were inspired by the SDS and should be analysed in the context of the student movement even if many members were later active in the New Women's Movement.[57] While Alice Schwarzer's anecdotes should thus not be mistaken for historical facts, she is certainly right in emphasizing that Frankfurt was a hotbed of militant feminist protest in the late 1960s and early 1970s. The scope and forms of feminist militancy in this context were shaped by both radical leftist ideas and feminist struggles.

Although it is widely acknowledged that the provocative protest by women on the radical Left in Frankfurt and West Berlin in the late 1960s and early 1970s provided vital impulses for feminist campaigns in West Germany,[58] it remains controversial whether this protest could and should be understood as the first chapter in history of the New Women's Movement. Some authors argue that the tomato attack on 13 September 1968 marks the 'birth of the New Women's Movement', and a number of testimonies support this conclusion.[59] Other accounts, however, challenge the assumption that there was a straight road from Crones' Councils and other women's groups on the radical Left into the New Women's Movement. Many of the actors involved were interested in discussing 'women's issues', but they considered the oppression of women to be a 'side contradiction' (*Nebenwiderspruch*). This means that it depends on the principle contradiction and will be resolved if the class system is overcome. Rather than getting involved in the feminist groups that formed in the early 1970s across the country, many women set up Marxist reading groups, joined leftist splinter parties or gave up on politics altogether. As the following chapter shows, Ulrike Meinhof and a few others took yet another path: they joined armed leftist groups to fight for a violent revolution in West Germany.

The 1970s

In the early 1970s, the New Women's Movement became a mass movement that mobilized women across the country. In March 1972, feminist groups in Frankfurt organized the first Federal Women's Congress (*Bundesfrauenkongress*), which was attended by approximately four hundred women.[60] The range of conference topics illustrates the depth and breadth of feminist activism in the early 1970s. In addition to planning further protest against the abortion ban, participants discussed reasons for and against an organization of women-only groups, the situation of women workers, the role of women in trade unions, the family as a social institution and solidarity campaigns with women in other countries.[61] Despite significant political and ideological differences among the conference participants and other women's groups in the Federal Republic, they worked together on campaigns on a number of issues including abortion, sexual health, domestic violence and rape.

In her seminal study of second-wave feminism in France and Germany, Kristina Schulz highlights that abortion was the first central topic in the New Women's Movement, and helped feminist activists in Frankfurt and West Berlin – mostly members of the highly educated middle class – to forge relationships with women from other social backgrounds.[62] According to paragraph 218 of the Criminal Code of the Federal Republic of Germany, abortion was a punishable act that could lead to a year-long prison sentence for the actors involved.[63] Taking inspiration from a similar project in France, Alice Schwarzer launched a provocative media campaign to encourage a public debate over a legal reform of paragraph 218. In June 1971, she published a manifesto against the ban on abortions in the magazine *Stern* that was signed by 374 German women. According to Schulz, the hostile responses to Schwarzer's campaign and the criminal investigations against the women involved raised awareness of reproductive rights and other women's issues and led to a wave of sympathy and solidarity within the population.[64] Moreover, 'the various groups demanding free abortion moved closer together and intensified communication and organization'.[65] In the following years, this social network proved vital not only for the mass mobilization against paragraph 218 but also for the organization of a range of other campaigns.

In her personal history of the Women's Movement in West Germany, the feminist activist and historian Frigga Haug notes that in the 1970s 'there was no town, indeed almost no village, without a women's group, no district that was not affected. It was like a bush fire'.[66] In the course of the 1970s, the New Women's Movement created a diverse network of local and national organizations, social centres, women's shelters, bookstores, publishing houses, magazines and other social platforms, where women met, discussed and organized campaigns.[67] The women's centre in West Berlin was one of the first alternative feminist spaces in the FRG. It was founded in 1973 on the initiative of Cristina Perincioli and other members of the women's group in the newly founded Homosexual Action West Berlin (*Homosexuelle Aktion Westberlin*).[68] In the same year, members of the second Crones' Council set up a women's space in Frankfurt.[69] Previous studies suggest that by 1974, there were up to two hundred women's groups in the FRG and more than twelve autonomous women's centres in West Germany.[70]

Soon, there was a range of local and national feminist magazines, publishing houses, educational projects and interest groups, which appealed to women with different political orientations and personal interests. While many of these projects had a rather short lifespan, some have established themselves and exist to the present day. Inspired by the Swiss magazine *Hexenpresse* (Witches' Press), which was first published in 1972, and feminist magazines in other countries, feminist activists in the FRG founded the magazine *Frauenzeitung: Frauen gemeinsam sind stark* (Women's News: Women together are strong). After the first issue in October 1973, there were seven more issues, which were edited by women's groups across the country.[71] In 1976, the feminist publishing house Frauenoffensive (Women's Campaign/Attack) published the second edition of the *Women's Yearbook*.

Founded in October 1975 by a group of feminist activists in Munich, Frauenoffensive was the feminist publishing house in the German speaking world.[72] One of the first and most successful books by the publishing collective was Verena Stefan's novella *Häutungen* (Sheddings), which 'was received as one of the first and most important manifestations of *Frauenliteratur* [women's writing]'.[73] Similarly popular was the first issue of Alice Schwarzer's magazine *Emma* in January 1977, which sold 300,000 copies.[74] While *Emma* tried to appeal to radical and moderate feminists, other magazines wanted to provide a platform for alternative political views and themes in the New Women's Movement. These periodicals included the radical leftist magazine *Schwarze Botin* (Black Messenger) (first published in 1976), the socialist feminist magazine *Courage: Berliner Frauenzeitung* (first published in 1977) and a range of other publications.[75]

Discussions in feminist publications from the 1970s illustrate that violence against women became a central topic in feminist circles in the FRG and other Western countries in the second half of the decade. From the very beginning, feminist debates on violence against women in West Germany were influenced by an active exchange with women in other countries. In 1974, more than five hundred women from twenty countries took part in the International Women's Congress in Frankfurt, where they discussed the possibility of using the opportunity of the 'International Year of the Woman' in 1975 to plan a critical feminist conference on violence against women. Soon, these plans became more concrete. In March 1976, the Russell Tribunal in Brussels provided a platform for two thousand feminists from forty countries to discuss different forms of violence against women.[76] Upon their return, German participants published their findings and created a national tribunal on violence against women.[77] In the following years, a range of feminist publications dealt with violence against women and possible ways of tackling the problem.[78] And feminists in West Germany did not leave it at theoretical debates. Inspired by similar projects in other countries, they created a network of resources and facilities for victims of domestic violence ranging from phone hotlines to advice centres and women's shelters.[79]

The second edition of the *Women's Yearbook* from 1976 included reports about some of these resources and personal testimonies from women who had experienced violence and abuse. One of the most striking contributions to the volume is a collection of essays by a feminist collective who took revenge for the brutal rape of two members by physically attacking and publicly denouncing the rapist. The authors do not comment on the question of whether their testimonies were factual or fictitious, but there is good reason to believe that they were based on real events. In a short epilogue to the testimonies, the women explain their reasons for sharing their story with other women: 'We have written this article, because there are many examples for the suffering, humiliation, exploitation and destruction of women, but there is little discussion about the ways in which women can fight back. We want to inspire other women to develop similar or completely different forms of resistance.'[80] Although there are only a few documented cases of actual violent attacks against alleged rapists, the discussion in chapter 4 shows that many individuals and groups in the New Women's Movement held the view that it could be legitimate and necessary for women to defend themselves against male violence and rape by violent means.

State violence and repression constituted a second focus in feminist debates on violence in the 1970s. The year 1978 saw two feminist conferences on violence – one on violence against women in Cologne,[81] and one entitled 'The Women's Movement and Repression' in Frankfurt.[82] Repression, in the context of this discussion, can be understood as 'the actual or threatened use of physical sanctions against an individual or organization within the territorial jurisdiction of the state, for the purpose of ... deterring specific activities and/or beliefs perceived to be challenging to government personnel, practices or institutions'.[83] In the spirit of the New Left, women in the New Women's Movement questioned the authority of the state and took a critical stance against the way in which state authorities responded to the threat posed by the RAF and other armed leftist groups. Unlike socialist and radical feminists, liberal and moderate feminists were not fundamentally opposed to the West German state. Yet they, too, criticized the state for curtailing the rights of alleged members and sympathizers of militant leftist groups.

Most groups and individuals in the New Women's Movement considered violence to be neither a legitimate nor a necessary response to repression and other forms of violence in West Germany.[84] In response to the escalating violence in the 1970s, a growing number of feminists publicly voiced this view. In October

1977, the feminist magazine *Courage* published the 'appeal to all women for the invention of happiness' by a group of women in Frankfurt. The authors of the short manifesto demanded release 'from the nation that created nothing but misery'. They claimed 'the fundamental right to laugh' and 'to invent happiness without being obstructed by murder and manslaughter, arrest and detention, raids and agitation'.[85] With a suggestion of irony, the women noted that they had to declare some 'great truths': 'you cannot shoot power, you cannot shoot countervailing power, you can only shoot people'.[86] The message was simple: violence is always destructive and will not help to create a better world. In their pursuit of happiness, many feminists distanced themselves not only from the state and the militant Left but also from all politics in the conventional sense. In line with the feminist principle that 'the personal is political', they focused their efforts in the second half of the 1970s increasingly on their own lives and immediate environments. Some parts of the New Women's Movement and groups in the radical Left criticized this development as a retreat into the private sphere (*Rückzug nach innen*).[87] Notions of feminist militancy evolved with and against these trends in the New Women's Movement.

The 1980s

It is a widespread misconception that the New Women's Movement in the FRG reached its peak in the 1970s and has been on the decline since. A recent study suggests that the level of mobilization grew more or less continuously from the late 1970s until 1990, remained constant until 1995, and has gradually declined since then.[88] According to Ilse Lenz, one of the reasons for the further spread of the movement in the 1980s was that many student activists who had been part of feminist struggles in the late 1960s and early 1970s started professional careers in this period and helped to spread the ideas and principles of the New Women's Movement beyond feminist circles. A few examples illustrate this development: in the late 1970s and early 1980s, feminism found its way into public institutions in West Germany. In 1979, the social-liberal government led by Chancellor Helmut Schmidt established a task force for women's issues. In 1986, the Federal Ministry for Health, Family and Youth received a new name and was expanded to include a department on gender equality and women's policy.[89] In 1980, the first institute for gender and women's studies (*Frauen- und Geschlechterforschung*) was founded in Bielefeld, and several more were set up in the course of the decade. A number of women's shelters and other feminist projects were state funded or received financial support from local authorities, and had salaried employees. As the transnational campaigns discussed in chapters 4 and 5 and other protest movements in this period illustrate, feminist activists and professionals forged alliances across political divisions, social sectors and national borders. Borrowing a term coined by political scientist Alison Woodward, Lenz describes these alliances as a 'velvet square', because they connected activists on the grassroots level with institution and association representatives, politicians and feminist academics.

Supported by feminist lawyers, journalists and politicians, activists in the New Women's Movement tried to improve the social status of women in West Germany and pushed for legal reforms. In the late 1970s, feminist activists set up the first political party in the FRG that was run for and by women.[90] On 23 June 1978, a group of feminist journalists and activists filed a complaint against the chief editor of the weekly magazine *Stern*. They argued that the sexualized images of women in *Stern* and other West German magazines constituted an offence against the freedom and dignity of all women as defined by the German Civil Code. Although the case was dismissed, it created attention for the objectification of women in the media and mobilized many women.

In 1987, Alice Schwarzer started a campaign for a law that defined pornography as a violation of women's civil rights. Although the draft law was rejected, Schwarzer continued her campaign against pornography and sexualized images of women in the media. Over time, she would win a number of prominent supporters, including leading politicians from all major parties, actors, filmmakers, writers and public intellectuals. The range of professions of Schwarzer's supporters substantiates the claim that feminism had arrived at the centre of German society. The question whether gender-based violence can and should be compared to hate crime motivated by racism or xenophobia was the subject of great controversy in feminist circles. Debates around this continued until 1998, when the lawyers and politicians Sabine Leutheusser-Schnarrenberger and Lore Maria Peschel-Gutzeit pushed for a legal recognition of misogyny as a motif for discrimination and violence against women.

While some feminists in the FRG began a long march through the institutions, others remained committed to the principle of autonomy and focused on grassroots activism. After the dark years of the German Autumn and its aftermath, the early 1980s were characterized by a 'new positive emphasis on political actions'.[91] In the first half of the 1980s, millions of people took to the streets to protest against the deployment of more nuclear weapons in Western Europe, which had been proposed by the North Atlantic Treaty Organization (NATO) in December 1979. Women on both sides of the Berlin Wall were directly affected by a growing militarization, and have played an active role in protests against rearmament plans and the deployment of nuclear weapons in Germany. One of the most active groups in the GDR was Women for Peace (*Frauen für den Frieden*), which had formed in 1982 in response to the government's decision to draft women into the military. Although the group faced constant surveillance and repression by state authorities, it was able to create networks of resistance that reached well beyond the iron curtain.

Women's peace groups in East and West Germany have developed feminist critiques of militarism and war. The historian Belinda Davis rightly emphasizes that the West German peace movement mobilized more feminists than the campaign against the abortion ban in the 1970s, and 'vast new populations constituted themselves as "feminist" – if often in contradiction with one another'.[92] Indeed, while many feminists argued that war and violence were inherently masculine and viewed women primarily or exclusively as victims of patriarchal violence, others emphatically rejected such claims. Most groups in the women's peace movement in Germany and in other countries drew primarily or exclusively on forms of protest and civil disobedience that they regarded as peaceful, but the activities of some groups were highly provocative and clearly intended to disrupt military operations. In 1983, a group of women set up a camp in the Hunsrück area in Rhineland-Palatinate to protest against the deployment of ninety-six cruise missiles at a local military base. The Women's Resistance Camp (*Frauenwiderstandscamp*) in 1983 was the first of eleven annual protest gatherings, which attracted up to two thousand women from West Germany and neighbouring countries.[93] According to Christiane Leidinger, the women engaged in a range of protest activities, and some were highly confrontational: 'They held vigils, spent nights in military bunkers, disturbed ceremonies and military manoeuvres, occupied construction cranes on the military base, carried out acts of sabotage on construction sites, blocked access roads, threw rugs on NATO-fences to access the base, put up memorial plaques at war cemeteries, demonstrated in villages, produced banners and flyers, sprayed political slogans on military barracks, and so much more.'[94]

Authorities responded to these activities with legal action and a wave of police repression: participants in the protests in 1984, for example, were charged with aggravated trespass, criminal damage, assault, civil disorder and a number of other offences.[95] Despite all tactical and political disagreements, activists in the New Women's Movement were united in their opposition to nuclear arms. When it came to other central questions, there was considerably less agreement. Some of the most disputed questions in feminist circles in the FRG in the 1980s included: Should women aspire to achieving equality to men in all regards (e.g. should they demand the right to join the military)? How can feminists account for forms of oppression and violence that many women in the FRG experienced in addition to gender-based discrimination in society? How can feminists address and tackle forms of discrimination and marginalization within the women's movement? And, how can they form alliances with women across national borders and political divisions to challenge these and other forms of oppression?

Lesbian activists, women from ethnic and religious minority groups and disabled women have been active participants in feminist protests in the FRG, and they have played a key role in addressing the questions of differences among women and intersecting forms of oppression in the New Women's Movement. As a result of their critical interventions and efforts to build independent networks, the German women's movement became noticeably more diverse and varied. Although these networks can be traced back further in history, they reached a new quality and visibility in the 1980s. A crucial moment in the formation of the German disability movement was the so-called crip tribunal,[96] which took place in Dortmund in 1981 on the occasion of the UN International

Year of Disabled Persons. According to Heike Raab, the tribunal in 1981 and the first national gathering of 'crip women' in 1982 in Marburg have inspired disabled women from across the country to form groups in which they could articulate and analyse the specific experiences of discrimination and violence that they made as women with disabilities.[97] In the same year, lesbian groups from West Germany and Berlin formed the umbrella organization 'Lesbian Circle' (*Lesbenring*) to better represent and defend their interests as lesbian women. In March 1984, migrant women organized the First Joint Women's Congress Against the Particular Oppression of Migrant Girls and Women (*Erster Gemeinsamer Kongress gegen die besondere Unterdrückung von ausländischen Mädchen und Frauen*) to draw attention to the multiple forms of discrimination and violence that they faced as female immigrants in the FRG. In the mid-1980s, Afro-German women began to set up their own platforms and networks (some of which are discussed in chapter 5).

Despite their different focal points, these groups and networks had a number of things in common: They provided platforms for women whose voices had been marginalized in German society and in the New Women's Movement. They were inspired by and associated with similar movements in a range of other countries and were profoundly transnational in scope. Rather than seeing gender-based oppression as a universal category that affected all women in the same way, they drew attention to the complex interplay of multiple forms of oppression and discrimination. The actors involved built activist networks and alliances that reached far beyond feminist circles. The New Women's Movement benefited from this process in two ways: on the one hand, the movement became more diverse, and feminist activists developed approaches to oppression and solidarity that paid greater attention to differences and inequalities among women; on the other hand, a growing number of women and men outside of the movement developed an interest in feminist ideas and campaigns.

The 1980s saw a wave of militant protest and acts of political violence with an explicitly feminist agenda. A significant part of these attacks was carried out by the radical women's group Red Zora, whose history and ideology will be discussed in more detail in the following chapter. Although most groups within the New Women's Movement opposed the use of confrontational and violent tactics for ethical and political reasons, the attacks discussed in the following chapters illustrate that some feminists made no secret of their 'joy' about some of the group's activities. A few women went as far as carrying out similar attacks.

Some of the most vocal supporters of the Red Zora and of feminist militancy were women in the Autonomen movement. Due to its heterogeneous and diffuse nature, the movement defies easy classification. According to George Katsiaficas, its 'political terrain lies somewhere between that of the Greens and the RAF, somewhere between parliamentary participation and guerrilla struggle'.[98] Like groups in the New Women's Movement, the Autonomen opposed central leadership structures, and fought for individual freedom, political self-determination, and organizational autonomy. One of the distinguishing features of the Autonomen movement was, as I have highlighted in the introduction, that militancy was not just a strategic question but played a crucial role in the self-image and public perception of the Autonomen movement. Patricia Melzer shows that women's groups in the Autonomen movement shared this militant stance, and at least some of them tried to combine autonomist and feminist principles.[99]

Developments since the 1990s

While militancy has remained a driving force in the Autonomen movement, confrontational and violent protest tactics have played a marginal role in the German women's movement since the early 1990s. This period saw drastic political changes that had a profound impact on feminist activism in the FRG and that have contributed to a reconfiguration of the continuum of feminist militancy. In 1990, East Germany joined the Federal Republic of Germany after more than forty years of separation. Although it is a subject of controversial debate whether the GDR should be understood as a totalitarian regime, there can be no doubt that life in the GDR was characterized by extensive surveillance, state repression and a profound lack of political freedom. Nevertheless, it is important to highlight that in many ways, women in the GDR were better off than their West German counterparts: the state propagated full-time employment for women and built the necessary infrastructure (e.g. nurseries); it was fairly straightforward for women in the GDR to get a divorce or to have an abortion, and there was no stigma attached to either. Already in the late 1980s, women in the political opposition in the GDR voiced the concern that reunification would have a negative impact on the situation of women in East Germany. Toward the end of 1989, 'women organized in virtually every city in the GDR'.[100] On 3 December 1989, more than 1200 women came together at the Volksbühne (People's Theatre) in Berlin, and founded the Independent Women's League (Unabhängiger Frauenverband) to represent the interests of women. One of the most influential contributions to the discussion at the gathering was Ina Merkel's manifesto, 'You can't make a state without women' (*Ohne Frauen ist kein Staat zu machen*). Merkel's statement, which was read by the actor Walfriede Schmidt, was an urgent warning that reunification would result in a backlash against women in East Germany. 'To put it bluntly', stated Merkel, reunification means: 'women back to the kitchen. It means: fighting once again for the right to employment, for a nursery school place, for school meals.'[101]

The consequences of the 'peaceful revolution' in the GDR exceeded some of the worst fears of feminists in the GDR. Poverty and unemployment among women in the former GDR rose dramatically.[102] Despite all efforts, East and West German feminists had little influence on the unification process, and found it difficult to find common ground for joint campaigns in the 1990s.[103] Although a range of new women's movements and feminist networks emerged in the 1990s, German reunification brought about the end of the New Women's

Movement. Since it was based on the experiences and aspirations of women in West Germany, it rose and declined with the Cold War. Women from the former GDR and from West Germany had different ideas about the scope and aims of feminist protest, and they had to re-orient themselves in a united country and in an increasingly connected and globalized world. In this context, many feminists pinned great hopes on global policies, and promoted reformist rather than confrontational tactics.

In 1995, women's groups from across the country drafted a joint statement for the fourth UN World Conference on Women in Beijing. Although most of the topics discussed – violence against women, sexual self-determination and reproductive choice, environmentalism and female poverty – had been recurring themes in the German women's movement for more than a century, the statement is expressive of a new transnational perspective on these issues.[104] The UN conference in Beijing and other global events in the 1990s led to new alliances and conflicts among feminist activists and scholars. While sharing a commitment to end violence against women and girls and to improve their social and legal status, participants in the Beijing conference had very different cultural backgrounds, political agendas and religious views. A number of central demands were not incorporated into the Beijing declaration from September 1995, because they met fierce resistance from some participants, and some of the terminology used was highly controversial. The use of the term 'gender' was particularly contentious.

In Germany, the term gained popularity in the 1990s. Particularly influential in this context was Butler's 1990 book *Gender Trouble: Feminism and the Subversion of Identity*, which was translated into German in 1991. As the translation of the title of Butler's book, *Das Unbehagen der Geschlechter*, illustrates, there is no German equivalent for 'gender'. The fact that the book received a mixed reception among feminist academics in the FRG did not impair the popularity of Butler's ideas – she became one of the icons of queer feminism in the FRG. Queer activism, theory and art seek to challenge practices normalizing the gender dichotomy, heteronormativity and multiple and intersectional discrimination. Unlike in the United States, where activists in the militant 'Bash Back' movement publicly declared that queer people had to use violence to defend themselves against the multiple forms of violence and discrimination they experienced in everyday life, there were no public statements of this kind by queer groups in the FRG.[105] Nevertheless, queer feminism remains one of the most diverse and vibrant strands of contemporary German feminism. In a book with the telling title *Welcome to Plurality*, feminist activists and scholars give an overview of this and a range of other feminist movements in Germany, including Islamic feminism, Marxist feminism, postcolonial feminism, Afro-German feminism and feminist disability studies.[106] Despite all claims that feminism is dead and that we are now living in a 'post-feminist' era, the authors show that there are thousands of young people in Germany who adopt and adapt feminist ideas and principles.

At the beginning of the twenty-first century, there is still a thriving feminist protest culture in Germany, and every year thousands of people take to the streets to protest against sexual violence, racism and sexism. Prominent examples include transnational events and movements like the 'slut-walk', 'laDIYfest' and 'International Women's Day' on 8 March. In recent years, a growing number of activists in German-speaking countries have begun to refer to the International Women's Day in the tradition of socialist feminists as '*Frauenkampftag*'. This name – the German word '*Kampf*' can be translated as 'struggle' or 'combat' – and the political self-understanding of some of the groups involved suggest that there are still (or again) feminist groups who believe that the struggle against sexist oppression requires a confrontational attitude.[107] Like in previous decades, feminist militancy manifests itself today in colourful protests, some of which involve property damage or clashes with police. Yet, the continuum of feminist militancy has evolved in response to technological developments and political changes. Many feminists are now using social media to plan and coordinate protest campaigns, and arson attacks and bombings with a feminist agenda seem to be a thing of the past. During the Cold War, discussions about feminist militancy evolved along different lines. As the next chapter illustrates, the continuum of militancy in this period needs to be understood within the context of the anti-authoritarian student movement and left-wing terrorism.

Notes

1. See e.g. Schlaeger and Vedder-Shults, 'The West German Women's Movement'; Altbach, 'The New German Women's Movement'; Heinrich-Böll-Stiftung and Feministisches Institut, *Wie weit flog die Tomate?*; Schulz, *Der Lange Atem der Provokation*; Notz, *Warum flog die Tomate?*; Hertrampf, 'Ein Tomatenwurf und seine Folgen'; Gerhard, 'Frauenbewegung'; Lenz, *Die Neue Frauenbewegung*.
2. H. Sander (1999), 'Rede des Aktionsrates zur Befreiung der Frauen', in A. Conrad and K. Michalik (eds), *Quellen zur Geschichte der Frauen*, Stuttgart: Reclam, 358–68.
3. Ibid.
4. Ibid.
5. 'stand da, mit ihrem grünen Kleid und den roten Haaren und dem dicken Bauch, und sah wunderbar aus. Und dann schmiß sie nacheinander zwei Pfund Suppentomaten, zuerst in vollkommene Stille und dann in Tumult'; H. Sander (1999), 'Der Seele ist das Gemeinsame eigen, das sich mehrt', in Heinrich-Böll-Stiftung und Feministisches Institut (eds), *Wie weit flog die Tomate? Eine 68erinnen-Gala der Reflexion*, Berlin: Heinrich-Böll-Stiftung, 43–56, here 52–53.
6. U. Helwerth (1988), 'Von der Panthertante zur Quotilde', interview with Sigrid Damm-Rüger, Margit Eschenbach and Ingrid Schmidt-Harzbach, *die tageszeitung*, 13 September 1988.
7. I. Lehmann (1999), 'Auf der Hut vor Nebenwidersprüchen', in Heinrich-Böll-Stiftung und Feministisches Institut (eds), *Wie weit flog die Tomate? Eine 68erinnen-Gala der Reflexion*, Berlin: Heinrich-Böll-Stiftung, 57–64, 64.

8. For a detailed discussion of this process, see Richter, 'Die Außerparlamentarische Opposition', 35–55.
9. U. Meinhof, 'Frauen im SDS oder in eigener Sache', *konkret*, 7 October 1968.
10. 'Die Konsequenz aus Frankfurt kann nur sein, daß mehr Frauen über ihre Probleme nachdenken, sich organisieren, ihre Sachen aufarbeiten und formulieren lernen und dabei von ihren Männern erstmal nichts anderes verlangen, als daß sie sie in dieser Sache in Ruhe lassen und ihre tomatenverkleckerten Hemden mal alleine waschen'; ibid.
11. Meinhof, 'Frauen im SDS'.
12. K. Schulz (2008), 'Ohne Frauen keine Revolution. 68er und Neue Frauenbewegung'. Retrieved 16 February 2015 from http://www.bpb.de/geschichte/deutsche-geschichte/68er-bewegung/51859/frauen-und-68?p=all.
13. M. Dehnavi (2013), *Das politisierte Geschlecht : biographische Wege zum Studentinnenprotest von '1968' und zur Neuen Frauenbewegung*, Bielefeld: transcript, 33.
14. The Provo movement was a political and artistic movement that tried to provoke consumers and political leaders in the Netherlands with spectacular happenings and disruptive protest. For a more detailed discussion, see R. Kempton (2007), *Provo: Amsterdam's Anarchist Revolt*, Brooklyn, NY: Autonomedia. M. Steffen (1998), 'SDS, Weiberräte, Feminismus?' in W. Kraushaar (ed.), *Frankfurter Schule und Studentenbewegung: Von der Flaschenpost zum Molotowcocktail 1946–1995*, vol. 3, Frankfurt: Rogner & Bernhard bei Zweitausendeins, 126–40.
15. FMT, PD-FB 01, 1968.
16. 'Befreit die sozialistischen Eminenzen von ihren bürgerlichen Schwänzen!'; ibid.
17. For two contrasting views, see Lehmann, 'Auf der Hut vor Nebenwidersprüchen', and Helwerth, 'Von der Panthertante zur Quotilde'.
18. See, e.g. M. Steffen (1984), 'Dekonstruktion feministischer Legendenbildung. Weiberräte contra Feminismus – Anfänge der autonomen Frauenbewegung', *die tageszeitung*, 17 October 1984.
19. FFBIZ, A Rep 400, Berlin 20 Aktionsrat, 'Resolution für die 23. O. DK des SDS. Vorgelegt vom Aktionsrat zur Befreiung der Frauen Berlin'.
20. Lenz, *Die Neue Frauenbewegung*, 23.
21. Susanne Rinner offers an insightful discussion of Morgner's Salman trilogy in the context of the cultural memory of 1968. S. Rinner (2013), *The German Student Movement and the Litarary Imagination: Transnational Memories of Protest and Dissent*, New York and Oxford: Berghahn Books, 67.
22. FFBIZ, A Rep 400, Berlin 20 Aktionsrat, 'Kurze Selbstdarstellung über die Entwicklung des Aktionsrats der Frauen', 1.
23. Ibid.
24. Sander (1999), 'Der Seele ist das Gemeinsame eigen, das sich mehrt', 47.
25. As Gisela Notz highlights, these anti-authoritarian child-care centres were often organized in vacant shops; Notz, 'Die autonomen Frauenbewegungen', 143.
26. C. Lord and R.N. Watkins (1973), *Storefront Day Care Centers: The Radical Berlin Experiment*, Boston: Beacon Press; J. Zipes (1973), 'Educating, Miseducating, Re-Educating Children: A Report on Attempts to Desocialize the Capitalist Socialization Process in West Germany', *New German Critique*, 142–59.
27. FFBIZ, A Rep 400, Berlin 20 Aktionsrat, Handapparat Tröger, Rundbrief vom 22. Juni 1968, 3.
28. The books were read and discussed in German. The original titles are *Die Frau und der Sozialismus, Der Ursprung der Familie, des Privateigenthums und des Staats* and *Zur Geschichte der proletarischen Frauenbewegung Deutschlands*.
29. FFBIZ, A Rep 400, Berlin 20 Aktionsrat, Handapparat Tröger.
30. Ibid.
31. Silies, 'Ein, zwei, viele Bewegungen?' 97.
32. For one of the first and most striking examples of such publications, see *Der Baader-Meinhof-Report. Dokumente, Analysen, Zusammenhänge*, 1972, Mainz: Hase und Koehler.

33. Hanshew, *Terror and Democracy*, 187.
34. Café Kranzler is a popular meeting point and tourist attraction in the centre of Berlin. It is located on the Kurfürstendamm, which became the scene of numerous student protests in the 1960s.
35. 'Wir aus dem Aktionsrat haben uns selbst als sehr militant empfunden, auch auf Demonstrationen. Das war Teilhabe an dem kleinen Machtrausch. Wenn wir in unseren farbenprächtigen Kleidern die Kreuzung vor dem "Kranzler" blockierten – dann hatten wir das Gefühl, die Straßen gehören uns'; Helwerth, 'Von der Panthertante zur Quotilde'.
36. 'Eier von links', *Der Spiegel*, 14 February 1966, 48.
37. Ibid.
38. Dehnavi, *Das politisierte Geschlecht*, 41–42.
39. 'Unsere Gedanken waren ein ganz merkwürdiger Cocktail: ein bißchen Marx, Lenin, Bakunin, Mao. Aber auch Rosa Luxemburg. Dann natürlich noch die verschiedenen Emanzipationstheorien, Wilhelm Reich und die Sexpol-Bewegung und eben Feminismus'; Helwerth, 'Von der Panthertante zur Quotilde'.
40. Dehnavi, *Das politisierte Geschlecht*, 42.
41. Wilma Aden-Grossmann's biography *Monika Seifert: Pädagogin der antiautoritären Erziehung* offers a detailed account of Seifert's life and work.
42. S. Binder, 'Erst das Kind und dann die Politik', *Die Zeit*, 24 January 1969.
43. The German titles were *Zur Geschichte der proletarischen Frauenbewegung Deutschlands*, *Der Freiraum* and *Frauenjahrbuch*.
44. Founded in Ukraine in 2008 by Anna Huzol and other activists, Femen has made headlines with topless protests across the world. It remains the subject of a controversial debate whether Femen could and should be considered a feminist organization. While Femen supporters claim that their 'method is to "defend with their breasts sexual and social equality in the world"', feminist critics claim that they 'simply . . . organise publicity stunts where they bare their breasts to capture the attention of the mainstream media'. T. O'Keefe (2014), 'My Body is My Manifesto! SlutWalk, FEMEN and Femmenist Protest', *Feminist Review* (107), 1–19, 8.
45. According to *Zeit* journalist Sepp Binder, the women were chanting: 'Meine Herren, heute sehen Sie uns nackt hier stehen / und wir zeigen unsere Brüste für jeden / Ihr, die Ihr voll Verdrängung und Komplexe seid / wißt, daß wer'n Weib sieht, schon verschoben ist / drum duldet Ihr uns nicht in Eurer Näh' / Ihr haltet Euch bei Tage an die Bibel / und streichelt lüstern höchstens mal das BGB / für uns gibt's Knast – für Euch ist das Moral.' S. Binder, 'Barbusig vor der Barriere', *Die Zeit*, no. 51, 20 December 1968.
46. T. Stelzer, 'Die Zumutung des Fleisches', *Der Tagesspiegel*, 7 December 2003.
47. Della Porta, *Social Movements*, 103.
48. Revolutionärer Kampf received widespread, albeit dubious, fame when it became known in 2001 that Joschka Fischer, at the time foreign minister and vice chancellor in the cabinet of Gerhard Schröder, was a former member of the group and had been involved in violent clashes with the police on the streets of Frankfurt.
49. 'Die Herrschaft der Schwänze hat ihre Grenze – Frauen gemeinsam sind stark', 'Im Kaufhaus, Büro und am Band, Frauen werden militant'; C. Bender (ed.) (1973), *Die Frauengruppe im Revolutionärer Kampf*, Frankfurt, 15, 45.
50. FMT, FB.05.175, 'Protestaktion gegen die Wahl der "Miß-Teenager-Beine" in Frankfurt'.
51. Ibid.
52. 'Abtreibung: Massenmord oder Privatsache?', *Der Spiegel*, 21 May 1973, 38–58.
53. Margit Eschenbach in Helwerth, 'Von der Panthertante zur Quotilde'.
54. Schwarzer, *So fing es an! 10 Jahre Frauenbewegung*, 40–41.
55. 'Wir deklarieren nicht den Mann zum Klassenfeind, wir können allerdings auch nicht umhin, die Auseinandersetzung mit der Härte zu führen, die notwendig ist, um ihm begreiflich zu machen, dass er sich in vielerlei Hinsicht zum Agenten des Klassenfeindes macht, einfach, indem er uns hindert, die Arbeit zu leisten, die geleistet werden muss, um eine sozialistische

Gesellschaft zu schaffen'; FFBIZ, A Rep 400, Berlin 20 Aktionsrat, 'Kurze Selbstdarstellung über die Entwicklung des Aktionsrats der Frauen', 7.
56. 'Es war nie die Absicht der Weiberräte des SDS, die Frauenwut auf feministische Mühlen zu lenken'; Steffen, 'Dekonstruktion feministischer Legendenbildung', 10.
57. Ibid.
58. See e.g. Schwarzer, *So fing es an*; Lenz, *Die Neue Frauenbewegung*; Frevert, *Frauen-Geschichte*.
59. Schulz, *Der lange Atem der Provokation*, 85.
60. Lenz, *Die Neue Frauenbewegung*, 71.
61. FMT, PD-FB 01, 1972, 'Protokoll zum Plenum des Bundesfrauenkongresses am 12. März 1972 in Frankfurt/M'.
62. Schulz, *Der Lange Atem der Provokation*, 29.
63. Ibid., 143.
64. See also Frevert, *Frauen-Geschichte*, 279.
65. K. Schulz (2004), 'Echoes of Provocation: 1968 and the Women's Movements in France and Germany', in G.R. Horn and P. Kenney (eds), *Transnational Moments of Change: Europe 1945, 1968, 1989*, Lanham: Rowman and Littlefield, 137–54, 140.
66. F. Haug (1986), 'The Women's Movement in West Germany', *New Left Review*, 50–74, 59.
67. Y.P. Doderer (1999), *Never Give Up! Zur Neuen Frauenbewegung*, Munich: Kunstverein, 6; Hertrampf, 'Ein Tomatenwurf und seine Folgen'.
68. C. Perincioli (2015), *Berlin wird feministisch. Das Beste, was von der 68er Bewegung blieb*, Berlin: Querverlag, 88.
69. Dehnavi, *Das politisierte Geschlecht*, 43.
70. Lenz, *Die Neue Frauenbewegung*, 73.
71. FMT, Z-Ü101.
72. 'Frauenoffensive', *Chronik der Neuen Frauenbewegung*. Retrieved 20 December 2015 from http://www.frauenmediaturm.de/themen-portraets/chronik-der-neuen-frauenbewegung/1975/frauenoffensive-presseinformation/.
73. A. Fiddler (2004), 'Subjectivity and women's writing of the 1970s and early 1980s', in G. Bartram (ed.), *The Cambridge Companion to the Modern German Novel*, 1st ed., Cambridge: Cambridge University Press. Retrieved 24 July 2015 from http://dx.doi.org/10.1017/CCOL0521482534, 249–265, 250.
74. '1977', *Chronik der Neuen Frauenbewegung*. Retrieved 20 December 2015 from http://www.frauenmediaturm.de/themen-portraets/chronik-der-neuen-frauenbewegung/1977/.
75. 'Kampf um Emma', *Der Spiegel*, 29 November 1976, 219–21.
76. E. Zellmer (2011), *Töchter der Revolte? Frauenbewegung und Feminismus in den 1970er Jahren in München*, Munich: Oldenbourg Verlag, 228.
77. For a detailed discussion, see Frauenzentrum (ed.), (1976), *Gewalt gegen Frauen in Ehe, Psychiatrie, Gynäkologie, Vergewaltigung, Beruf, Film und was Frauen dagegen tun: Beiträge zum Internationalen Tribunal über Gewalt gegen Frauen, Brüssel März 1976*, Berlin: Agit Druck.
78. See e.g. E. Fischer, B. Lehmann and K. Stoffl (1977), *Gewalt gegen Frauen*, Cologne: Kiepenheuer & Witsch; I. Boettcher (1978), *Frauen gegen Männergewalt: Berliner Frauenhaus für Mißhandelte Frauen*, Berlin: Frauenselbstverlag; Notruf und Beratung für vergewaltigte Frauen (ed.) (1979), *Gewalt gegen Frauen und was Frauen dagegen tun*, Berlin: Wagenbach.
79. Notz, 'Die autonomen Frauenbewegungen', 138–39.
80. 'Wir haben den Artikel geschrieben, weil es hauptsächlich nur Beispiele von Leid, Erniedrigung, Ausbeutung und Zerstörung von Frauen gibt, jedoch sehr wenig Möglichkeiten aufgezeigt werden, wie Frauen sich wehren können. Wir wollen andere Frauen anturnen, ähnliche oder ganz andere Formen der Gegenwehr zu entwickeln'; 'Antwort auf eine Vergewaltigung', in Jahrbuchgruppe des Münchner Frauenzentrums (eds), *Frauenjahrbuch '76*, Munich: Frauenoffensive, 1976, 216.
81. S. Plogstedt (1978), 'Die Gewalt in unseren Köpfen: Kölner Kongreß', *Courage: Berliner Frauenzeitung* 6(3), 7–8.

82. T. Bührmann (1978), 'Kongress in Frankfurt: die Arbeitsgruppen; was heißt hier "politisch"?' *Courage: Berliner Frauenzeitung* 1978, 5; S. Plogstedt (1978), 'Rückzug der Frauenbewegung?' *Courage: Berliner Frauenzeitung* 1978, 7.
83. C. Davenport (2007), 'State Repression and Political Order', *Annual Review of Political Science* 10(2007), 2.
84. I. Bandhauer-Schöffmann (2009), '"Emanzipation mit Bomben und Pistolen"? Feministinnen und Terroristinnen in deutschsprachigen Sicherheitsdiskursen der 1970er Jahre', *L'Homme* (20), 84.
85. 'Wir nehmen uns das elementare Recht, in der Erfindung des Glücks nicht dauernd durch Mord und Totschlag. Gefangennahme und Gefängnis, Fahndung und Hetze behindert zu werden'; 'Aufruf an alle Frauen zur Erfindung des Glücks', *Courage: Berliner Frauenzeitung* 1977, 10.
86. 'Hört, wir verkünden hiermit folgende große Wahrheiten: Die Macht lässt sich nicht erschießen. Die Gegenmacht lässt sich nicht erschießen. Erschießen lassen sich nur Menschen'; ibid.
87. Gerhard, 'Frauenbewegung', 204.
88. Lenz, *Die Neue Frauenbewegung*, 22.
89. C. Wippermann (2012), '25 Jahre Bundesfrauenministerium. Von der Frauenpolitik zu einer nachhaltigen Politik der fairen Chancen für Frauen und Männer', Berlin: Bundesministerium für Familie, Senioren, Frauen und Jugend, 7. Retrieved 20 December 2015 from http://www.bmfsfj.de/RedaktionBMFSFJ/Broschuerenstelle/Pdf-Anlagen/25-Jahre-Bundesfrauenministerium,property=pdf,bereich=bmfsfj,sprache=de,rwb=true.pdf.
90. S. Plogstedt (1979), 'Wir haben gegründet und sind von Herzen froh darüber: Frauenpartei', *Courage: Berliner Frauenzeitung* 4(12), 4–5.
91. Della Porta, *Social Movements*, 43.
92. B. Davis (2005), '"Women's Strength Against Crazy Male Power": Gendered Language in the West German Peace Movement of the 1980s', in J.A. Davy, K. Hagemann and U. Kätzel (eds), *Frieden – Gewalt – Geschlecht. Friedens- und Konfliktforschung als Geschlechterforschung*, Essen: Klartext Verlag, 244.
93. C. Leidinger (2010), '11 Jahre Widerstand Frauenwiderstandscamps in Reckershausen im Hunsrück von 1983 bis 1993', in *Wissenschaft & Frieden* 2010-2, 47–50. Retrieved 11 November 2015 from http://www.wissenschaft-und-frieden.de/seite.php?artikelID=1620.
94. 'Sie hielten Mahnwachen, übernachteten an Bunkern, störten Fahnenweihen und Manöver, schnitten Absperrungszäune durch, besetzten Baukräne auf Militärgelände, sabotierten militärische Baustellen, blockierten Zufahrtsstraßen, überwanden Nato-Draht mit Teppichen, stellten Gedenktafeln an Kriegsgräbern auf, demonstrierten in Dörfern, produzierten Transparente und Flugblätter, sprühten Parolen im militärischen Absperrgebiet und vieles andere mehr'; ibid.
95. Ibid.
96. Similarly to queer activists in the 1990s, disabled groups tried to appropriate and re-signify the derogative term '*Krüppel*' (cripple).
97. H. Raab (2014), 'Dis/Ability, Feminismus und Geschlecht', in Y. Franke et al. (eds), *Feminismen heute. Positionen in Theorie und Praxis*, Bielefeld: transcript, 101–14, 104.
98. G. Katsiaficas (1997), *The Subversion of Politics: European Autonomous Social Movements and the Decolonialization of Everyday Life*. Atlantic Highlands, NJ: Humanities Press, 277.
99. Melzer, 'Frauen gegen Imperialismus und Patriarchat', 162.
100. B. Young (1999), *Triumph of the Fatherland: German Unification and the Marginalization of Women*, Ann Arbor: University of Michigan Press, 3.
101. 'es hieße überspitzt gesagt: Frauen zurück an den Herd. Es hieße: wieder kämpfen um das Recht auf Arbeit, kämpfen um einen Platz für den Kindergarten, um die Schulspeisung'; I. Merkel (2010), 'Ohne Frauen ist kein Staat zu machen', in I. Lenz (ed.), *Die Neue Frauenbewegung in Deutschland: Abschied vom kleinen Unterschied: Eine Quellensammlung*. 2nd rev. edn, Wiesbaden: VS-Verlag, 879.

102. I. Lenz, *Die Neue Frauenbewegung*, 955.
103. For a detailed discussion of the relationship between feminists from East and West Germany in the unification process, see Young, *Triumph of the Fatherland*.
104. For details of the statement, see Lenz, *Die Neue Frauenbewegung*, 923–34.
105. K. Karcher (2016), 'How (not) to "Hollaback": Towards a transnational debate on the "Red Zora" and militant tactics in the feminist struggle against gender-based violence', *Feminist Media Studies* 16(1), 80.
106. Y. Franke et al. (eds) (2014), *Feminismen heute: Positionen in Theorie und Praxis*. Bielefeld: transcript.
107. The Hanover-based group Riot statt Rosen (Riot not Roses) is an illustrative example. On their website, the activists involved write: 'In our view, fighting for feminism means that we have to attack sexist and racist power structures' ('Feministisch kämpfen bedeutet für uns, sexistische und rassistsiche Herrschaftsverhältnisse anzugreifen'). Retrieved on 18 June 2016 from http://frauenkampftag2015.de/.

Chapter 2

TERRORISM, FEMINISM AND THE POLITICS OF REPRESENTATION

Speculation over the links between the New Women's Movement and female participation in left-wing terrorism in West Germany can be traced back to 1970 and the first incident of an armed attack by a militant leftist group. On 14 May 1970, a group of women and one man liberated at gunpoint the prisoner Andreas Baader from the German Central Institute for Social Issues in Berlin. Retrospectively, Astrid Proll – who drove the getaway car – noted that the event 'marked the birth of the RAF'.[1] As Jeremy Varon emphasizes, 'the birth of the Red Army Faction was both slow and sudden'.[2] Indeed, although evidence suggests that the attack was rather spontaneous and ill prepared, the founding members of the RAF did not radicalize overnight. Before participating in the attack, most of the perpetrators had been actively involved in the student and protest movement in West Germany, where discussions about violence and counter-violence intensified in the late 1960s as a response to police repression during demonstrations and polemical attacks in the media.

In 1968, Andreas Baader and Gudrun Ensslin were among the first people in the radical Left in West Germany to carry out a politically motivated arson attack. Together with two acquaintances, Horst Söhnlein and Thorwald Proll, Baader and Ensslin started fires in two department stores in Frankfurt on the night of 2 April 1968. Shortly after the arson attack, the police arrested all four perpetrators. After a few months in jail and a spectacular court case, they were sentenced to three years in prison in October 1968.[3] One of the lawyers defending the arsonists was Horst Mahler, who – after playing an active role in violent protests in Berlin – was charged with different crimes himself.[4] In

---

Notes for this section begin on page 63.

detention, Ensslin gave an interview to Ulrike Meinhof.[5] Apparently, the writer was impressed by Ensslin and considered her a 'partner in thought' (*Partnerin im Denken*).[6] Due to an appeal on points of law, Baader, Ensslin, Söhnlein and Proll were temporarily released in June 1969. Restored to freedom, the couple started to work on a social project with young people in Frankfurt. However, in November of the same year the Federal Court of Justice refused the appeal, which meant that the four perpetrators had to spend up to twenty-two more months in prison.[7]

Söhnlein and Proll followed the demand note by the Federal Court of Justice and surrendered to the police. Ensslin and Baader, however, refused to serve the rest of their sentence and went underground. This choice implied for both a radical break with their previous lives but also with legality and society as a whole.[8] After travelling for several weeks in France and Italy, Baader and Ensslin returned – accompanied by Thorwald Proll's sister Astrid – to Germany. In March 1970, they moved into Meinhof's flat in Berlin. There, the couple joined forces with Mahler, who was as keen as Baader and Ensslin to found a militant underground organization. According to Proll, the group consisted in spring 1970 of six or seven people and was dominated by women.[9] Their first efforts to form an organization based on the model of the Latin American urban guerrilla in Berlin, however, ended abruptly when Baader was arrested on 4 April 1970.[10]

Soon after Baader's arrest, Ensslin and Mahler began to make plans for his liberation. Since Ensslin was still wanted by the police for arson, she could not contact Baader openly. Meinhof, however, had no criminal record and was a respected journalist. She requested to meet the prisoner in the German Central Institute for Social Issues in Berlin to do literary research for a co-authored book about marginalized adolescents.[11] The governor of the prison in Berlin Tegel refused this request at first, but eventually gave his consent after an intervention by Mahler.[12] It was, after all, not exceptional for detainees to participate in activities outside prison under the surveillance of police officers. According to an unofficial report, 1012 detainees from prisons in Berlin were escorted to external events in 1969, and only 9 of them attempted to escape.[13]

At 9:45 AM on 14 May, Baader arrived at the library in the company of two male police officers. Meinhof awaited him with the documents she had requested in the reading room.[14] In an internal report, a librarian stated that he found nothing suspicious about the guests. According to the employee of the Institute, the 'pale' (*blasse*) prisoner looked 'very harmless' (*sehr harmlos*) and smoked a lot.[15] In front of the reading room, he noticed 'two young girls, who . . . , if I remember rightly, wore green glasses, who seemed strangely nervous and stressed, and who both had a notably large bag next to them at all times'.[16] The 'nervous girls' were Meinhof's acquaintances Irene Goergens and Ingrid Schubert, who had registered under false names, and pretended to look for literature for a research project on therapies for criminal youths. Employees of the Institute asked them to wait in the entrance hall for as long as Baader and Meinhof were working in the reading room.[17]

At approximately 11:00 AM, the young women took guns out of their bags and opened the front door for a third intruder. This person was of male sex and wore a balaclava that showed only his eyes.[18] Initially, the police suspected that the man was the artist and journalist Peter Homann, a friend of Meinhof's. Later investigations, however, revealed that the third intruder was the 31-year-old mechanic Hans-Jürgen Bäcker.[19] Attracted by the noise in the entrance hall, Georg Linke – the door attendant at the Institute – entered the scene. Without any warning, the man in the balaclava fired at him from close range, seriously wounding the 62-year-old.[20] The armed intruders proceeded to storm the reading room, where they attacked the two surprised police officers. The masked man disabled one of Baader's guards by shooting him in the face with a gas pistol.[21] The other police officer struggled with Schubert, but she managed to get away and escaped with the other group members through a window into the garden behind the library.[22] Proll waited for them nearby in a stolen car, in which the group drove away.[23]

Only a few hours after the attack, police issued an arrest warrant for Meinhof. She was charged with attempted murder and the liberation of a prisoner. Both of these crimes were said to have been committed in complicity with at least two other perpetrators.[24] The authorities chose not to specify the sex of the other participants in the attack in the arrest warrant or in other documents that they released immediately after the attack. It seems, however, that they quickly realized that women had greatly outnumbered men among Baader's liberators. Allegedly, one of the first police officers to arrive at the Institute for Social Issues on the day of the attack said: 'It seems that we are dealing primarily with a "ladies squad".'[25]

Shortly after the attack, the police initiated a thorough search that, since the armed intruders were not yet identified, focused on the only known participant in the attack: Ulrike Meinhof. Shortly after the liberation of Andreas Baader, the chief public prosecutor authorized a nationwide search with a reward of 10,000 deutschmarks (DM) for information leading to the arrest of Meinhof – the first instance of such a reward being offered in Germany since WWII.[26] A number of biographical and journalistic accounts indicate that Meinhof had not intended to play an active role in Baader's rescue and took the decision to escape with the rest of the group only in the heat of the moment.[27] Regardless of all situational and unintentional dynamics during Baader's rescue, the police investigations after the attack focused at first almost exclusively on Meinhof. The journalist was now pursued for attempted murder, and her name and face featured prominently on wanted posters on advertising pillars throughout West Germany.

Most journalists referred to Meinhof's accomplices as 'gangsters', 'masked perpetrators' (*maskierte Täter*), 'armed terrorists' (*bewaffnete Terroristen*), 'wig wearers' (*Perückenträger*) and, particularly creatively, as 'Beatle haircuts' (*Pilzköpfe*). The focus of most news reports, however, was not on the armed intruders and their behaviour during the attack. Rather, journalists speculated about the political and ideological background of Baader and Meinhof. Accounts in conservative and right-wing newspapers in particular, framed Baader as an 'APO arsonist' – a label that misleadingly associated the extra-parliamentary opposition as a whole with arson and presented Baader as a member of the New Left.[28]

Unlike Baader's arson in 1968, Meinhof's role in his rescue in 1970 required explanation, at least in the eyes of many journalists. Most articles presented Meinhof as a radical leftist author-activist. Some reports, however, attacked her on a more personal level. A *Bild* article, for instance, claimed that Meinhof's personality changed due to brain surgery in 1962. The author noted that 'Ulrike – who had always been intelligent but highly nervous and very erratic – was afterwards often absentminded. In addition to her clumsy choice of dress, she began to look unkempt.'[29] Not only did the journalist pathologize Meinhof, he also depicted her as an unpredictable woman who let herself go after her divorce. In addition, this article and several other reports depoliticized Meinhof's participation in the attack by suggesting that she had acted out of love for her 'fiancé' Baader.[30] These and other personal attacks against Meinhof in the German media confirm Gisela Diewald-Kerkmann's claim that authors presented her behaviour as irrational and pathological.

Two studies have shown that Meinhof was neither the first nor the last woman to, allegedly, 'let herself go' and resort to violence because of romantic feelings for a man. Based on an empirical analysis of articles in several major newspapers in West Germany between 1970 and 1977, Hanno Balz concludes that journalists tended to pathologize and sexualize women in the RAF and, at least initially, in particular Meinhof and Ensslin.[31] However, Balz rightly emphasizes that the association of female criminality with deviant forms of femininity and sexuality did not emerge with female participation in left-wing political terrorism but can be traced back much further in history.[32] In her study of representations of violent women in the West German press in the 1960s and 1970s, Clare Bielby comes to a similar conclusion. She finds that the image of the 'terrorist woman' in the media served 'to pathologize, feminize, and hence to discredit left-wing political violence per se' and helped 'the West German state to construct and maintain itself as rational and masculine'.[33] However, on the basis of the case of Vera Brühne, charged with incitement to murder in 1962, Bielby illustrates that 'female empowerment was causing anxiety and gender trouble long before terrorist violence and the women's movement captured the public imagination'.[34]

Although speculation over links between the emancipation of women and female violence were thus by no means limited to left-wing terrorism, they reached a new level in the public debate surrounding the RAF in the 1970s. As early as 1971, the future president of the Federal Criminal Police Office, Günther Nollau, suggested that female involvement in the RAF constituted an 'excess' of women's liberation.[35] The 1972 book *Der Baader-Meinhof-Report. Dokumente, Analysen, Zusammenhänge* went even further. It offered a pseudo-scientific analysis of data collected by the Federal Office for the Protection of the Constitution (Bundesverfassungsschutz).[36] The report suggests that women in the RAF were psychologically disturbed, lesbian or bisexual, violent and 'overemancipated' (*überemanzipiert*).[37]

Although Ulrike Meinhof's writings and the theory and practice of the RAF had an impact on militant feminist activism in the FRG in the 1970s and 1980s, the feminist image of the RAF is not the product of a feminist agenda. Rather, it reflected resentments towards the New Women's Movement in West Germany. Vojin Saša Vukadinović rightly argues that 'the female RAF member became the negative emblem of women's liberation, as West German men fearfully imagined it: armed and invisible in the underground, uncompromisingly militant in prison'.[38] Dominique Grisard's lucid analysis of the gendered discourse on left-wing terrorism in Switzerland shows that the association of feminism and female participation in political violence was not limited to West Germany. Her findings support Vukadinović's claim that the prominent role of feminism in terrorism discourses in the 1970s had more to do with a 'systematic anti-feminism of state, science, clergy and the media' than with the political stance of women in the RAF.[39] According to Grisard, anti-feminist, anti-terrorist and racist discourses at the time intersected and jointly produced an image of the female terrorist as the antithesis to the white heterosexual male citizen.[40]

The Late 1960s in Berlin: The Radical Left, Political Violence and 'Anti-Zionism'

In the late 1960s, the movement experienced an increasing fragmentation and polarization. According to a report by the Federal Office for the Protection of the Constitution, by the end of 1970, there were more than 250 radical leftist groups in the country.[41] While most of these groups were orthodox communists, there were also a few Maoist, Trotskyite and anarchist organizations. Berlin had been the centre of student protests in the 1960s, and became the hotbed of militant leftist violence in the late 1960s and early 1970s. As the student movement in West Berlin was on the decline, a less political and more hedonistic subculture emerged, which became known as the 'Berlin Underground'.[42] Against the social background of Berlin's quickly growing drug scene, a number of small militant networks such as the Black Rats (*Schwarze Ratten*) and the Central Council of the Roaming Hash Rebels (*Zentralrat der umherschweifenden Haschrebellen*) developed. Most of these networks had very short life spans and were composed of similar if not the same circles of friends and acquaintances.

While the Berlin Underground was clearly dominated by men, there were exceptions. The Women's Liberation Front (*Frauenbefreiungsfront*), for instance, was a short-lived alliance of women who promoted a violent struggle against the oppression of women in society at large and in leftist groups.[43] Taking inspiration from figures as diverse as Valerie Solanas, Emma Goldman and Leila Khaled, the Women's Liberation Front claimed in 1969: 'We fight against hierarchy, [i.e.] the domination of humans by other humans. This struggle can only be fought by women, because even the most oppressed proletarian is still also the oppressor of his wife and children and of any girl on the street.'[44] Although the members of the Women's Liberation Front and the Berlin Action Council (discussed in the previous chapter) had similar ideas about the liberation of women, they adopted different forms of action. According to a former acquaintance, two future members of the armed leftist group the Movement of June 2nd, Angela Luther and Verena Becker, were among the members of the Women's Liberation Front. They were the first activists in Berlin to carry out violent attacks against perceived patriarchal oppressors. Apparently, they attacked the property of misogynist gynaecologists with butyric acid and paint.[45]

In July 1969, militant leftist activists from Berlin and West Germany – among them a number of future members of the RAF and other armed leftist groups – gathered in the small Frankish town of Ebrach to campaign for the release of a detained comrade.[46] More than a few of the participants had personal contacts with leaders of the Popular Front for the Liberation of Palestine (PFLP). After the gathering in Erbrach, the communards Dieter Kunzelmann, Lena Conradt, Ina Siepmann, Adalbert Fichter and Georg von Rauch travelled further to Jordan and received military training in a PFLP camp (note that this was almost a year before the RAF's first visit to a Palestinian training camp).[47]

After their return, the 'Palestine Faction' (*Palästina Fraktion*) urged the formation of an urban guerrilla group in West Berlin.[48] Jointly with a few other militants in Berlin, they created the Tupamaros West Berlin (TW). As the name indicates, the group sought to follow the armed struggle of the Tupamaros in Uruguay and other revolutionary movements in the Third World. The Tupamaros West Berlin was the first self-declared urban guerrilla group in West Germany.[49] In February 1969, more than a year before the RAF committed its first attack, members of the TW made plans to kill US President Richard Nixon during a visit to West Berlin.[50] On 9 November in the same year, they planted a bomb in a Jewish community centre. Both bombings failed, probably due to dysfunctional explosive devices provided by the agent provocateur Peter Urbach.[51] Like other attacks by militant leftist groups in the late 1960s, these two actions did not claim any lives, but they illustrate that some factions in the radical Left no longer shied away from violence against people and that the RAF was neither the first nor the only leftist group to take up arms in this period.

While distancing itself emphatically from the anti-Semitism of the Third Reich, the Tupamaros West Berlin carried out an attack against a Jewish community centre on the anniversary of the Jewish pogrom in 1938. On the same night, the group painted pro-Palestinian slogans on Jewish memorials in Berlin. Apparently, the attackers felt compelled to ignore the enormous complexity of questions of anti-Semitism in the German context. In claiming responsibility, they called for an end to the 'neurotic-historicist process of coming to terms with the past'[52] and for 'true anti-fascism', by which they meant 'clear and simple solidarity with the fighting *Fedayeen*'.[53] The members of the TW considered their politics not anti-Semitic but anti-fascist and anti-Zionist.

A growing number of people in the radical Left, including most founding members of the RAF and other armed leftist groups in the FRG, saw anti-Zionism in the late 1960s as a political imperative.[54] Among other factors, the Six-Day War in June 1967 fuelled anti-Zionist tendencies in the New Left. 'The Six-Day War ... and its portrayal in the German media', writes Volker Weiss, 'caused a break between the "old" and "new" Left with regard to the attitude towards Israel.'[55] While critical of Israel's war efforts and news coverage in the West German media, groups and individuals associated with the 'old' Left emphasized the need for solidarity with Jewish people in Israel and in other parts of the world. Many people in the New Left, by contrast, considered Israel a fascist state. More than a few strongly supported Palestinian fighters and had personal contacts with leaders of the PFLP.

Drawing on some of these contacts, the founding members of the Red Army Faction and the Movement of June 2nd had learned to use weapons in Palestinian military camps in the Middle East. In the 1960s, Ulrike Meinhof had called for solidarity with the Jewish people. As part of the RAF, she openly supported fatal attacks such as the kidnapping and murder of Israeli athletes during the 1972 Olympic Games in the FRG by the militant Palestinian group Black September.[56] In a statement from November 1972, the RAF claimed that the attack in Munich was 'anti-imperialist, anti-fascist and internationalist' (*anti-imperialistisch, antifaschistisch und internationalistisch*). [57] On several occasions, members of the RAF and other armed leftist groups in the FRG carried out joint attacks with the PFLP and other militant groups in the Middle East, and members of the militant leftist network Revolutionary Cells (RC) attacked several Israeli institutions and companies in the FRG.[58] Against this background, it is understandable that the British journalist Jilian Becker labelled the RAF 'Hitler's children'.[59] The history of the RAF, as Sarah Colvin highlights, 'is a history of violence and killing that is uncomfortably difficult to separate from another history of violence and killing – the Nazi regime between 1933 and 1945'.[60] While RAF members presented themselves as both fighters against and victims of a fascist state, scholarship has critically examined the cultivation of these images.[61]

Women + Political Violence = Feminism?

To develop a better understanding of the social background and motives of those carrying out acts of political violence in the Federal Republic of Germany, the federal minister of the Interior mandated an ambitious research project. Based on police records and biographical data of 250 persons who were associated with militant leftist or rightist groups, an interdisciplinary team of researchers analysed the causes and the effects of the armed struggle in West Germany. The people in the centre of the study were men and women against whom the West German police had issued an arrest warrant for support or membership of a terrorist organization before January 1979. Of this sample, 219 people were associated with the RAF or the Movement of June 2nd, eight were members of the Revolutionary Cells and the remaining twenty-three were part of militant rightist groups.

Based on this data, sociologist Friedhelm Neidhardt estimates that militant leftist groups in West Germany carried out 385 attacks between 1968 and 1980.[62] Among the militant leftist organizations that were active in this period, the RAF pursued by far the most brutal strategy. It was responsible for forty-six of sixty-nine political assassinations and other attacks against people carried out by the left wing in the FRG between 1968 and 1980.[63] As the name 'Red Army Faction' indicates, the founding members of the group wanted to form the military wing of a not-yet existing revolutionary communist party. The RAF understood itself as avant-garde and expediting a revolution, which it expected to be carried out by the working class and other oppressed groups across the globe. Due to its ideology and theoretical background, the group quickly earned the reputation of 'Leninists with guns'.[64] While identifying with the marginalized and oppressed, most group members came from relatively privileged backgrounds. For the greater part, members of the RAF originated in the upper middle class and were current or former university students.[65] This applies in particular to female group members. According to Gerhard Schmidtchen's survey, 60 per cent of the women in militant leftist groups came from wealthy backgrounds, while this applies only to 39 per cent of their male counterparts.[66]

After the liberation of Andreas Baader, the police started a thorough search for the actors involved, which increased the pressure on the whole Left in West Berlin. In December 1971, Georg von Rauch, one of the leading figures of the TW, was killed in a shootout with plainclothes officers.[67] In January 1972, some of the remaining TW members and several other small militant leftist groups founded the MJ2. They chose the name 'Movement of June 2nd' to commemorate the killing of student Benno Ohnesorg during a demonstration in West Berlin in 1967. The founding members of the MJ2 rejected the avant-gardist position of the RAF. They identified with the '*lumpenproletariat*' and hoped to mobilize revolutionary forces in the working class by adopting a more populist line than the RAF.[68] While not all members of the MJ2 came from working-class backgrounds, there is evidence that most were younger and less privileged than members of the RAF.[69] Also, the internal structure of the group differed from that of the RAF. The RAF was a hierarchical and centralist organization and, after Baader's rescue in 1970, operated entirely underground.[70] The founding members of the MJ2, in contrast, avoided going underground for as long as possible. Moreover, they aimed to create a less hierarchical, horizontally connected network of local groups.[71]

Unlike the RAF, the MJ2 sought to focus on attacks against property rather than actions against people. However, as Della Porta highlights, they did not stick to this principle.[72] In fact, the very first attack by the newly founded group resulted in a casualty. On 2 February 1972, MJ2 members planted bombs in the British yachting club in Berlin and in two cars belonging to the Allied forces. The attack was a rather spontaneous and ill-prepared response to the events during 'Bloody Sunday' on 30 January in Northern Ireland.[73] One civilian died while trying to deactivate one of the explosive devices. This fatal accident did not keep the group from executing dozens of other attacks including bombings, abductions and bank robberies. After the first group members were arrested, the MJ2 focused – similarly to the RAF – a great part of its energy on the liberation of imprisoned comrades.[74] Many attacks continued to be of a more spontaneous nature and most did not result in casualties. Throughout its existence, the members of the MJ2 killed three people. The RAF, by contrast, was responsible for more than thirty deaths. Two years after their last strike in 1978, a portion of the group declared the end of the MJ2 and joined the RAF.[75]

According to Schmidtchen's evaluation of the previously mentioned data sample of 250 political extremists, all members of right-wing groups were male, while 33 per cent of the members of militant leftist groups were women.[76] The data suggests that 34 per cent of the members of the RAF were female and that women constituted 39 per cent of the MJ2.[77] A recent study indicates that the percentage of women in the RAF and MJ2 was significantly higher than Schmidtchen's survey suggests. Based on an analysis of wanted posters and Interpol alerts, the historian Gisela Diewald-Kerkmann concludes that women constituted 48 per cent of RAF and MJ2 members.[78]

In a study of forty-four court cases against members of the RAF and MJ2, Diewald-Kerkmann analyses public reactions to female participation in the two groups. Rather than understanding the active involvement of women in leftist political violence as a result of political considerations, Diewald-Kerkmann reasons, researchers, journalists and legal authorities have drawn on three problematic arguments to explain it. According to the first one, women are naturally inclined to use violence. Diewald-Kerkmann highlights that the journalists and legal authorities who drew on this model usually evoked stereotypical notions of femininity, for example, by depicting women in militant leftist groups as irrational, emotional and dependent on men.[79]

A second – and no less problematic – line of argumentation presents female perpetrators of violence as deviant women, i.e. morally bad, mentally ill or otherwise different from 'normal' women. This line of argumentation can be traced back to Cesare Lombroso and Guglielmo Ferrero's *Criminal Woman, the Prostitute, and the Normal Woman* (first published in 1893) and the work of other pioneers in the field of criminology.[80] Diewald-Kerkmann uses the case of Ulrike Meinhof to illustrate this line of argumentation. Several authors and public authorities have claimed that Meinhof's decision to join the armed struggle was related to brain damage caused by a surgery during her pregnancy.[81] According to this model, Meinhof was literally out of her mind.

Drawing on a third explanatory model, authors and self-proclaimed experts on female terrorism have argued that women joined militant leftist groups because they were feminists.[82] Since the early 1970s, feminist activists, journalists and scholars have firmly rejected claims that female participation in militant leftist groups was a result of the women's movement. Apart from wanting to correct factually inaccurate claims, they saw a political need to oppose a criminalization and demonization of the feminist struggle as a whole. In 1978, the editor of the feminist anthology *Frauen und Terror*, Susanne von Paczensky, pointed out that 'it is not enough to dismiss the link between terror and emancipation. For the sake of our conflicting loyalties, we have to examine it closely and carefully.'[83]

While condemning sexist attacks against women in militant leftist groups by journalists and other public authorities, the contributors to *Frauen und Terror* made clear that they considered women in the RAF neither feminist nor emancipated. In her contribution to the volume, Margarete Fabricius-Brand argues 'women who join terrorist groups live in circumstances in which they must radically deny their economic, cultural and psychological needs. . . . Therefore, they fully correspond to the image of the unemancipated woman.'[84] The sociologist Lieselotte Süllwold came to a similar conclusion. According to her, the 'overzealous conformity' and 'cold perfectionism' of women in the RAF and other armed leftist groups were indicative of a complete disavowal of the emancipation of women.[85] A number of recent studies have adopted and developed the arguments in *Frauen und Terror*.[86] In 2009, Irene Bandhauer-Schöffman concluded that 'the link to the women's movement was externally imposed on female terrorists in the 1970s'.[87] Charity Scribner's recent discussion of feminism and women in the RAF echoes this view: 'Although the RAF put a kind of subconscious feminism into practice by placing women in the lead, the group's deliberate violence and withdrawal from larger social issues corrupted any viable political program.'[88]

Despite all of this criticism, a number of feminist activists and scholars have suggested that the armed struggle of the RAF and the MJ2 had a feminist potential. Even Scribner acknowledges that 'the RAF women's deadly commitment to militancy helped to widen the space for political action' for feminists and other political activists.[89] While she leaves no doubt that the feminist potential of the militant Left was unhinged by the RAF's escalating violence, Patricia Melzer comes to a very different conclusion. In her book *Death in the Shape of a Young Girl: Women's Political Violence in the Red Army Faction*, Melzer argues that female participation in leftist political violence in West Germany could and should be understood as a feminist practice, even if many of the actors involved did not identify with the aims and principles of the women's movement. According to Melzer, it is necessary to abandon the definition of feminist politics as a form of activism in which feminist subjects engage. Rather than limiting feminism to identity politics, she suggests, we should consider all ideas and practices that have a destabilizing effect on gender norms as potential feminist practices. Feminist practices, as defined by Melzer, 'need not be "consciously" feminist in their orientation; they have discursive effects and shape power in ways that undermine essentialist notions of femininity and masculinity'.[90]

While Melzer's study offers critical insights into the subversive potential of female participation in leftist political violence, her notion of feminist practices makes it difficult if not impossible to distinguish feminist from other political struggles. What, if any, difference is there between feminist and queer practices, if queer is defined in similarly broad terms as everything that is at 'odds with the normal, the legitimate, the dominant'?[91] How can we account for the fact that women have participated in armed political struggles for a range of reasons, and they have identified with different theoretical and ideological positions, including feminist ones? To account for these differences, I understand feminism, following bell hooks, as a joint 'struggle to end sexist oppression'.[92] This definition is useful, because it allows me to distinguish between militant feminist protest and other forms of political militancy. Although the latter have influenced and shaped the continuum of feminist militancy, they did not have the objective of ending sexist oppression. Another advantage of hooks's definition is that it acknowledges that there are many different feminist positions and tactics. Hooks rejects definitions that present feminism as 'a movement that aims to make women the social equals of men', as these limit feminism to the position of liberal feminists and do not address differences among women, and among men.[93] To overcome these limitations, she suggests a broad characterization of feminism as a 'political movement that aims to have a radical transformational impact on society'.[94] According to hooks, feminism must be a 'revolutionary struggle' that tackles not only sexism but also imperialism, racism and capitalism.[95] Although women in the RAF were committed to a revolutionary struggle against imperialism and capitalism, they distanced themselves from the aims and principles of feminism.

Feminism in the Red Army Faction and in the Movement of June 2nd

Although two of the RAF's leading theoreticians (Ulrike Meinhof and Gudrun Ensslin) were women, gender-based discrimination and sexist oppression in West Germany and in other geopolitical contexts was of little interest to the group. In 1970, the founding members of the RAF referred to (working) women in West Germany as potentially revolutionary elements. In 1993, the third generation of the RAF declared that it found inspiration in the women's movement. In the entire twenty-three years between these two statements, however, the RAF consistently neglected women's issues. Before she went underground, Ulrike Meinhof had made important contributions to debates and campaigns in the New Women's Movement in the FRG.[96] After joining the RAF, however, feminist politics played an increasingly reduced role in her thinking. Domestic violence, sexual abuse, abortion and other central themes in the New Women's Movement were of no relevance to the RAF, since the group focused almost exclusively on state repression and violence.

The first generation of the RAF depicted the issue of women's rights in an orthodox Marxist vein as a side contradiction, and the following generations of fighters did not challenge this approach. Monika Berberich, a former member of the group, elaborated on their gender politics: 'Even if, in the eyes of Gudrun [Ensslin], women were predestined for guerrilla warfare because they could only fulfil themselves by fighting against dominant beliefs: We were not about the liberation of women, we were about the liberation of humans.'[97] Berberich's statement and other personal accounts by women in the RAF give important insights into the group's views on women's liberation. The founding members of the RAF were convinced that women had to take up arms to liberate themselves. Secondly, personal accounts by women in the RAF indicate that they felt liberated, because they considered themselves equal to their male comrades in every way.[98] Thirdly, it seems that women in the RAF were convinced that a revolution would miraculously do away with all forms of oppression including sexism and racism. However, neither the perceived gender equality within the illegal group nor the utopian vision of a postrevolutionary world without gender norms had practical value for interactions in the existing social world.

While sharing the RAF's interest in gender equality, the Movement of June 2nd rejected the 'rigid' approach, the elitism and the centralized structure of the RAF.[99] When asked about internal hierarchies in an interview in 1978, founding members Ronald Fritzsch and Ralf Reinders claimed half in jest, half seriously: 'In the MJ2, women oppress men, proletarians oppress students and the other way around.'[100] In his autobiography, former MJ2 member Till Meyer made a similar statement. According to him, the group laughed when a hostage asked to talk to their 'boss', and they informed the man: 'In our group, there is no such thing as a chief.'[101] Autobiographical accounts by female members of the MJ2 indicate that they felt equal to their male comrades in every respect.[102] 'There was no chief in our clan', asserts Gabriele Rollnik.[103] Inge Viett commends in her autobiography 'the vehement development of the autonomy of us women'.[104]

Previous research suggests that the power structure in the MJ2 was indeed 'considerably more balanced' than relations in the RAF.[105] Tobias Wunschik goes as far as to claim that women long set the agenda in the MJ2.[106] Jo Groebel and Hubert Feger come to a similar conclusion and acknowledge an equality between men and women even 'when it came down to "hard" activities' ('*harte' Aktivitäten*) such as armed attacks.[107] However, even if MJ2 statements occasionally mentioned women's issues, the group did not have a feminist agenda. In an interview in 1997, Viett stressed this point clearly: 'None of us had a background in the feminist scene. . . . We did not deliberately choose to go through a process of liberation as women. . . . We simply made a decision and then we fought and did the same things as men. For us, that was no man-woman question. Underground, the old role models were irrelevant to us.'[108] Viett's statement indicates that, like female RAF members, women in the MJ2 wanted to be equal to their male comrades in all regards, but they did not identify as feminists.

Neither Melzer nor Scribner claim that the RAF and MJ2 pursued a feminist agenda. Yet, both come to very different conclusions regarding the feminist potential of female participation in leftist violence in the West Germany. Drawing on Jean Luc Nancy's work on violence, Melzer argues that women's political violence in the two groups constituted 'true violence' (because it harmed people and caused material damage) and revealed a 'violent truth', because it exposed and challenged a violent gender regime.[109] Since 'the gender regime's disciplinary technologies already inflict violence on lives', Melzer argues that female participation in left-wing violence in the FRG can be understood as a form of feminist 'counter-violence'.[110] Scribner, by contrast, considers it a key achievement of feminism in West Germany that most individuals and groups in the New Women's Movement distanced themselves from terrorist violence and were striving towards nonviolent modes of resistance and forms of political subjectivity. In her study of literary and artistic representations of the RAF, she discusses Yvonne Rainer's film *Journeys from Berlin/1971* and other feminist artworks as exemplary of a 'resistant post-militancy'.[111] The fact that Scribner and Melzer come to such different conclusions about the relationship between feminism and political violence in post-WWII Germany shows that this relation remains a subject of controversial debate. It is regrettable that this debate has so far focused almost exclusively on the RAF, with the consequence that scholars have neglected the only two armed leftist groups in the FRG who adopted the central topics and aims of the New Women's Movement: the Revolutionary Cells and the Red Zora.

Feminism in the Revolutionary Cells

Unlike the RAF and the MJ2, which originated in West Berlin, the first Revolutionary Cell was founded in Frankfurt.[112] So far, little is known about the history and membership of the group, and state and police authorities have long underrated the expansion and strength of this militant leftist network.[113] Allegedly, it was the sociology student Wilfried Böse who came up with the idea to create the group in 1973.[114] Like Brigitte Kuhlmann and other founding members of the RC, Böse was associated with the leftist publishing house Red Star in Frankfurt.[115] As the name of the group indicates, the founding members of the RC set out to create a network of loosely connected autonomous revolutionary cells. This structure was fundamentally different to that of the RAF, which had been cut to the quick by the arrest of its leading members in 1972. Another crucial difference between the groups was that most members of the RC did not go underground. Instead, they tried to combine illegal activities with legal forms of protest and with everyday activities. Unlike the MJ2, most members of the RC did actually remain true to this principle. For this reason, the group is sometimes referred to as an 'after-work guerrilla' (*Feierabend-Guerilla*).[116]

Similarly to the MJ2, the RC rejected the dogmatism and elitism of the RAF. In an interview, a group member explained that the RC wanted to 'create small nuclei of resistance, who work autonomously in different spheres of society, and who fight, intervene, act as a protection, [and] form a part of the political mass movement'.[117] Throughout the history of the RC, members of the group participated in a range of local and national protest movements and political subcultures including the New Women's Movement, the squatting scene, the Spontis and the anti-nuclear movement.[118] Between 1973 and 1993, the RC carried out more than 180 attacks to publicize and assert the demands of the groups and movements that they wanted to support and to spread militant tactics among their members. Unlike women in the RAF and in the MJ2, a number of the women in the RC identified as feminists and committed the first attack in the history of political violence in West Germany that had a distinctively feminist agenda. On 5 March 1975, a group calling itself Women of the Revolutionary Cell (WoRC) planted a bomb at the Federal Court of Justice to protest against the court's decision on the abortion ban, which is discussed in more detail in the following chapter.

The RC is best known for two fatal attacks: a raid during a conference of the Organization of the Petroleum Exporting Countries (OPEC) in Vienna in 1975 and the joint hijacking of an Israeli passenger flight with members of the Popular Front for the Liberation of Palestine (PLFP) in July 1976, which became the bloodiest attack in the history of the RC. Dozens of people, including one Israeli soldier, all hijackers, four hostages and an unconfirmed number of Ugandan soldiers were killed.[119] Yet these fatal attacks are hardly representative of its overall activities. While there were exceptions (e.g. the attack on the Hessian politician Heinz-Herbert Karry in 1981), most attacks by the RC did not result in casualties. Overall, the tactics of the RC tended to be less brutal than those of the RAF. 'They avoided', as Della Porta notes, 'using guns and sophisticated explosives, and stated that they wanted to carry out their revolution using (with imagination) "everyday" materials – such as glue to destroy the much hated ticket machines or other easy-to-find ingredients for small "home-made" bombs.'[120] Doubtlessly, such strikes caught fewer headlines than abductions and political assassinations. In an interview from 1975, one member of the RC argued, '90 per cent of our work is invisible and makes no noise'.[121]

The first edition of the illegally printed and disseminated RC-zine *Revolutionärer Zorn* (Revolutionary Rage) illustrates that, in contrast to the RAF and the MJ2, the RC quickly espoused the cause of women's liberation. Here, the RC declared, as mentioned previously, that supporting 'the struggles of workers, young people and women' constituted a priority for them.[122] In 1986, former member Enno Schwall explained that 'the RC tried to include a feminist dimension from the very beginning'.[123] According to Schwall, feminism was not merely an additional area of politics for the RC; it also inspired a part of the group to form an autonomous women's guerrilla organization that was based on feminist principles.[124]

While the data collected for this study supports Schwall's claim, it also indicates that the history of feminism in the RC was far more complex than his statement suggests. The group was generally open to feminist ideas, but the views of members differed considerably when it came to the question of what it meant to include 'a feminist dimension' in their politics. It seems that most men in the RC were indifferent to feminist ideas or simply supported them largely in principle rather than in practice. They left it to women in the group to plan and carry out attacks with a feminist agenda. It is important to note that not all women in the RC identified as feminists, and only some of those who did wanted to organize in a separate group. To contribute to a better understanding of the complex role of feminism in the RC, I want to distinguish between three positions among female members of the RC. These positions coexisted in the group until 1984, when the women's group Red Zora, who had previously formed the feminist wing of the militant network, left the RC.

A first position on feminism in the RC was that of the (female) militant. The word 'female' is placed in parentheses here because female group members with this stance understood themselves not primarily as women but as revolutionaries. In many respects, this position is comparable to the stance of many women in the RAF and MJ2. While they did not identify as feminists and did not actively participate in the Women's Movement, female militants in the RC saw equality between men and women in the group as a matter of course. Like their male comrades, female militants performed a range of roles in the group, and they were involved in the struggles of a range of groups (e.g. protests by migrants and workers or the anti-nuclear movement). Although the ideas and actions of female militants in the RC and other armed groups have influenced feminist militancy in the FRG, they were not part of the feminist struggle to end sexist oppression.

The feminist militant is a second position that existed among women in the RC. Group members with this stance engaged with feminist ideas, and they wanted to see women's issues on the political agenda of the RC. Feminist militants were also among the women who participated in the group's first attack with an explicitly feminist agenda. To protest against the enforcement of the ban on abortions in West Germany by the Federal Court of Justice in February 1975, a group of women in the RC planted a bomb at the highest German court a few weeks after the judgement (the next chapter offers a detailed discussion of this attack). Feminist militants in the RC wanted to support the struggles of women, but that was neither their only nor their main priority. Evidence suggests that some women in fact supported attacks that were at odds with their feminist principles. The ideas and practices of feminist militants in the RC have had a decisive influence on feminist militancy in West Germany, even if they were sometimes at odds with the ethics and principles of activists in the New Women's Movement.

RC co-founder Brigitte Kuhlmann provides a good example of this feminist militant stance. Apparently, she introduced ideas and politics of the New Women's Movement to the group and tried to put them into practice in her personal relationships. According to former RC member Magdalena Kopp and other friends and acquaintances, Kuhlmann identified as a feminist. However, Kopp also confirmed that Kuhlmann's highest priority – the liberation of Ulrike Meinhof and other 'political prisoners' – was not related to the New Women's Movement.[125] To force the release of imprisoned comrades, Kuhlmann supported activities and alliances that seem difficult to reconcile with her feminist principles: for example, she was actively involved in the planning and execution of joint attacks with hierarchical, male-dominated groups, such as Carlos the Jackal's Organization of Armed Struggle. In her eyes, 'anti-Zionist' and 'anti-imperialist' campaigns were as important as, if not more important than feminist campaigns.

In the eyes of militant feminists in the RC, the feminist politics of Kuhlmann and other women in the group did not go far enough. Like feminist militants, militant feminists in the RC identified with the women's movement and its aims. They, too, considered a confrontational approach essential for the success of the struggle against sexist oppression, and they used tactics that were widely regarded as violent. Their first attack was the bombing at the Federal Court of Justice, which they planned jointly with feminist militants in the RC. Yet in contrast to the feminist militants who participated in the attack, the militant feminists held radical feminist views. In 1999, Yvonne P. Doderer aptly characterized this branch of feminism in the context of the New Women's Movement in Germany as follows:

> Radical feminism prioritizes the gender issue, which means in this context the oppression of women through an appropriation of their sexuality and the exploitation of their reproductive capacities by individual men and by patriarchy. Radical feminists found that men with leftist views and their theories were not necessarily reflective and critical of these oppressive [patriarchal] structures. A central assumption in radical feminism is that all women are affected by sexist oppression and that all need to liberate themselves from dependencies on men.[126]

Since radical feminists consider misogyny and sexism to be structural problems rather than remediable defects within the prevailing social order, their thinking is characterized by a more confrontational attitude than that of liberal feminists and other feminists with a reformist agenda. Yet, it is important to stress that a radical feminist stance by no means implies a propensity to violence. As discussed in the previous chapters, Alice Schwarzer and other radical feminists in the FRG have drawn on highly provocative yet explicitly nonviolent tactics to fight against sexist oppression.

In line with radical feminist ideas, militant feminists in the RC considered the exploitation of women to be one of the earliest and most universal forms of oppression and a governing principle in Western societies.[127] According to them, occasional campaigns on women's issues alone could hardly challenge patriarchal structures within the group and in society at large. They argued that feminist politics had to be put into practice at all levels of the armed struggle, including personal relationships, ideology, structure, tactics and targets. Many men in the RC, however, were – at least according to their radical feminist comrades – not willing or able to question their politics or 'patriarchal identity' (*patriarchale Identität*) in such a radical way.[128]

The Militant Feminist Group Red Zora

Partly in response to the perceived lack of support in the RC, partly because they wanted to create a group based on radical feminist principles, militant feminists in the RC formed an autonomous feminist cell within the militant leftist network. From 1977, this group operated under the name Red Zora. While it seems that most founding members of the RZ had been part of the Women of the Revolutionary Cell, three former group members explained to me in an interview that the membership of the RZ was not identical with that of the WoRC.[129] A statement from 1993 supports this claim. Here, the group mentions that it had recruited members not only in the RC but also in the women's movement.[130]

The founding members of the group chose the name Red Zora (Rote Zora) for two reasons. Firstly, in German the name has the same initials as the RC, indicating the groups' shared ideological and structural principles. The name Red Zora also refers to a children's book from 1941, which the group saw as a source of inspiration for its politics. *The Red Zora and her Gang* (Die Rote Zora und ihre Bande) tells the story of a wild gang of street children led by a young girl. Like the RC, the RZ wanted to create a network of autonomous groups who fought with everyday materials rather than firearms or sophisticated bombs. But the RZ had a radical feminist philosophy. 'Our dream', explained two group members in 1984, 'is that there are small gangs of women everywhere; and that a rapist, trafficker of women, wife batterer, porn dealer, creepy gynaecologist must fear that a gang of women finds him, attacks him and humiliates him in public.'[131] As this statement indicates, the RZ understood itself as a militant part of the women's movement.

From 1977 until 1984, the RZ continued to operate as a part of the wider RC network. Members tried to balance campaigns on women's issues with other 'general' campaigns of the RC. Looking back on this period in 1993, however, RZ members explained that they became unhappy with this arrangement: 'When confining ourselves to "women's issues", we excluded a part of our identity, which we could not yet relate to "women's issues". When working on so-called "general" topics, we disappeared with our identities as women behind the men and behind a political orientation which was embedded in patriarchal structures.'[132] According to the Red Zora, the distinction between 'women's issues' and 'general topics' in the RC led to a gendered division of labour in the militant leftist network. They felt that male group members dominated discussions and campaigns on so-called general or universal topics while showing little interest in the campaign against paragraph 218 and other 'women's issues', leaving these topics almost entirely to feminists in the RC. Over the years, the Zoras became increasingly frustrated with the gender politics of the RC as they came to realize that they could not break the distinction between 'women's issues' and 'general topics'.

In 1984, the Red Zora split off from the Revolutionary Cells to form an independent women's guerrilla group. While the separation from the RC never led to a complete break, members of the Red Zora emphasize that the autonomy they gained was of vital importance for their personal development and their political struggle.

> A joint organizational structure with men does not only imply that we spend a considerable part of our energy to assert our positions as women/lesbians[133] in continual arguments, it also confines us to a discursive field that is created by men, and it orientates us again and again towards male norms, which we have often deeply internalized. They block our thinking and our development, and they are a bar to the development of a revolutionary-feminist perspective.[134]

Retrospectively, members of the Red Zora described the theory and practice of the militant Left and of the New Women's Movement in West Germany as two 'different poles' in their thinking.[135] Both had emerged from the student and protest movement in the 1960s and shared a number of theoretical influences (e.g. Marxism, Anarchism and existentialism), guiding principles (e.g. 'the personal is political', anti-fascism, anti-authoritarianism, solidarity with people in the Third World, etc.) and common aims (e.g. the liberation of oppressed groups). Despite these similarities, the New Women's Movement and the militant Left in West Germany set different priorities and soon evolved in very different directions. One constitutive difference was the prevailing approach to violence. The Red Zora drew on, adapted and challenged the politics of the New Left and the New Women's Movement by trying to develop a distinctively feminist notion of counter-violence.

As highlighted previously, Rudi Dutschke and other leading thinkers in the anti-authoritarian wing of the student movement considered the use of violence legitimate, if it was a response to a greater form of violence, if it was limited to situations in which other means of protest are futile, and if it took the form of a symbolic provocation rather than being an end in itself. Although Dutschke opposed the use of violent tactics in West Germany, he argued that political activists were sometimes left with no other option but to use violence to defend themselves.[136] The murder of Benno Ohnesorg on 2 June 1967, an attempt on Dutschke's life by a right-wing extremist in April 1968 and other events in the late 1960s contributed to the radicalization of some student activists in West Germany. These men and women took up arms and endorsed a notion of counter-violence that was not limited to symbolic attacks and that included violence against people.

Similar to Dutschke, the RZ held the view that violent protest was legitimate only if it was a response to a greater form of violence, and had the clear objective to overcome existing forms of oppression and violence. Like many student activists in the 1960s, the Red Zora actively supported '*Gewalt gegen Sachen*' but had an ambivalent relationship to '*Gewalt gegen Menschen*'. Contrary to the RAF and other militant leftist groups in West Germany, the RZ focused on small-scale attacks against property and made it a priority not to hurt or kill people in their attacks. According to former group members, their approach to violence was as much the result of personal ethics as of the life-affirming politics of the women's movement.[137] The RZ set itself the objective to convince other women that it was possible to fight back against everyday violence and abuse, and wanted to challenge the commonly held view that violent tactics were irreconcilable with feminist politics.

In the context of the Red Zora's ideological framework, counter-violence had a double meaning. On the one hand, it implied recourse to violence for defensive rather than aggressive reasons. According to the RZ, women were left with no other option but to use violence to defend themselves against the open and hidden forms of violence they faced in a patriarchal society. On the other hand, it signalled the group's opposition to 'macho-militancy' (*Mackermilitanz*) on the radical Left.[138] The RZ made the criticism that 'the decision to join an armed struggle is often mystified as a revolutionary act per se. To understand this form of struggle as particularly radical without considering the subject matter, however, contributes to a mystification of violence that does not break with the dominant definition of violence.'[139] The Red Zora opposed the prevailing notion of violence, because it did not tackle 'the structural, subtle and direct violence that constitutes and reinforces patriarchy'.[140] As long as the militant Left did not challenge the prevailing concept of violence, argued the Red Zora, it would try to seize power within the existing patriarchal structures rather than helping to overcome them.

Between 1977 and 1988, the RZ claimed responsibility for forty-five arson attacks and bombings, most of which took place in the 1980s,[141] and a few more followed in the 1990s. Most but not all of these attacks were carried out with the intention to support feminist struggles, including feminist campaigns against the abortion ban, sexual exploitation, trafficking and genetic engineering.[142] Although the Red Zora did not succeed in spreading violent tactics in the New Women's Movement, the following chapters show that some of its attacks sparked vivid debates on the scope and limits of feminist protest. The first major campaign in which feminists in the FRG drew on highly confrontational tactics to fight against sexist oppression was one that can be traced back into the early twentieth century: the movement against the abortion ban.

Notes

1. A. Proll (2004), *Hans und Grete: Bilder der RAF 1967–1977*, Berlin: Aufbau-Verlag, 11.
2. Varon, *Bringing the War Home*, 62.
3. W. Winkler (2007), *Die Geschichte der RAF*, Berlin: Rowohlt, 127.

4. M. Jander (2006), 'Horst Mahler', in W. Kraushaar (ed.), *Die RAF und der linke Terrorismus*, Hamburg: Hamburger Edition, 372–373, 379.
5. Compared to other group members, Ulrike Meinhof has certainly attracted the most attention from journalists and scholars. An in-depth discussion of her life and work goes beyond the scope of this chapter but can be found elsewhere. See e.g. M. Krebs (1988), *Ulrike Meinhof: Ein Leben im Widerspruch*, Reinbek: Rowohlt; A. Prinz (2003), *Lieber wütend als traurig: Die Lebensgeschichte der Ulrike Marie Meinhof*, Weinheim: Beltz und Gelberg; J. Ditfurth (2007), *Ulrike Meinhof: Die Biografie*, Berlin: Ullstein; S. Colvin (2009), *Ulrike Meinhof and West German Terrorism: Language, Violence and Identity*, Rochester, NY: Camden House.
6. J. Seifert (2006), 'Ulrike Meinhof', in W. Kraushaar (ed.), *Die RAF und der linke Terrorismus*, Hamburg: Hamburger Edition, 350–71, 366.
7. S. Bressan and M. Jander (2006), 'Gudrun Ensslin', in W. Kraushaar (ed.), *Die RAF und der linke Terrorismus*, Hamburg: Hamburger Edition, 398–429, 413.
8. Ibid., 414.
9. U. Edschmid (2001), *Frau mit Waffe: Zwei Geschichten aus terroristischen Zeiten*, 1st edn, Frankfurt: Suhrkamp, 123–25.
10. Baader was arrested when he and Mahler tried to find a secret arms depot in a cemetery in Berlin-Buckow that Peter Urbach, an undercover agent for the Federal Office for the Protection of the Constitution, had mentioned to them. According to Martin Jander and other authors, the police had not yet confirmed Baader's identity when Mahler made the naïve mistake of calling to ask for the whereabouts of Andreas Baader; Jander, 'Horst Mahler', 381–82. However, it should be added that Urbach's own account as quoted in a report by the Federal Criminal Police Office does not confirm this anecdote; *Der Baader-Meinhof-Report*, 26–28.
11. H.D. Nagel (1970), 'Schwurgerichtsanklage', RAF collection at the International Institute of Social History in Amsterdam (IISH), 37–41. Retrieved 1 July 2011 from labourhistory.net.
12. Ibid., 41–46.
13. *Der Baader-Meinhof-Report*, 36.
14. Nagel, 'Schwurgerichtsanklage', 53.
15. H.J. Schneider (1970), 'So fing es an . . .', unpublished report from the archive at the Institute for Social Issues, Berlin, 2.
16. 'zwei junge Mädchen, . . . die, wenn ich mich recht erinnere, beide grüne Brillen trugen, beide merkwürdig nervös und abgespannt wirkten, und beide eine auffallend große Tasche ständig neben sich hatten'; ibid., 1.
17. Nagel, 'Schwurgerichtsanklage', 56.
18. Ibid., 57–59.
19. Ten months after Baader's rescue, the leading prosecutor Nagel informed the public during the fifth day of the trial against Mahler, Goergens and Schubert that Bäcker, not Homann, had been involved in the attack; H.E. Schultz, 'Justizbeamte sollten Baader ohne Waffen ausführen. Angeklagte von Institutsangestellten "mit 99 prozentiger Sicherheit" erkannt', *Der Abend*, 19 March 1971.
20. Nagel, 'Schwurgerichtsanklage', 59.
21. Ibid., 61.
22. Ibid., 62–63.
23. Ibid., 64.
24. BAK, B 131/173 M-157.018, arrest warrant, 14 May 1970.
25. 'Es scheint, wir haben es hauptsächlich mit einer Damenriege zu tun'; *Der Baader-Meinhof-Report*, 38.
26. B. Peters (1991), *RAF: Terrorismus in Deutschland*, Stuttgart: Deutsche Verlags-Anstalt, 81.
27. Edschmid, *Frau mit Waffe*, 125; Ditfurth, *Ulrike Meinhof*, 13; Winkler, *Die Geschichte der RAF*, 163; M. Sontheimer (2010), *Natürlich kann geschossen werden. Eine kurze Geschichte der Roten Armee Fraktion*, Munich: Deutsche Verlags-Anstalt, 15.

28. Although Baader participated in a number of protests and demonstrations, biographical accounts argue that he was known neither as a committed leftist theorist nor as an activist; see e.g. G. Koenen (2009), *Vesper, Ensslin, Baader: Urszenen des deutschen Terrorismus*, 3 edn, Frankfurt: Fischer Taschenbuch Verlag, 106–13; K. Wieland (2005), 'A.', in W. Kraushaar, K. Wieland and J.P. Reemtsma (eds), *Rudi Dutschke, Andreas Baader und die RAF*, Hamburg: Hamburger Edition, 51–99, 67.
29. 'Hinterher war Ulrike – stets schon hochnervös-intelligent und ungeheuer sprunghaft – "häufig abwesend". Zu ihrem Ungeschick, sich anzuziehen, kam ein leichter Touch zur Ungepflegtheit'; L. Horst, 'Die Rote Ulrike ist mit der Gewalt verheiratet', *Bild*, 16 May 1970.
30. See e.g. 'Ruf nach mehr Härte in Berlin', *Süddeutsche Zeitung*, 16 May 1970.
31. H. Balz (2008), *Von Terroristen, Sympathisanten und dem starken Staat: Die öffentliche Debatte über die RAF in den 70er Jahren*, Frankfurt and New York: Campus, 198–231.
32. Ibid., 202.
33. C. Bielby (2012), *Violent Women in Print: Representations in the West German Print Media of the 1960s and 1970s*, Rochester, NY: Camden House, 96.
34. Ibid., 3.
35. 'Löwe Los', *Der Spiegel*, 22 February 1971, 26–34.
36. The fact that the book draws on a substantial amount of confidential police files led some authors to the conclusion that it was authored by employees of the Federal Office for the Protection of the Constitution, but it was no official report, and its origin is unknown.
37. *Der Baader-Meinhof-Report*, 113.
38. 'Das weibliche RAF-Mitglied wurde zum negativen Emblem der Frauenbefreiung, wie sie sich westdeutsche Männer ängstlich ausmalten: Bewaffnet und unsichtbar im Untergrund agierend, im Gefängnis dann unbeugsam weiterkämpfend'; S.V. Vukadinović (2004), 'Der unbegründete Feminismusverdacht. Die RAF und die Frage der Frauenemanzipation', in K. Hentschel and T. Hensch (eds), *Terroristinnen – Bagdad '77*, Berlin: Edition Der Freitag, 85–106, 86.
39. S.V. Vukadinović (2010), 'Feminismus im Visier. Zur Verknüpfung von Linksterrorismus und Feminismus in der BRD', *Ariadne*, 54–59, 54–55.
40. D. Grisard (2011), *Gendering Terror: Eine Geschlechtergeschichte des Linksterrorismus in der Schweiz*, Frankfurt: Campus, 13.
41. BAK, 'Linksradikale Bestrebungen in den Jahren 1969 und 1970 (Fassung des DMI)', 1.
42. Kraushaar, 'Die Tupamaros', 514.
43. Antiquariat Schwarzer Stern (ed.) (1982), *Der Blues gesammelte Texte der Bewegung 2. Juni*, Dortmund, 85.
44. 'Wir bekämpfen die Hierarchie, die Herrschaft von Menschen über Menschen. Dieser Kampf ist nur uns Frauen möglich, weil auch der unterdrückteste Prolet immer noch Unterdrücker seiner Frau und Kinder und jedes Mädchens auf der Straße bleibt'; C. Perincioli (1999), 'Anarchismus -> Lesbianismus -> Frauenzentrum. Warum musste die Tomate so weit fliegen?' Heinrich-Böll-Stiftung and Feministisches Institut (eds), *Wie weit flog die Tomate?* Berlin: Heinrich-Böll-Stiftung, 98–117, 101.
45. Ibid., 103.
46. Claessens and de Ahna, 'Das Milieu', 119.
47. The communards wanted to promote and practice a revolutionary lifestyle, which implied a radical opposition to capitalism, individualism and the 'bourgeois' model of the nuclear family. According to Dieter Claessens and Karin de Ahna, the objectives of the commune movement were the elimination of possessive behaviour of all kinds, the collective analysis of problems and the planning of joint political activities. The first and, beyond doubt, most famous commune in West Berlin was the 'Kommune 1' (K1). Inspired by political avant-garde movements such as the 'Situationist International' and literature, activists from Berlin and Munich founded the K1 in January 1967. The occupants of the K1 soon attracted media attention with remarks about 'orgasmic dysfunctions' rather than more conventionally political demands.

48. Kraushaar, 'Die Tupamaros', 518.
49. Ibid., 526.
50. Wunschik, 'Die Bewegung 2. Juni', 542–43.
51. K. König (2006), 'Zwei Ikonen des bewaffneten Kampfes', in W. Kraushaar (ed.), *Die RAF und der linke Terrorismus*, Hamburg: Hamburger Edition, 430–71, 441–42; Wunschik, 'Die Bewegung 2. Juni', 544.
52. 'Die neurotisch-historizistische Aufarbeitung'.
53. 'Der wahre Antifaschismus ist die klare und einfache Solidarisierung mit den kämpfenden *Fedayeen*'; quoted after W. Kraushaar (2005), *Die Bombe im Jüdischen Gemeindehaus*, Hamburg: Hamburger Edition, 48. *Fedayeen*, literally 'those who sacrifice', is an Arabic word for militants, commonly used for Palestinian fighters in this period.
54. Ibid., 74.
55. 'Anläßlich des Sechstagekriegs im Jahre 1967 und dessen Rezeption in den deutschen Medien kam es hinsichtlich der Haltung gegenüber Israel zum Bruch zwischen "alter" und "neuer Linker"'; V. Weiss (2005), '"Volksklassenkampf" – Die Antizionistische Rezeption des Nahostkonflikts in der militanten Linken der BRD', *Tel Aviver Jahrbuch für deutsche Geschichte*, 214–38, 223.
56. For a detailed discussion of the Munich Games and their political repercussions, see K. Schiller and C. Young (2010), *The 1972 Munich Olympics and the Making of Modern Germany*, Berkeley: University of California Press.
57. M. Hoffmann (ed.) (1997), *Rote Armee Fraktion: Texte und Materialien zur Geschichte der RAF*, Berlin: ID Verlag, 151.
58. For a detailed overview of these attacks, see K. Karcher (2013), 'Sisters in Arms? Female Participation in Leftist Political Violence in the Federal Republic of Germany Since 1970', unpublished PhD thesis, University of Warwick, Department of German Studies.
59. J. Becker (1977), *Hitler's Children: The Story of the Baader-Meinhof Terrorist Gang*, Philadelphia, PA: Lippincott.
60. Colvin, *Ulrike Meinhof*, 8.
61. See e.g. D. Hauser (2006), 'Deutschland, Italien, Japan. Die ehemaligen Achsenmächte und der Terrorismus der 1970er Jahre', in W. Kraushaar (ed.), *Die RAF und der linke Terrorismus*, Hamburg: Hamburger Edition, 1272–98; C. Schneider (2006), 'Omnipotente Opfer. Die Geburt der Gewalt aus dem Geist des Widerstands', in W. Kraushaar (ed.), *Die RAF und der linke Terrorismus*, Hamburg: Hamburger Edition, 1328–42.
62. F. Neidhardt (1982), 'Linker und rechter Terrorismus. Erscheinungsformen und Handlungspotentiale im Gruppenvergleich', in W. von Baeyer-Katte (ed.), *Gruppenprozesse, Analysen zum Terrorismus 3*, Opladen: Westdeutscher Verlag, 433–76, 437.
63. Neidhardt, 'Linker und rechter Terrorismus', 437.
64. 'Rote Armee Fraktion: Leninisten mit Knarren', *Agit 883*, 6 December 1971, 8–9.
65. G. Schmidtchen (1981), 'Terroristische Karrieren. Soziologische Analyse anhand von Fahndungsunterlagen und Prozessakten', in H. Jäger, G. Schmidtchen and L. Süllwold (eds), *Lebenslaufanalysen*, Opladen: Westdeutscher Verlag, 14–77, 21, 24.
66. Ibid., 21.
67. The Tupamaros West Berlin was one of several militant leftist networks that developed against the social background of Berlin's quickly growing drug scene. Most of these networks had very short lifespans and were composed of similar if not the same circles of friends and acquaintances. The members of these groups bought, took and sold drugs in particular places and bars in Berlin, where they frequently clashed with the police. As Klaus Weinhauer highlights, this recourse to violence was mostly spontaneous and defensive; K. Weinhauer, J. Requate and H.G. Haupt (2006), *Terrorismus in der Bundesrepublik: Medien, Staat und Subkulturen in den 1970er Jahren*, Frankfurt and New York: Campus, 225.
68. M. Baumann (1980), *Wie alles anfing*, Munich: Trikont, 56.
69. Schmidtchen, 'Terroristische Karrieren', 24.

70. Kraushaar, 'Die Tupamaros', 512.
71. Wunschik, 'Die Bewegung 2. Juni', 557.
72. Della Porta, *Social Movements*, 125.
73. On 30 January 1972, British soldiers killed and wounded twenty-six unarmed protesters during a demonstration in Derry, Northern Ireland; D. Walsh (2000), *Bloody Sunday and the Rule of Law in Northern Ireland*, Basingstoke: Palgrave Macmillan, 10. Retrieved 12 January 2013 from http://public.eblib.com/choice/publicfullrecord.aspx?p=736411. For a detailed discussion of the events on that day and their relevance to the Irish Troubles, see P. Hayes and J. Campbell (2005), *Bloody Sunday: Trauma, Pain and Politics*, London: Pluto Press; M. Alison (2009), *Women and Political Violence: Female Combatants in Ethno-National Conflict*, London and New York: Routledge.
74. Wunschik, 'Die Bewegung 2. Juni', 539.
75. Die Bewegung 2. Juni (1980), 'Auflösungspapier Bewegung 2. Juni'. Retrieved 16 February 2013 from http://bewegung.nostate.net/mate_aufloesung.html.
76. Schmidtchen, 'Terroristische Karrieren', 23.
77. Ibid., 24.
78. Diewald-Kerkmann, *Frauen, Terrorismus und Justiz*, 275.
79. Ibid., 5.
80. Cf. C. Lombroso and G. Ferrero (2004), *Criminal Woman, the Prostitute and the Normal Woman*, translated and with a new introduction by N. Hahn Rafter and M. Gibson, Durham, NC: Duke University Press. See also Grisard, *Gendering Terror*, 37, 41; Bielby, *Violent Women in Print*, 75.
81. Diewald-Kerkmann, *Frauen, Terrorismus und Justiz*, 6.
82. Ibid., 6–7.
83. 'Es genügt nicht, den Zusammenhang zwischen Terror und Emanzipation einfach zurückzuweisen, um unserer eigenen Loyalitätskonflikte willen müssen wir ihn genau und gewissenhaft untersuchen'; S. von Paczensky (ed.) (1978), *Frauen und Terror: Versuche, die Beteiligung von Frauen an Gewalttaten zu erklären*, Reinbek: Rowohlt, 12.
84. 'Frauen, die sich terroristischen Gruppen angeschlossen haben, leben unter Bedingungen, in denen sie ihre ökonomischen, kulturellen und psychischen Bedürfnisse radikal verleugnen müssen . . . Insofern entsprechen sie voll dem Bild der unemanzipierten Frau'; ibid., 67.
85. L. Süllwold (1981), 'Stationen in der Entwicklung von Terroristen. Psychologische Aspekte biographischer Daten', in H. Jäger, G. Schmidtchen and L. Süllwold (eds), *Lebenslaufanalysen*, Opladen: Westdeutscher Verlag, 80–116, 106.
86. Bandhauer-Schöffmann, 'Emanzipation mit Bomben und Pistolen'; Vukadinović, 'Der unbegründete Feminismusverdacht' and 'Feminismus im Visier'; Grisard, *Gendering Terror*; Bielby, *Violent Women in Print*.
87. 'war der Konnex zwischen Terroristinnen der 1970er Jahre und der Frauenbewegung ein von außen herangetragener'; Bandhauer-Schöffmann, 'Emanzipation mit Bomben und Pistolen', 84.
88. Scribner, *After the Red Army Faction*, 93.
89. Ibid., 202.
90. Melzer, *Death in the Shape of a Young Girl*, 237.
91. D.M. Halperin (1997), *Saint Foucault: Towards a Gay Hagiography*, New York: Oxford University Press, 62.
92. Hooks, *Feminist Theory*, 28.
93. Ibid., 18–19. In her critical discussion of liberal feminism, bell hooks argues that a focus on equality between men and women fails to consider race, class and other differences among women *and* among men. 'Since men are not equals in white supremacist, capitalist, patriarchal class structure', asks hooks provocatively, 'which men do women want to be equal to?' Ibid., 19.
94. Ibid., 30.
95. Ibid.

96. Meinhof's journalistic work from the 1960s featured prominently on the reading list of the 'Action Council for the Liberation of Women' and other feminist groups in the FRG. Her dictum, 'Protest is, if I say, I don't want to accept this and that. Resistance is, if I ensure that that what I don't want to accept will no longer happen' ('Protest ist, wenn ich sage, das und das paßt mir nicht. Widerstand ist, wenn ich dafür sorge, daß das, was mir nicht paßt, nicht länger geschieht'), became a popular slogan for the radical Left, and featured prominently in the first theory paper of the Red Zora.
97. 'Auch wenn Gudrun [Ensslin] die Frauen als prädestiniert für die Guerilla ansah, weil sie sich nur gegen die herrschenden Vorstellungen verwirklichen können: Es ging uns nicht um die Befreiung der Frauen, sondern um die Befreiung der Menschen'; Berberich quoted after T. Stelzer, 'Die Waffen der Frauen', *Die Zeit*, 27 September 2007.
98. 'Frauen im Untergrund – "Etwas Irrationales"', *Der Spiegel*, 8 August 1977, 22–33, 25; M. Schiller (2001), *Es war ein harter Kampf um meine Erinnerung: Ein Lebensbericht aus der RAF*, Munich: Piper; O. Tolmein and I. Möller (2005), *'RAF – Das war für uns Befreiung': Ein Gespräch mit Irmgard Möller über Bewaffneten Kampf, Knast und die Linke*, Hamburg: Konkret Literatur Verlag, 68–69; G. Ensslin, C. Ensslin and G. Ensslin (2005), *'Zieht den Trennungsstrich, jede Minute': Briefe an ihre Schwester Christiane und ihren Bruder Gottfried aus dem Gefängnis 1972–1973*, Hamburg: Konkret Literatur Verlag, 138.
99. G. Rollnik and D. Dubbe (2004), *Keine Angst vor Niemand: Über die Siebziger, die Bewegung 2. Juni und die RAF*, Hamburg: Edition Nautilus, 24; K. Viehmann, R. Fritzsch and R. Reinders (1980), 'Zu der angeblichen Auflösung der Bewegung 2. Juni'. Retrieved 16 February 2013 from http://bewegung.nostate.net/mate_nichtaufloesung.html; Fritzsch and Reinders, *Die Bewegung 2. Juni*, 36.
100. 'Beim 2. Juni unterdrücken die Frauen die Männer und die Proleten die Studenten, sowie umgekehrt'; R. Fritzsch and R. Reinders (1995), *Die Bewegung 2. Juni: Gespräche über Haschrebellen, Lorenzentführung, Knast*, Edition ID- Archiv: Berlin, 120.
101. 'Einen Chef, so etwas gibt es bei uns nicht'; T. Meyer (2008), *Staatsfeind Erinnerungen*, Berlin: Rotbuch, 28.
102. Rollnik and Dubbe, *Keine Angst vor Niemand*; I. Viett (1997), *Nie war ich furchtloser*, Hamburg: Edition Nautilus.
103. 'Bei uns gab es keinen Häuptling'; Rollnik and Dubbe, *Keine Angst vor Niemand*, 23.
104. 'die vehemente Entfaltung der Eigenständigkeit von uns Frauen'; Viett, *Nie war ich furchtloser*, 176.
105. 'wesentlich ausgeglichener'; J. Groebel and H. Feger (1982), 'Analyse von Strukturen terroristischer Gruppierungen', in W. von Baeyer-Katte (ed.), *Gruppenprozesse, Analysen zum Terrorismus 3*, Opladen: Westdeutscher Verlag, 393–431, 413.
106. Wunschik, 'Die Bewegung 2. Juni', 556.
107. Groebel and Feger, 'Analyse von Strukturen', 415.
108. 'Wir sind alle nicht aus der feministischen Bewegung gekommen. . . . Wir haben nicht bewusst so einen Frauenbefreiungsprozess für uns durchleben wollen. . . . Wir haben uns einfach entschieden, und wir haben dann gekämpft und dieselben Dinge getan wie die Männer. Es war für uns keine Frage Mann-Frau. Das alte Rollenverständnis hat für uns in der Illegalität keine Rolle gespielt'; Viett quoted after G. Diewald-Kerkmann (2007), 'Frauen in Der RAF', in *'Wer wenn nicht wir'*. Retrieved 12 January 2013 from http://www.bpb.de/gesellschaft/ kultur/filmbildung/43364/frauen-in-der-raf?p=all.
109. Melzer, *Death in the Shape of a Young Girl*, 11–12.
110. Ibid., 12.
111. Ibid., 5.
112. A.S. Markovits and P.S. Gorski (1993), *The German Left: Red, Green and Beyond*, Cambridge: Polity Press, 73.
113. G. Langguth (1983), *Protestbewegung: Entwicklung, Niedergang, Renaissance: Die Neue Linke seit 1968*, Cologne: Verlag Wissenschaft und Politik, 224; W. Kraushaar (2006), 'Im Schatten

der RAF. Zur Entstehung der Revolutionären Zellen', in W. Kraushaar (ed.), *Die RAF und der linke Terrorismus*, Hamburg: Hamburger Edition, 583–601, 595.
114. Ibid., 593.
115. Ibid., 590.
116. Ibid, 593.
117. 'Gegenmacht in kleinen Kernen zu organisieren, die autonom in den verschiedenen gesellschaftlichen Bereichen arbeiten, kämpfen, intervenieren, schützen, ein Teil von der politischen Massenarbeit sind'; ID Verlag (ed.) (1993), *Die Früchte des Zorns*, Amsterdam: ID Verlag, 81.
118. Langguth, *Protestbewegung*, 224.
119. F. Anders and A. Sedlmaier (2013), '"Unternehmen Entebbe" 1976: Quellenkritische Perspektiven auf eine Flugzeugentführung', *Jahrbuch für Antisemitismusforschung* 22, 267–289, 269.
120. Della Porta, *Social Movements*, 125.
121. '90 % unserer Arbeit sieht und hört man nicht'; ID Verlag, *Die Früchte des Zorns*, 79.
122. 'Kämpfe von Arbeitern, Jugendlichen, Frauen'; ibid., 62.
123. 'In der RZ hat es von Anfang an den Versuch gegeben den feministischen Aspekt mit einzubeziehen. Nicht nur als einen zusätzlichen politischen Bereich, sondern das war immer verbunden damit, dass sich innerhalb der RZ, später unter dem Namen "Rote Zora" Frauen zusammengesetzt haben und versucht haben ein Guerillakonzept unter feministischer Perspektive zu entwickeln'; E. Schwall (1986), 'Gespräch Mit Enno Schwall'. Retrieved 3 November 2012 from http://www.freilassung.de/prozess/ticker/history/rz/hinter/enno1.htm.
124. Ibid.
125. Interview with Magdalena Kopp, 30 October 2011.
126. 'Der Radikalfeminismus setzte die Geschlechterfrage an erste Stelle, womit die Unterdrückung von Frauen durch die Aneignung ihrer Sexualität durch die Ausbeutung ihrer Reproduktionskräfte durch einzelne Männer und das Patriarchat gemeint ist. Von diesen Unterdrückungsstrukturen und –mechanismen waren, so erkannten, die Radikalfeministinnen, auch die linken Männer und ihre Theorien nicht ausgenommen . . . Zentral . . . ist weiterhin der Ausgangspunkt, dass alle Frauen von der Geschlechterfrage betroffen sind und dass sich alle aus Abhängigkeiten von Männern befreien müssen'; Doderer, *Never Give Up!*, 7
127. ID Verlag, *Die Früchte des Zorns*, 209–11.
128. Die Rote Zora, 'Mili's Tanz auf dem Eis'.
129. Focus group with three former members of the Red Zora, 17 August 2012.
130. Die Rote Zora, 'Mili's Tanz auf dem Eis'.
131. 'Unser Traum ist, daß es überall kleine Frauenbanden gibt – wenn in jeder Stadt ein Vergewaltiger, ein Frauenhändler, ein prügelnder Ehemann, ein frauenfeindlicher Zeitungsverleger, ein Pornohändler, ein schweinischer Frauenarzt damit rechnen und sich davor fürchten müßte, daß eine Bande Frauen ihn aufspürt, ihn angreift, ihn öffentlich bekannt und lächerlich macht'; ID Verlag, *Die Früchte des Zorns*, 462.
132. 'Bei der Beschränkung auf "frauenspezifische" Themen grenzten wir einen Teil unserer Identität aus, den wir noch nicht so recht als durchaus auch "frauenspezifisch" begreifen konnten. Bei den sog. "allgemeinen" Themen verschwanden wir mit unserer Frauenidentität hinter den Männern bzw. einer patriarchal eingebetteten politischen Ausrichtung'; Die Rote Zora, 'Mili's Tanz auf dem Eis'.
133. The term 'women/lesbians' was used by Red Zora and other women's groups in West Germany to draw attention to the fact that the position of women and lesbians was related yet not always identical; ibid.
134. 'Gemeinsame Organisierung mit Männern bindet nicht nur unsere Energien in der ständigen Auseinandersetzung um die Behauptung von FrauenLesbenpositionen, sondern sie bindet uns auch in von Männern gesetzte Diskussionsprozesse ein, bringt uns immer wieder auf das Gleis der Orientierung an männlichen Normen, die wir selbst oft tief verinnerlicht

haben. Sie blockiert uns damit in unserem Denken und unserer Entwicklung und steht der Herausbildung einer revolutionär- feministischen Perspektive ständig im Wege'; ibid.
135. Ibid.
136. Dutschke, 'Wir fordern die Enteignung Axel Springers'.
137. Focus group with three former members of the Red Zora, 17 August 2012.
138. Ibid.
139. '[die] Entscheidung für "bewaffneten Kampf" wird oft als revolutionäres Handeln per se mystifiziert. Die Kampfform an sich als besonders radikal zu sehen, losgelöst vom Inhalt, arbeitet einer Mystifizierung von Gewalt zu, die mit der herrschenden Definition von Gewalt nicht bricht'; Die Rote Zora, 'Mili's Tanz auf dem Eis'.
140. 'die strukturelle, subtile und direkte Gewalt, die das Patriarchat ausmacht und stützt'; ibid.
141. S. Deckwerth. 'Geständnis nach 20 Jahren', *Berliner Zeitung*, 12 April 2007.
142. Die Rote Zora, 'Mili's Tanz auf dem Eis'.

Chapter 3

Militant Feminist Protest against the Abortion Ban

On 6 June 1971, 374 women caused a public outcry in West Germany by declaring in a joint manifesto in the weekly magazine *Stern* that they had all had illegal abortions. According to paragraph 218 of the Criminal Code of the Federal Republic of Germany, abortion was a punishable act that could lead to a year-long prison sentence for the actors involved. This legislation was based on the Reich Penal Code from 1871, which punished abortions with prison sentences of up to five years. Although socialist and liberal members of the Reichstag called for legal reform, and mass protests were held against the abortion ban in the late Weimar Republic, the law remained unchanged until the National Socialists came into power.[1] During the Third Reich, women who were considered healthy and German could face the death penalty if they had an abortion, while others were forced to have abortions or sterilized against their will. After the end of the Second World War, the Allied Powers revoked this legislation and reintroduced a slightly amended version of the law from 1871. By the late 1960s, even supporters of the abortion ban acknowledged that reform was needed, because the law was applied inconsistently and clearly failed to prevent illegal abortions.[2] Every year, hundreds of thousands of women in the FRG had abortions, often under insanitary and dangerous conditions.[3] By declaring publicly and collectively that they had gone through this experience, the 374 signatories of the *Stern* manifesto broke the taboo surrounding the issue of abortion and underlined the need for legal reform. The women claimed that they would not accept a 'reform in instalments' (*Reform auf Raten*) and demanded comprehensive sex education, unrestricted access to contraceptives and a complete deletion of paragraph 218.[4]

Notes for this section begin on page 86.

The *Stern* manifesto took inspiration from a similar campaign in France. In April 1971, the French magazine *Nouvel Observateur* published a statement in which 343 women, including a number of famous personalities, had made the same declaration. The German journalist Alice Schwarzer, at that time a foreign correspondent in Paris, followed the campaign closely and decided to initiate a similar project in West Germany. She contacted groups in the New Women's Movement, where her plan met with a divided response. Some activists argued that Schwarzer's plan was not confrontational enough and rejected it as 'reformist' and 'apolitical'.[5] Many others, however, felt that the campaign would help increase the pressure for an urgently needed reform of the abortion legislation. Within a few weeks, Schwarzer and her supporters collected 374 signatures in West Berlin, Frankfurt, Cologne and other West German cities.

Signatories of the statement included the actresses Romy Schneider and Senta Berger, the fashion model Veruschka von Lehndorff and several other famous personalities, but the campaign mainly focused on the views and experiences of secretaries, housewives, students and other 'ordinary' women. The youngest woman to sign the petition was twenty-one, the oldest seventy-seven.[6] Testimonies from participants show that they saw their self-denunciation not as a personal confession but as a political act and as an expression of solidarity with other women, which is also illustrated by the fact that a number of signatories had not actually had an abortion.[7] From the very beginning, the campaign was thus characterized by a strong sense of solidarity that connected the participants with each other and with other women in the FRG.

With their public self-denunciation, the signatories of the *Stern* manifesto adopted a highly provocative and confrontational tactic to make their voices heard in a reform debate, from which women had been largely excluded. Their violation of law met with a great amount of sympathy and support. Polls from 1971 indicate that 83 per cent of women in West Germany declared themselves in favour of a deletion of paragraph 218.[8] Yet, this demand met with fierce opposition from church authorities, who argued that the issue of abortion was no matter of policy but a question of morality. In 1973, the chairman of the German Bishops' Conference emphasized that 'whatever the German Bundestag decides regarding the reform of paragraph 218, the German bishops will not cease from calling abortion an unjustified act of murder'.[9]

Until the early 1970s, the public debate over the reform of paragraph 218 in West Germany was dominated by legal experts, medical associations and conservative politicians who shared this harsh view of abortion. The *Stern* manifesto challenged this position and confronted state authorities with the lived experience of many women. Due to the public nature of Schwarzer's campaign, it was difficult for politicians and public prosecutors to turn a blind eye to this obvious violation of law. Yet, they were aware of the fact that a hard course of action against the signatories of the manifesto would have been extremely unpopular and could potentially spark further protest. The state response to the *Stern* manifesto illustrates this dilemma: although police authorities initiated investigations against many of the women involved, none of these cases ended up in court.[10]

It is widely acknowledged that the *Stern* manifesto played a vital role in the development of the New Women's Movement. According to Kristina Schulz, the hostile responses to Schwarzer's campaign and the criminal investigations against the women involved had a positive effect on the Women's movement in West Germany because they attracted public support and strengthened social cohesion within the movement. The manifesto led to a wave of sympathy and solidarity within the population. Within a few weeks, 3000 other women publicly admitted to having had abortions, and 86,000 people expressed solidarity with the signatories.[11] The following years saw further self-denunciations, e.g. when 329 medics, out of opposition to paragraph 218, publicly announced in the weekly *Spiegel* that they had helped women with abortions and would continue to do so.[12] These and other protest activities in the early 1970s brought the various groups who campaigned for a decriminalization of abortion closer together and helped them to create local, national and transnational networks.[13] In the following years, these networks proved vital not only for the mass mobilization against paragraph 218 but also for the organization of a range of other campaigns.

Previous studies of the New Women's Movement argue that the *Stern* manifesto is exemplary of feminist protest in West Germany. Schulz concludes that Schwarzer's campaign was a provocation 'par excellence', because it tied in with existing political debates, involved an element of surprise and was conflict-oriented.[14] According to Ilse Lenz, the manifesto provides a powerful example of the use of self-denunciation as a nonviolent tactic of political resistance.[15] While Schulz and Lenz emphasize the provocative nature of Schwarzer's campaign, neither of them reads it as an expression of feminist militancy. This is surprising, because Alice Schwarzer and other former participants explicitly acknowledge the militant nature of the *Stern* manifesto and other feminist protest in the early 1970s.

1971–1975: Campaigning for a New Law

In the early 1970s, feminist activism on the issue of abortion in West Germany focused on three main areas: publicity and lobbying activities, information and support for women who experienced unwanted pregnancies and protest against institutions and groups who supported the abortion ban. While some groups focused on a particular area, most campaigns involved activities in two or more. Although the actors involved employed different tactics and had different political backgrounds, they shared a common goal: free and safe abortions. The Frankfurt-based Frauenaktion 70 was one of the first women's groups in West Germany to publicly campaign for sex education, wider access to contraceptives and a complete deletion of paragraph 218.[16] As early as 1970, the group organized a teach-in with 120 participants, a go-in at a campaign rally of the Social

Democratic Party and other events in Frankfurt. The women also collected more than one thousand signatures for a public letter to Federal Minister of Health Käte Strobel demanding a decriminalisation of abortion.[17] In a public letter to the German Bishops' Conference, members of Frauenaktion 70 criticized the position of the Church on the issue of abortion as classist, misogynist and sexually oppressive.[18]

The *Stern* manifesto brought a new intensity to feminist protest against paragraph 218, and women's groups from Berlin and West Germany decided to form a national umbrella organization, AKTION 218, to coordinate and synchronize protest activities in different parts of the country. In the early 1970s, these activities took a range of forms: women leaving the church en masse, tribunals, go-ins at political events, church services and medical conferences, national demonstrations, street theatre and teach-ins at universities and community centres. In addition to these activities, feminists tried to offer practical support for women who experienced unwanted pregnancies. In 1972, the women's group Bread & Roses published a handbook on abortion and contraception and offered a counselling and support service for pregnant women in the first women's centre in West Berlin.[19]

Due to its high visibility and growing popularity, the feminist campaign against paragraph 218 further increased pressure on the social-democrat/liberal government. In 1972, Minister of Justice Gerhard Jahn proposed a reform that decriminalized all abortions during the first trimester of pregnancy, the so-called time-phase solution (*Fristenlösung*), which had been adopted in several countries, including East Germany. After several versions of the bill had been rejected, the Bundestag approved the reform with a narrow majority in 1974. Church representatives and conservative politicians condemned this decision, which constituted in their eyes a legalization of murder.[20] Immediately after the parliamentary vote, members of the CDU appealed against the reform at the Federal Court of Justice. On 25 February 1975, the highest German court declared the legislation void. The judges found the reform incompatible with the sanctity of human life as defined by the constitution.[21] They ruled: 'The protection of the foetus, as a matter of principle and for the entire duration of the pregnancy, has priority over the self-determination of the pregnant woman and must not be called into question for any period of time.'[22]

The decision on paragraph 218 troubled the judges at the Federal Court of Justice and divided the country. After the president of the court, Ernst Benda, had read the judgement, two members of the court, including the only female judge, announced their dissent. One of the majority judges then left the room as a show of discontent with the two dissenters. This unusual conduct was seen as an offence to his colleagues, and constitutes a unique act in the history of the court.[23] To add to the scandal, the court's internal negotiations leaked to the public more than a week before the judgement. While representatives of the Catholic and the Protestant Churches, the CDU and the German Medical Association all welcomed the judgement, liberal and progressive politicians and medics in West Germany, who had supported a legal reform, criticized the decision.[24] The decision by the judges in Karlsruhe, however, was incontestable. This meant that the many opponents of paragraph 218 were left with no legal means to proceed against the abortion ban. The ruling was a hard blow to all women who had campaigned for years to achieve a decriminalization of abortion.

In February 1976, the parliament passed a modified version of the law that it had adopted in 1974. The new legislation exempted abortions within the first three months from punishment if pregnant women could persuade independent medical experts that their situation was so dreadful that they could not be expected to continue the pregnancy. In the eyes of many women, the so-called indication model (*Indikationsmodell*) was a weak compromise, because it was yet another law that denied women the right to self-determination. After reunification in 1990, East and West Germany kept applying different abortion laws until the Federal Court of Justice passed a law that was mandatory for the entire Republic in 1992.[25] Prior to the court's decision, the former East German States continued to apply the 'time-phase solution'. In 1995, the parliament passed an adapted version of paragraph 218 that is still valid to this day.

Although feminist protest against paragraph 218 continued well into the 1990s, it reached a peak of militancy in the mid-1970s. When the decision by the Federal Court of Justice leaked to the public, women's groups organized protests in several German cities, including Bonn, Berlin, Hamburg, Munich and Karlsruhe, that were characterized by a highly confrontational approach.[26] The women who participated in these demonstrations made no secret of their disappointment over the decision and their anger towards the authorities and institutions that they deemed responsible for it: the Federal Court of Justice, the Churches and the German Medical Association. Some of this protest caused minor property damage. On 16 February, women poured red paint on the stairs of the Kaiser Wilhelm Memorial Church, a famous church in Berlin. They had chosen 'red paint as a symbol for blood, the blood of the women who die during illegal abortions'.[27] Church authorities condemned the event and called on the state to protect their churches against such radical protests.[28] In Frankfurt, police attacked participants in a demonstration with batons and tear gas, allegedly because the crowd tried to prevent officers from arresting a young man who had been caught writing on a wall. During the same demonstration, a group of women burnt three rag dolls – one dressed as a clergyman, one as a medic and one as a judge.[29] Apparently, this symbolic act of violence was no isolated event. According to *Der Spiegel*, protesters in other German cities had carried out similar actions for the day of the judgement.[30]

In July 1975, feminist activists began to organize coach trips to abortion clinics in the Netherlands. Like the *Stern* manifesto in 1971, these trips constituted a highly provocative form of 'limited violation of rules' (*begrenzte Regelverletzung*) and resulted in criminal proceedings for some of the actors involved.[31] While the organizers of these trips regarded them as a nonviolent form of direct action with the aim of helping female victims of institutionalized sexism and male violence, state and church authorities considered their conduct accessory to murder. Criminal charges, however, did not stop feminist groups from supporting women who wanted to have abortions. In November 1976, the newsmagazine *Spiegel* reported that in some parts of the country it was virtually impossible for women from poorer backgrounds to have an abortion even if they were legally entitled to do so.[32] To help these women, feminist groups in several German cities continued to offer cheap coach trips to abortion clinics in the Netherlands, even if this involved the risk of legal proceedings.

On at least two occasions in the mid-1970s, women expressed their disgust for the abortion ban through physical attacks against the Federal Court of Justice in Karlsruhe. In 1969, the court had moved from its previous seat, the Prinz-Max Palais, into a newly constructed building less than a kilometre away. The new complex had a light and open design to suggest 'democratic transparency'.[33] It was clothed almost entirely in glass and consisted of five parts connected with glass bridges. At the heart of the 20 million DM construction was a three-storey building that accommodated the courtroom, a reception lobby and several conference rooms.[34] This part of the court was designed as a meeting point for journalists, visitors and members of the court. It was open to the public during the day. Night and day, two police officers guarded the building, typically from within a sentry box positioned sixty meters from the building. The officers inspected vehicles that approached the court. Pedestrians, however, could access the court through the surrounding Schlossgarten, without having to pass any controls. On at least two occasions, women used this entrance to carry out attacks against the highest German court to protest against the abortion ban. The first attack on the court caused only minor damage. Apparently, a group of feminist protesters entered the compound during opening hours. One observer reported that some of the women distracted the guards, while others wrote 'My belly belongs to me!' (*Mein Bauch gehört mir!*) in big letters on the glass façade of the reception hall.[35] The second attack against the Federal Court of Justice took feminist militancy to an entirely new level and shall therefore be discussed in detail.

A Feminist Bomb at the Federal Court of Justice

On 4 March 1975, a group of women planted a bomb at the Federal Court of Justice. It is not clear when and how the perpetrators entered the compound, but there is good reason to believe that they walked into the Schlossgarten in the middle of the day and passed as ordinary visitors. Unnoticed by the two police officers, they attached a time bomb with magnets to one of the steel girders at the glass facade of the reception hall. At 8:07 PM, the explosive device detonated. Since no employees or visitors were in the building at this time of day, the bomb did not hurt or kill anyone. It did however cause substantial material damage: forty-seven linear metres of glass – the entire façade on the ground level and several windows on the first floor of the building – shattered under the pressure of the detonation. Moreover, the bomb destroyed parts of the floor and the ceiling in the entrance hall as well as furniture in the foyer.[36] Overall, the estimated damage to the building amounted to 150,000 DM.[37]

One day after the bombing, the editors of several West German newspapers and a publishing house in Berlin received envelopes with photocopies of a typed letter.[38] Further copies of the statement were found in the following days in a leftist bookstore in Heidelberg and in a telephone booth in Cologne.[39] In the short text, the Women of the Revolutionary Cell claimed responsibility for the attack. After inspecting the crime scene and examining the claim of responsibility, police authorities declared that they considered the claims to be legitimate, as members of the Revolutionary Cell had executed similar attacks in the past.[40] Indeed, a comparison with previous bombings by the RC reveals that the attack in Karlsruhe was typical of the approach of the group for a number of reasons.

Firstly, all bombings that the RC carried out between 1973 and 1975 were directed against buildings in publicly accessible areas. Secondly, the group placed the bombs in locations that could easily be reached without entering the buildings – usually a window on the ground level. In some cases, including the attack at the Federal Court of Justice, the perpetrators attached a bomb with magnets to a steel girder at a front window.[41] Thirdly, the bombs were homemade and had the same components: as much as one thousand grams of strong explosives, conventional batteries and an electric alarm clock that the perpetrators had converted into a time fuse. This detail is significant because, at the time, the RC was the only militant leftist group in West Germany who used bombs of this design.[42] Finally, the bombs were detonated at times of the day when no staff or visitors were using the facilities – typically in the evening or the early morning hours. As a result, none of the RC attacks prior to the bombing at the Federal Court of Justice hurt or killed people. Evidence in the Federal Archives suggests that these previous attacks had caused property damage totalling at least 850,000 DM. Since the bombing in Karlsruhe complied with all four features, it was perfectly in line with the RC tactics.

The feminist agenda of the attack, however, constituted a novelty in the history of the RC. While the RC wanted to intervene in a range of local and international struggles, there is no evidence that group members were directly affected by any of the oppressive structures that they denounced. Prior to the bombing in Karlsruhe, as a means of expressing solidarity with workers and the local youth, members of the RC had committed arson attacks against the cars of a factory owner and of a politician who wanted to shut down a youth centre in Berlin. They had planted bombs at Chilean institutions and US companies to protest against the dictatorship in Chile, and they had attacked Israeli institutions to express solidarity with the Palestinian people. The Women of the Revolutionary Cell were the first group members who fought for themselves and emphasized the personal dimension of their violent protest. Rather than claiming to fight for workers, people in the Third World or other oppressed people, the perpetrators made demands as women and acted on their own behalf. To this extent, the attack can be understood as one of the first practical applications of the previously mentioned feminist principle that 'the personal is political' in the militant Left in West Germany.

In the claim of responsibility, the Women of the Revolutionary Cell adopted a position that might be described as anarchist feminist. They claimed that it made no difference to them whether six judges or six hundred members of parliament made decisions regarding women's reproductive rights and other important issues, as they were opposed to all forms of political representation. Contrary to other critics of paragraph 218, the WoRC emphasized that they did not understand the court's decision as a misinterpretation of the constitution. Rather, the group considered the constitution itself to be an effective tool of state oppression. The women explained that they had planted the bomb:

> 'Not to protect the constitution against the Federal Court of Justice . . . , but to protect *us* from the constitution; a constitution that provides the legal framework for the daily exploitation, attrition and psychological breakdown of millions of women and men. A constitution that illegalizes women and that incites the death of many women who do not want to accept that the mafia of medics and judges decides about their relations to their own bodies and the number of children they have.'[43]

In line with many other women in West Germany, the WoRC demanded the right to decide freely about their bodies and sexuality and criticized the position of judges, medics and clerics who opposed a decriminalization of abortions. However, their tone was more aggressive than that of most opponents of the abortion ban. They referred to politicians and judges as 'sleazebags' and encouraged women to publicly shame and beat up medics who made money with illegal abortions. The WoRC accused the Church of being a 'fascist institution' (*faschistische Struktur*) dividing women into 'mothers and whores, "purified" by or punished for their sexuality with pregnancy',[44] and referred to priests as 'pitiful chickenfuckers' (*armselige Hühnerficker*). 'We have not forgotten', declared the group, 'that, in the Middle Ages, they [i.e. churchmen] burnt our feminist sisters at the stake.'[45] While their name identifies them as part of the Revolutionary Cell, their statement suggests that the perpetrators also identified as feminists.

The attack itself and the claim of responsibility indicate that the Women of the Revolutionary Cell deemed violence a legitimate and necessary means to overcome patriarchal structures. Even if the perpetrators minimized the risk of casualties by detonating the bomb at the courthouse at a time when nobody was in the building, they were not opposed to violence against people. In the claim of responsibility, they expressed solidarity with all women who 'got rid of the men who exploit them',[46] and they openly called for attacks against medics who earned money with illegal abortions and other 'enemies of the people' (*Volksfeinde*) – capitalists, clergymen, politicians, judges and members of the press.[47] According to the WoRC, the state could not protect all public authorities, and they mentioned the abduction of the politician Peter Lorenz by members of the MJ2 a few days before their own attack as a case in point.[48] They tried to encourage workers, students and women to follow their example by forming guerrilla groups and asserting their demands by force. The claim of responsibility ended with the following sentence: 'The day will come, when women will rise up . . . but only if we get things moving today.'[49]

In the first issue of the illegally printed and distributed RC magazine *Revolutionärer Zorn* (Revolutionary Rage), the Women of the Revolutionary Cell expanded on their motives and aims. Here they declared that they had attacked the Federal Court of Justice for two reasons. Firstly, they sought to defend themselves against 'the constitution of this imperialist state, to fight against this shameful verdict of class justice and the hypocrisy of priests and medics'.[50] Secondly, they wanted to convince other feminists that 'consciousness-raising groups, women's shops, self-help (abortion) etc. are not sufficient to stop the dreadful activities of medics, priests and notorious chauvinists',[51] unless they were combined with militant and violent protest. Both the claim of responsibility and the short statement in *Revolutionary Rage* illustrate that it was a principal aim of militant feminists and feminist militants in the RC to spread militant forms of protest in the New Women's Movement.

'A Substitute for the Slacking 218 Movement'? Responses to the Bombing

It is difficult to draw a nuanced picture of the reactions and discussions that the bombing in Karlsruhe and the statements by the Women of the Revolutionary Cell sparked in West Germany. The claim of responsibility received virtually no attention in the West German media, and most newspapers ignored the attack or mentioned it only in passing.[52] Only the *Frankfurter Rundschau* and a few newspapers from the Karlsruhe area went into more detail about the bombing. Most of these reports were based on information that Federal Minister of Justice Hans-Jochen Vogel had provided in a press conference the day after the attack. At this conference, Vogel posted an award of 50,000 DM for information that would lead to the arrest of the perpetrators, who had disappeared without a trace.[53] He left no doubt that he understood the bombing as a 'challenge to the state' and as an attack 'against the constitutional principle that this institution engendered'.[54] An article in the *Frankfurter Rundschau* echoed this view: 'The attack in Karlsruhe did not destroy a random building. The bombing was directed against an institution that represents the state. The Federal Court of Justice, a centrepiece of this democracy and accorded great significance by the constitution, became the object of fanaticism that could express itself no longer in anything but blind hatred.'[55]

In the radical Left, the court bombing received little attention. The editors of the Frankfurt based Sponti newspaper *Wir Wollen Alles* (We Want Everything) reprinted the claim of responsibility without adding any comments or discussing the statement any further.[56] In the following years, the magazine's editors took a more explicit stance on the politics of the RC and criticized the group openly.[57] A prison note from Ulrike Meinhof indicates that the detained founding members of the RAF were also dismissive of the tactics of the RC in general and of the bombing at the Federal Court of Justice in particular. Meinhof's scathing criticism read as follows: 'Their [i.e. the WoRC] action against the Federal Court of Justice was shit, a substitute for the slacking 218 movement, which cannot be revived with such an action; especially because they have chosen the wrong target.'[58] Although this might have been lost in translation, Meinhof used a strikingly phallic metaphor to comment on the development of the feminist movement in the FRG.[59]

Given that the ban on abortion was a central topic in the New Women's Movement, it is interesting that there were hardly any public feminist responses to the attack at the Federal Court of Justice.[60] On 6 March, the newspaper *Die Welt* reported that thirteen women's groups had distanced themselves resolutely from the bombing.[61] The editors of the fifth issue of the autonomous feminist magazine *Frauenzeitung: Frauen gemeinsam sind stark* (Women's Newspaper: Women Together Are Strong) chose a different path. Rather than condemning or endorsing the bombing, they reprinted the full claim of responsibility by the Women of the Revolutionary Cell and confined themselves to the following comment (capitalized in the original):

AFTER THE EDITORIAL DEADLINE FOR THIS ISSUE, WE RECEIVED THE FOLLOWING DECLARATION BY THE WOMEN OF THE REVOLUTIONARY CELL THAT WE PRINT WORD-FOR-WORD FOR DOCUMENTARY REASONS. PLEASE SEND LETTERS AND CONTRIBUTIONS TO A DISCUSSION ABOUT THE TEXT OF THESE COMRADES TO THE EDITORS OF THE NEXT ISSUE![62]

The next issue of the *Frauenzeitung*, however, included neither readers' letters nor a discussion of the claim of responsibility.[63] Whether there was simply nothing to publish, or the editors decided not to include the contributions they had received, the effect was the same. The discussion (or lack of such) in the *Frauenzeitung* is expressive of the public silence with which the bombing in Karlsruhe seems to have been met in the New Women's Movement.

Feminist activists and scholars have critically examined obvious and hidden power structures that marginalize and silence women in patriarchal societies, and they have documented and analysed the voices and experiences of women across the globe. Yet, it is important to acknowledge that there are many reasons for and forms of silence. Róisín Ryan-Flood and Rosalind Gill rightly emphasize that 'one may silence or be silenced, keep silent out of respect, rage, fear or shame, or even as a mode of resistance'.[64] Since all research involves silences of various kinds, feminist scholars have to pay careful attention to the context in which moments of silence occur in the research process and distinguish between manifestations of restrictive silence (e.g. as a result of censorship or shame) and forms of engaged or oppositional silence (e.g. during silent vigils or protests).

Moreover, we have to be aware of the fact that feminist discourses, too, can marginalize and silence certain views and experiences. Although the lack of public feminist responses to the courtroom bombing and other acts of political violence with a feminist agenda does not necessarily reflect a lack of discussion within feminist circles, it is symptomatic of a wider silence on feminist political violence. Previous research on feminism in West Germany has reinforced rather than challenged this silence.[65]

There are many reasons for the silence around militant feminist protest in the FRG. State and police authorities still know very little about the structure and activities of the Red Zora and other militant feminist groups, and former members and sympathizers of the groups have been anxious not to reveal information that could incriminate themselves or others. As a result, many feminists today are simply not aware of the fact that they existed. Another reason is that highly confrontational protest was the exception rather than the rule, and it is a widespread belief that it had little or no impact on feminist campaigns in the FRG. Ideological differences are a third reason why most groups in the New Women's Movement have paid little attention to feminist ideas and activities in the militant Left: they considered violent protest irreconcilable with feminist politics. One of the main objectives of the Red Zora was to convince other feminists of the worth of confrontational tactics.

The Red Zora: Bombs and Poems against the Abortion Ban

As highlighted in the previous chapter, the Red Zora formed in the mid-1970s as a women's group in the militant leftist network Revolutionary Cells. In April 1977, the group carried out a first attack under the name Red Zora. Like the bombing at the Federal Court of Justice, this attack was directed against an institution that the women deemed responsible for the insistence on the abortion ban: the headquarters of the German Medical Association in Cologne. Shortly after the attack, they released a claim of responsibility that featured, for the first time in history, the name and logo of the Red Zora (see figure 3.1).

The short statement was characterized by an aggressive tone similar to that of the claim of responsibility for the attack in Karlsruhe. The text referred to medics as 'pigs' (*Schweine*) and 'rapists in white coats' (*Vergewaltiger in weißen Kitteln*) and attacked the German Medical Association sharply for its insistence on the abortion ban.[66] 'Worried about losing the lucrative business of illegal abortions, they [the medics] have successfully opposed the deletion of paragraph 218 with their all-pervading power over the human body.'[67] However, rather than identifying themselves as part of the militant Left – as the Women of the Revolutionary Cells had done – the Zoras presented themselves as 'ordinary' women with an active interest in the New Women's Movement.[68] The claim of responsibility for the bombing at the German Medical Association did not mention the activities of other militant leftist groups, and the authors did not endorse

frauen erhebt euch und die welt erlebt euch!

Am 28.4.1977 haben wir uns eine Nacht zurückerobert:die Bundesärztekammer in Köln kann nach unserer Vorarbeit jetzt ihren Frühjahrsputz halten.
Die Bundesärztekammer vereint die Macht der gesamten Ärzteschaft: die Landesärztekammern,verschiedene Ärzteverbände (z.B. den Hartmannbund)und die Kassenärztliche Vereinigung.

Das war unser Beitrag zur Walpurgisnacht.In der Walpurgisnacht zum 1.Mai demonstrieren überall in der BRD Frauen gegen Vergewaltigung - eine Form der Gewalt,die wir Frauen tagtäglich in der Familie, in der Werbung,im Betrieb,auf der Straße und beim Frauenarzt erleben.

Wir verstehen die Bundesärztekammer als Vertreter der Vergewaltiger in weißen Kitteln,die sich über unser Selbstbestimmungsrecht hinwegsetzen und mit unseren Körpern Profit machen wie die großen Chemiekonzerne.Die Handlanger der Chemiekonzerne in Gestalt der Arzneimittelkommission sitzen unter einem Dach mit dem Ärztepack.

Besorgt um den Verlust ihrer Einnahmen durch illegale Abtreibungen und um ihre Allmacht über den menschlichen Körper wehren sie sich bis heute erfolgreich gegen eine Streichung des § 218.

Vor der "Reform" riet uns der Hartmannbund:"Treibt doch mit dem Schürhaken ab!" (anläßlich eines go-ins in Oberursel)

Nach der "Reform" sind wir Frauen vollends des Ärzten ausgeliefert:
- 2/3 der Ärzte boykottieren die Abtreibungen
- Gutachten über die soziale Notlage werden von vielen Chefärzten nicht anerkannt

Gleichzeitig soll auf unsere Kosten gespart werden:die Kassenärztliche Vereinigung fordert aus dem Hinterhof der Bundesärztekammer heraus die Streichung der Mutterschaftsvorsorge und die Streichung sachfremder Ausgaben,die durch den § 218 entstehen.

Dabei geht es den meisten Ärzten schon lange nicht mehr um das gesundheitliche Wohlbefinden ihrer Patienten:ihnen geht es vielmehr darum,die Leute fit für die Arbeit zu halten.Der Vorsitzende der Kassenärztlichen Vereinigung Nord - Württemberg:"Im Krankheitsfall sollte sich in den ersten sechs Wochen zunächst einmal die Einkommenssituation verschlechtern,damit ein Anreiz zum Gesundwerden da ist."

Damit die Ärzte pro Jahr und Nase durchschnittlich 170.000 DM einstreichen können,geht jede 9. von uns verdiente Mark an die Krankenkassen.

Die Schweine haben Namen.Frauen,sucht euch die Adressen,z.B. in Telefonbüchern ! Frauen,denkt an Sewering,Alt - Nazi und SS - Mitglied seit 33,heute CSU - Mitglied und Präsident der Bundesärztekammer ! Ihm widmen wir die folgenden Zeilen:

ES SCHÜTZT DICH KEINE MAUER
WIR LIEGEN AUF DER LAUER
DIE ROTEN ZORAS WERDEN TRAINIEREN
UND AUCH DIR DIE FRESSE POLIEREN
DAS AUTO FLAMBIEREN
DEN GARTEN SEZIEREN
DIE VILLA DEMOLIEREN

Rote Zora

GRÜNDET EURE EIGENEN BANDEN - GRUSS UND KUSS DIE

Figure 3.1 First claim of responsibility by the Red Zora. Courtesy FrauenMediaTurm, Cologne (FB.07.102).

fatal attacks against perceived oppressors. Although less than a page long, the flyer addressed several central themes in the New Women's Movement: rape and violence against women, reproductive rights, paragraph 218 and the gendered nature of poverty.

The spirit and purpose of the first RZ statement were clearly inspired by the New Women's Movement. The title ('Women rise up, and the world will see you'[69]) was a quote from a giant banner at the Federal Women's Conference in March 1972, the first event where women from towns and cities across West Germany discussed aims and politics of the women's movement. It was also a quote from a song by the Flying Lesbians, the first female rock band in West Germany.[70] By presenting the bombing as a contribution to the feminist Walpurgisnight, which will be discussed in more detail in the following chapter, the Red Zora associated itself with a transnational feminist protest campaign. On 30 April 1977, women's groups across West Germany organized colourful demonstrations and parties on the streets to 'reclaim the night' and to protest against sexual violence against women and girls.[71] A comparison between a flyer for the feminist Walpurgisnight by an autonomous women's centre in Berlin and the first RZ statement shows similarities in tone and style (see figure 3.2). Using short sentences and a language that can be easily understood, the women's collective in Berlin urged women to reclaim the night and to fight back against violence and rape. Like the RZ statement, the Walpurgisnight flyer featured a poem and a variation of the Venus symbol.

The claim of responsibility indicates that the Red Zora wanted to follow up on previous protest against paragraph 218. The text explicitly mentions a feminist 'go-in' during a meeting of the German Medical Association in 1973 that was met with great hostility by participants.[72] The text concluded with a poem. Addressed to the president of the German Medical Association, it noted: 'No wall will protect you / We're on the lookout / The Red Zora will train hard / To smash your face in / To flambé your car / To dissect your garden / To demolish your villa.'[73] While aligning themselves with feminist activists who drew on explicitly nonviolent protest in the struggle against paragraph 218, the authors called for actions with a significantly higher degree of confrontation. This position isolated the Red Zora in feminist circles in the FRG. The only group who had called for similarly confrontational tactics in the campaign for free and safe abortions was the Women of the Revolutionary Cell.

One of the few studies on political violence in the FRG that mention that there was militant and violent protest against the abortion ban suggests that the groups behind the bombing at the Federal Court of Justice in 1975 and at the German Medical Association in 1977 were identical,[74] but there is no clear evidence supporting this claim. In 1984, a member of the Red Zora responded to the question 'What have you done so far and against which background?' as follows: 'The Women of the Revolutionary Cell started with a bombing at the Federal Court of Justice in 1974 [sic], because we all wanted the abolition of paragraph 218 and not the easily manipulable indication model.[75] On Walpurgisnight 1977, we planted a bomb at the German Medical Association, because it blocked even this reduced reform of the abortion law.'[76]

The prominent error in the statement (the bombing at the Federal Court of Justice happened in 1975 not in 1974) makes it unlikely that the respondent was

Frauen, wir erobern uns die Nacht zurück!

35.000 Frauen werden jährlich in der BRD und West-Berlin vergewaltigt, weil sie

- nachts alleine auf der Strasse waren,
- angeblich aufreizende Kleidung trugen,
- Autostop gemacht haben,
- alleine in eine Kneipe gingen,
- sich von Bekannten nach Hause fahren liessen,
- mit der U-Bahn fuhren,
- im Hinterhaus wohnen,
- bei offenem Fenster schlafen,
- Schichtdienst haben,
- einen Bekannten in die Wohnung liessen,
- Freunde besuchten,
- weil niemand auf ihre Hilferufe reagierte, Nachbarn und Passanten nicht eingegriffen haben, weil sie meinen, daß die Frauen ihre Situation selbst verschulden.

Das bedeutet: 51% der Bevölkerung haben abends Ausgangssperre, nämlich alle Frauen, vom kleinen Mädchen bis zur Rentnerin.
Von frühester Kindheit an wird uns eingebleut, daß wir uns vor Männern in Acht nehmen sollen. Diese Angst hindert uns, uns frei zu bewegen, lähmt uns, wenn wir uns wehren sollten, – sie ist unser unsichtbares Gefängnis.

Frauen, hören wir auf, dies als selbstverständlich hinzunehmen:

schreien wir zurück,
schlagen wir zurück,
wehren wir uns gemeinsam!

FRAUENZENTRUM, Berlin 61
Stresemannstr.40, Tel.251.09.12

Wenn Frauen NEIN sagen, dann meinen sie auch NEIN!

Setzen Frauen sich zur Wehr, gibt es Vergewaltigung nicht mehr

Frauen, hört Ihr Frauen schrein, lasst die andere nicht allein!

Mit uns gemeinsam demonstrieren heute nacht Frauen in vielen Städten der BRD. Ausgangssperre bei Dunkelheit, ist das Los der Weiblichkeit!

Frauen, leistet Widerstand gegen Vergewaltiger im Land schliesst Euch fest zusammen!

Frauen·Nacht·Demo: 30.4.77 Savignyplatz 20⁰⁰

Figure 3.2 Flyer for the first Walpurgisnight protest in Berlin. Courtesy FrauenMediaTurm, Cologne (FB.07.104).

directly involved in the attack. However, it is worth noting that she mentions the bombing in Karlsruhe, refers to the WoRC and RZ as 'we all' and emphasizes that both groups had a common goal – the decriminalization of abortions. Due to the lack of data, it is difficult to prove or challenge any claim about the membership of the WoRC and the founding members of the RZ, but there is good reason to believe that both groups were not completely identical. The three women interviewed for this study signalled that they were not in a position to comment on the formative years of the RZ, but they assumed that the founding members of the RZ included not only members of the RC but also feminist activists from outside the group.[77]

What distinguished members of the Red Zora from most other feminists in West Germany was their belief that violence was essential to the liberation of women. In 1993, members of the Red Zora explained why:

> But every woman who once threw a stone, who did not quietly accept sexual assault but hit back instead, will understand how liberated we felt when we destroyed sex shops or planted a bomb in front of the Federal Court of Justice on the occasion of the judgement on paragraph 218. In this society, liberation requires destruction. We need to destroy the structures that chain us to the role of the woman; and we can only destroy these structures if we attack the conditions that seek to destroy us. These attacks have to be consistent with our intransigent hatred against this society, but they can take many different forms. Even if this position is hardly developed in the women's movement, we consider armed attacks an essential part of the women's struggle.[78]

The Red Zora considered violent protest legitimate from a feminist point of view for a number of reasons. Firstly, they argued that the existing political regime was sexist and imperialist to the core, and that many women had no other option but to use violent means to defend themselves against legal and illegal forms of exploitation and abuse.[79] Secondly, the RZ claimed that the use of violent tactics could have an empowering effect on women. In a theory paper from 1981, the group criticized how passivity and submissiveness were instilled in women from an early age. According to the RZ, women had to stop thinking of themselves as mere victims of patriarchy and stand up to fight for themselves and other people to challenge the existing power structures.[80]

Drawing on their own experiences, the Zoras claimed that the use of violent tactics could help women to overcome fear, powerlessness and resignation and to challenge repressive (gender) norms.[81] To the extent that the bombing at the Federal Court of Justice, attacks against sex shops, violent resistance against sexually abusive men and other violent acts by women break with the notion of woman as caring and nurturing mother (to be), as passive victim and as object of male desire, the Red Zora considered them active steps towards the liberation of women. Finally, the RZ claimed that, as part of broader protest campaigns, violent attacks could play a vital role in feminist solidarity campaigns if they took the form of feminist 'counter-violence'. While this approach met with little support in the feminist campaign against paragraph 218, it attracted significantly more attention and sympathy in the movement against violence against women.

Notes

1. D. Rucht (1991), 'Soziale Bewegungen, Gegenbewegungen und Staat: Der Abtreibungskonflikt in den USA, Frankreich und der Bundesrepublik Deutschland', *Forschungsjournal Neue Soziale Bewegungen* 2, 33.
2. Ibid.
3. Previous research suggests that there were between 86,000 and 1,000,000 abortions per annum. See Lenz, *Die Neue Frauenbewegung*, 70; Schulz, *Der Lange Atem der Provokation*, 157.
4. 'Wir haben abgetrieben', *Stern*, no. 24, 6 June 1971, 16–23.
5. A. Schwarzer (1981), *So fing es an! 10 Jahre Frauenbewegung*, 24; C. Schäfer and C. Wilke (2000), *Die Neue Frauenbewegung in München 1968–1985. Eine Dokumentation*, Munich: Buchendorfer Verlag, 170.
6. Schwarzer, *So fing es an! 10 Jahre Frauenbewegung*, 24.
7. A number of testimonies are presented in the *arte*-documentary 'Wir haben abgetrieben' (dir. by Birgit Schulz and Annette Zinkant) from 2011. See also J. Kramm, 'Sie war eine der Frauen, die vor 30 Jahren bekannten: "Wir haben abgetrieben!" Heute, in der Gendebatte [sic], fällt Nori Möding das Argumentieren schwerer: Zwei Leben', *Berliner Zeitung*, 6 June 2001.
8. 'Der Aufstand der Frauen', *Emma*, no. 6, 1991, 16–21, 18.
9. The quoted passage is from a public letter by Cardinal Julius Döpfner featuring a close-up image of an embryo in the tenth week of pregnancy. 'Wie immer die Entscheidung im Deutschen Bundestag zur Änderung des § 218 ausfällt, die deutschen Bischöfe werden nicht aufhören, . . . die Abtreibung als ungerechtfertigte Tötung menschlichen Lebens zu bezeichnen.' Source: public letter from 28 March 1973, FFBIZ, A Rep. 400, Berlin, 20 FZ (1–3).
10. Schulz, *Der Lange Atem der Provokation*, 151.
11. Kramm. 'Sie war eine der Frauen, die vor 30 Jahren bekannten'.
12. 'Hiermit erkläre ich . . .', *Der Spiegel*, 11 March 1974.
13. Schulz, 'Echoes of Provocation', 140.
14. Schulz, *Der Lange Atem der Provokation*, 108.
15. Lenz, *Die Neue Frauenbewegung*, 77.
16. Frauenaktion 70 was a group of socialist and liberal women that had formed in the context of a project on women's emancipation in the citizens' initiative Humanistische Union in 1969. See R. Scheunemann and K. Scheunemann (1971), 'Die Kampagne der "Frauenaktion 70" gegen den § 218. Ein Versuch zur Emanzipation durch Selbsttätigkeit', in H. Grossmann (ed.), *Bürgerinitiativen: Schritte zur Veränderung?* Frankfurt: Fischer, 71–84.
17. Ibid., 79.
18. Ibid., 82.
19. Schulz, *Der Lange Atem der Provokation*, 148.
20. Frevert, *Frauen-Geschichte*, 279.
21. G. Helwig (1997), 'Frau und Gesellschaft', in Bundeszentrale für politische Bildung (ed.), *Frauen in Deutschland – Informationen zur politischen Bildung*. Retrieved 10 October 2015 from http://www.bpb.de/publikationen/D6SSWQ,0,0,Frau_und_Gesellschaft.html#art0.
22. 'Der Lebensschutz der Leibesfrucht genießt grundsätzlich für die gesamte Dauer der Schwangerschaft Vorrang vor dem Selbstbestimmungsrecht der Schwangeren und darf nicht für eine bestimmte Frist infrage gestellt werden'; Deutsche Welle, KalenderBlatt, '25.2.1975: Urteil zum "Abtreibungsparagrafen" 218'. Retrieved 15 June 2015 from http://www.kalenderblatt.de/index.php?what=thmanu&lang=de&manu_id=123&sdt=20120225&maca=de-podcast_kalenderblatt-1086-xml-mrss.
23. R. Lamprecht (2011), *Das Bundesverfassungsgericht: Geschichte und Entwicklung*, Bonn: Bundeszentrale für Politische Bildung, 157–58.
24. R. Strobel (2004), 'Die Neue Frauenbewegung', in W. Faulstich (ed.), *Die Kultur der 70er Jahre*, Munich: Wilhelm Fink, 259–72.

25. C. Usborne (2007), *Cultures of Abortion in Weimar Germany*, New York: Berghahn Books, 6.
26. 'Selbstherrlich und zynisch', *Der Spiegel*, 17 February 1975.
27. 'rote Farbe als Symbol für Blut, für das Blut der Frauen, die bei illegalen Abtreibungen ums Leben kommen'; D.E. Zimmer, 'Denunzieren wider Willen', *Die Zeit*, 7 March 1975.
28. 'Von hinten gegriffen', *Der Spiegel*, 24 February 1975.
29. Ibid.
30. 'Selbstherrlich und zynisch'.
31. I. Münzing, 'Ärzte-Anzeige gegen Münchner Frauenzentrum', *Abendzeitung München*, 15 July 1975.
32. '§218: "Mit sozialer Notlage ist nichts drin"', *Der Spiegel*, no. 49, 29 November 1976, 75.
33. On its official website, the Federal Court of Justice states: 'Die offene Bauweise soll den Eindruck demokratischer Transparenz vermitteln'; 'Gebäude'. Retrieved 20 December 2015 from http://www.bundesverfassungsgericht.de/DE/Gebaeude/gebaeude_node.html.
34. 'Ein Bauwerk mit Anspruch auf Qualität', *Badische Neueste Nachrichten*, 6 May 1969.
35. Lamprecht, *Das Bundesverfassungsgericht*, 159.
36. BAK, B 362/7379, letter from the state criminal police Baden-Wuerttemberg from 29 April 1975, 3.
37. H. Kühnert, 'Vogel: Anschlag auf Rechtsstaatlichkeit', *Süddeutsche Zeitung*, 6 March 1975.
38. According to a letter from the state criminal police of Baden-Wuerttemberg from 29 April 1975, the perpetrators posted their declaration to the editors of *Der Spiegel*, *Stuttgarter Zeitung*, *Kölner Stadtanzeiger*, *Frankfurter Rundschau* and to the Axel Springer publishing house (BAK, B 362/7379, 4).
39. Ibid.
40. 'Spuren zum BVG-Anschlag', *Badische Neueste Nachrichten*, 7 March 1975.
41. BAK, B 362/7379, letter from the state criminal police Baden-Wuerttemberg from 29 April 1975.
42. BAK, B 362/7383, 'telefax des bka, abt. sg., bonn bad godesberg', 18 November 1973.
43. 'Nicht, um die Verfassung gegen das Verfassungsgericht zu schützen, wie Herr Abendroth meint, sondern um uns vor der Verfassung zu schützen. Einer Verfassung, die den legalen Rahmen liefert für die tagtägliche Ausbeutung, Zermürbung und psychische Zerrüttung von Millionen Frauen und Männern. Einer Verfassung, die Frauen illegalisiert viele in den Tod treibt wenn sie sich nicht von der Ärzte- und Richtermafia ihre Sexualität, den Umgang mit ihrem eigenen Körper, die Zahl ihrer Kinder vorschreiben lassen'; FMT, PD-SE.11.15, 'Erklärung der REVOLUTIONÄREN ZELLE zu ihrem Anschlag auf das Bundesverfassungsgericht', in *Frauenzeitung*, no. 5.
44. 'entweder Mütter oder Huren, geläutert bzw. bestraft für ihre Sexualität durch Schwangerschaft'; FMT, PD-SE.11.15, 'Erklärung der REVOLUTIONÄREN ZELLE', 2.
45. 'Wir haben nicht vergessen, dass sie unsere feministischen Schwestern im Mittelalter auf dem Scheiterhaufen verbrannt haben'; ibid. .
46. 'die sich ihren Unterdrücker vom Hals schaffen'; ibid.
47. Ibid.
48. Ibid.
49. 'Der Tag wird kommen, wo die Frauen sich erheben . . . aber nicht, ohne daß wir uns heute schon bewegen'; ibid.
50. 'um uns gegen die Verfassung dieses imperialistischen Staates zu schützen, um gegen dieses Schandurteil der Klassenjustiz, gegen die Heuchelei von Pfaffen und Kurpfuschern vorzugehen'; ibid.
51. 'dass Selbsterfahrungsgruppen, Frauenläden, Selbsthilfe (Abtreibung) usw. nicht genügen, daß Ärzte, Pfaffen, notorische Chauvinisten nicht länger ihr Unwesen treiben dürfen'; ibid., 64.
52. A few hours after the bomb had exploded at the Federal Court of Justice, Peter Lorenz regained his freedom after six days of captivity in a basement in Berlin-Kreuzberg. In the following

days, the cover pages of national and local newspapers were preoccupied with the kidnapping in Berlin. Due to the media hype surrounding this attack, the courthouse bombing received very little attention in the German press. While attacks against property attracted generally less media interest than assassinations, kidnappings and other attacks against people, the bombing in Karlsruhe received considerably less attention than similar attacks in the history of the RC. Only the *Frankfurter Rundschau* and a few newspapers from the Karlsruhe area went into more detail about the bombing.

53. BAK, B 106/106662, 'Auslobung', 5 March 1975.
54. 'Herausforderung des Staates', 'der das rechtsstaatliche Grundprinzip, das sich in dieser Institution verkörpere, treffen sollte'; 'Anschlag in Karlsruhe noch ungeklärt', *Frankfurter Rundschau*, 6 March 1975; Kühnert, 'Vogel: Anschlag'.
55. 'Der Karlsruher Anschlag zertrümmerte nicht ein beliebiges Gebäude. Die Bombe sollte eine Institution treffen, sichtbare Repräsentanz des Staates. Das Bundesverfassungsgericht, ein Kernstück dieser Demokratie und durch das Grundgesetz mit hohem Rang versehen, ist das Objekt eines Fanatismus geworden, der sich nur noch in blindem Hass zu artikulieren vermag'; 'Blinder Hass', *Frankfurter Rundschau*, 6 March 1975.
56. FMT, PD-SE.11.15, *WIR WOLLEN ALLES*, no. 26, March 1975.
57. Some of the most vocal critics of the politics of the Revolutionary Cell and other militant leftist groups in the Sponti-scene in Frankfurt were the future politicians Daniel Cohn-Bendit and Joschka Fischer. For a detailed description of the position of both, see A.M. Siemens (2006), 'Durch die Institutionen oder in den Terrorismus: Die Wege von Joschka Fischer, Daniel Cohn-Bendit, Hans-Joachim Klein und Johannes Weinrich', PhD thesis, Ludwig-Maximilians-University-Munich.
58. 'ihre aktion gegen den BVG war scheiße, substitut der abschlaffenden 218-bewegung, die so nicht hochzukriegen ist. zumal der addressat der falsche war'; HIS, Me, U/008,003.
59. In a more detailed analysis of Meinhof's writings, Sarah Colvin highlights that the word 'cunt' (*Votze*) was 'standard terminology' in the RAF; Colvin, *Ulrike Meinhof*, 208–9.
60. I have consulted the following archives: the Spinnboden archive and the FFBIZ in Berlin, the Frauenmediaturm in Cologne and the 'Auszeiten' archive in Bochum. I have also searched for responses to the attack in the Papiertiger archive in Berlin, in the Federal Archives, the IISH in Amsterdam, the HIS archive in Hamburg and in the newspaper department of the Staatsbibliothek Berlin.
61. 'Frauen bekennen: Wir legten die Bombe', *Die Welt*, 6 March 1975. Alas, the unidentified author decided not to specify this claim any further or to mention the names of the thirteen groups.
62. 'NACH REDAKTIONSSCHLUSS ... GING UNS FOLGENDE ERKLÄRUNG DER FRAUEN DER REVOLUTIONÄREN ZELLE ZU, DIE WIR AUS DOKUMENTARISCHEN GRÜNDEN IM WORTLAUT ... ABDRUCKEN. ZUSCHRIFTEN UND DISKUSSIONSBEITRÄGE ZU DIESEM PAPIER DER GENOSSINNEN SCHICKT AN DIE READAKTIONSGRUPPE DER NÄCHSTEN FZ!' FMT, PD-SE.11.15, 'Erklärung der REVOLUTIONÄREN ZELLE', 1.
63. I owe this insight to Jasmin Schenk from the FrauenMediaTurm, who assisted me with the research.
64. S. Malhotra and A. Carrillo Rowe (2013), *Silence, Feminism, Power: Reflections at the Edges of Sound*, New York: Palgrave Macmillan, 1.
65. See e.g. Schlaeger and Vedder-Shults, 'The West German Women's Movement'; Altbach, 'The New German Women's Movement'; Frevert, *Frauen-Geschichte*; Haug, 'The Women's Movement in West Germany'; Schulz, *Der lange Atem der Provokation*; Marx Ferree, *Varieties of Feminism*.
66. Die Rote Zora (1977), 'Frauen erhebt euch und die Welt erlebt euch!' FMT, FB.07.102.
67. 'Besorgt um den Verlust ihrer Einnahmen durch illegale Abtreibungen und mit ihrer Allmacht über den menschlichen Körper, wehren sie sich bis heute erfolgreich gegen eine Streichung des 218'; ibid.

68. In contrast to other militant leftist groups in West Germany, the members of the Red Zora spoke openly about their personal living conditions, circumstances and sexual orientation. A statement from 1984 suggests that the RZ had both heterosexual and lesbian members. In an interview for the feminist magazine *Emma*, the Red Zora introduced itself as a group of 'women between 20 and 51, some of us sell our labour on the market of possibilities, some take what we want, others have not yet fallen through the social net. Several women have children, many others don't. Some women are lesbian, others love men. We shop in terrible supermarkets, we live in ugly houses, we enjoy going for walks or to the cinema, to the theatre, to the discothèque. We like having parties and enjoy doing nothing' ('Frauen zwischen 20 und 51, einige von uns verkaufen ihre Arbeitskraft auf dem Markt der Möglichkeiten, einige nehmen sich, was sie brauchen, andere sind noch nicht durchs soziale Netz gefallen. Einige haben Kinder, viele andere nicht. Manche Frauen sind lesbisch, andere lieben Männer. Wir kaufen in ekelhaften Supermärkten, wir wohnen in hässlichen Häusern, wir gehen gerne spazieren oder ins Kino, ins Theater, die Disco, wir feiern Feste, wir pflegen das Nichtstun'; ID Verlag, *Die Früchte des Zorns*, 457).
69. 'Frauen erhebt euch und die Welt erlebt euch.'
70. In their book *Lesbian Peoples: Material for a Dictionary*, Monique Wittig and Sande Zweig describe the Flying Lesbians as a 'tribe of companion lovers who, as their name indicates, are wanderers. The Flying Lesbians come from Germany and have companion lovers everywhere. Singers and musicians, they owe their celebrity to the fact that they were the first group of wandering lesbians in the raving that began the Glorious Age'; M. Wittig and S. Zweig (1979), *Lesbian Peoples: Material for a Dictionary*, New York: Avon, 56.
71. Chapter 4 offers a more detailed discussion of the feminist Walpurgisnight marches.
72. According to an article in the news magazine *Spiegel*, medics told the women to go home and to abort with an iron poker; 'Abtreibung: Massenmord oder Privatsache'.
73. 'Es schützt Dich keine Mauer / Wir liegen auf der Lauer / Die Roten Zoras werden trainieren / Um auch Dir die Fresse zu polieren / Das Auto flambieren / Den Garten sezieren / Die Villa demolieren'; ibid.
74. G. Boeden (1989), 'Die Herausforderung unseres demokratischen Rechtsstaates durch den linksextremistischen Terrorismus', in Bundesminister des Innern (ed.), *Extremismus und Terrorismus*, Bonn: Bundesminister des Innern, 63–79, 71.
75. The 'indication model' (*Indikationsmodell*) exempted abortions within the first three months from punishment if pregnant women could persuade independent medical experts that their situation was so dreadful that they could not be expected to continue the pregnancy.
76. 'Angefangen haben die Frauen der RZ 1974 mit einem Bombenanschlag auf das Bundesverfassungsgericht in Karlsruhe, weil wir ja alle die Abschaffung des 218 wollten und nicht diese jederzeit manipulierbare Indikationslösung. In der Walpurgisnacht 77 haben wir einen Sprengsatz bei der Bundesärztekammer gezündet, weil von dort aus selbst diese reduzierte Abtreibungsreform mit allen Mitteln hintertrieben wurde'; ID Verlag, *Die Früchte des Zorns*, 458.
77. Focus group with three former members of the Red Zora on 17 August 2012.
78. 'Aber jede Frau, die schon einen Stein geworfen hat, die auf Anmache von Männern nicht mit Rückzug reagiert, sondern zurückgeschlagen hat, wird unser Gefühl von Befreiung nachvollziehen können, das wir hatten, als wir Sexshops zerstörten oder eine Bombe anläßlich des Urteils zum § 218 vor dem Bundesverfassungsgericht zündeten. Befreiung hat in unserer Gesellschaft etwas mit Zerstörung zu tun. Zerstörung der Strukturen, die uns an die Frauenrolle ketten wollen. Und diese Strukturen lassen sich nur zerstören, wenn wir die Verhältnisse, die uns kaputtmachen wollen, angreifen. Angreifen in den vielfältigsten Formen, aber immer verbunden mit unserem unversöhnlichen Haß auf diese Gesellschaft. Die bewaffnete Form des Angriffs ist für uns ein unverzichtbarer Teil des Frauenkampfes. Diese Position ist wie wir beschrieben haben in der Frauenbewegung kaum entwickelt'; ID Verlag, *Die Früchte des Zorns*, 214.
79. Ibid., 460.
80. Die Rote Zora, 'Mili's Tanz auf dem Eis'.
81. Ibid.

Chapter 4

WOMEN FIGHTING BACK
Feminist Responses to Violence against Women

According to a recent survey, 40 per cent of women in Germany are or have been victims of physical violence or sexual abuse since the age of sixteen.[1] The first representative survey on violence against women in the FRG, commissioned by the Federal Ministry of Family Affairs, Senior Citizens, Women and Youth in 2003, came to similar findings. Although these statistics indicate that violence against women remains a problem that affects significant parts of the population, the very fact that they exist can be considered a concession to the New Women's Movement. They show that violence against women is not limited to physical acts of aggression by strangers. Informed by feminist theory and practice, recent studies try to document and tackle a range of forms of violence and intimidation, including domestic violence, street harassment and psychological violence. Although violence against women had been an issue in earlier feminist movements in Germany, the New Women's Movement brought about a new understanding of the gravity of this problem.

While groups in the bourgeois women's movement in the early twentieth century tended to see domestic violence and rape as '*Sittlichkeitsverbrechen*' (crimes against public decency), feminist activists in the New Women's Movement regarded both as structural problems in a patriarchal social order. Based on this analysis, their aim was to set up feminist support networks for female survivors of violence and abuse that sought to challenge the prevailing social order rather than fill gaps in existing welfare policy. A first step in this process was that feminist activists tried to find new ways of discussing and defining violence against women in the early 1970s. Due to a strong focus on the oppression of the working class

---

Notes for this section begin on page 110.

in the student movement, there was little awareness of and interest in gender-based violence and discrimination. As highlighted in chapter 1, many men and women in the student movement in West Germany considered the oppression of women to be a 'side contradiction' (*Nebenwiderspruch*), which would be resolved if the class system could be overcome.

The sexual revolution of the 1960s and the liberalization of the pornography legislation in 1975 had a profound impact on the public debate surrounding sexuality in West Germany.[2] In her insightful analysis of political pornography in West Germany, Mia Lee shows that although sex was seen as 'a vehicle of protest' in the late 1960s, it soon became apparent that 'it could neither vanquish authoritarianism nor deliver equality'.[3] In the late 1960s, publishers from across the political spectrum tried to boost their sales by including sexually explicit images in their publications. As a result, pictures of scantily dressed and naked women featured prominently in Klaus Röhl's *konkret* and other leftist magazines as well as in Axel Springer's tabloid *Bild*. In the 1970s, West German cinemas screened a wave of soft-porn and erotic films. In 1975, the controversial film *The Story of O* (Die Geschichte von O.) attracted 2 million more viewers than Volker Schlöndorff's screen adaptation of Heinrich Böll's *Die Verlorene Ehre der Katharina Blum*.[4] Based on a book that French author Anne Cécile Desclos published under the pseudonym Pauline Réage in 1954, *The Story of O* tells the story of a young woman who seems to enjoy being tortured, raped and humiliated by men.

Women's groups in West Germany responded to the first screenings of *The Story of O* in November 1975 with angry protests. According to film critic Stefan Volk, the most spectacular protests took place in West Berlin, Aachen, Bonn and Frankfurt where feminists expressed their opposition to the film by urinating in the cinema auditoriums and by pelting the screen with eggs and stink bombs.[5] In the eyes of the troublemakers (and many other feminists), *The Story of O* promoted rape because it gave the impression that women enjoyed male violence and forced sexual intercourse, even if they protested otherwise. One of the first public statements about gender-based violence in the New Women's Movement from the mid-1970s, a flyer by a women's group from Frankfurt, illustrates this point. Five years before radical feminist Robin Morgan coined the phrase 'pornography is the theory, rape is the practice',[6] the authors of the short statement claimed that the objectification and commodification of the female body in popular culture, and the sexualized images of violence against women in *The Story of O* and other films, 'prepared the ground' for violence against women.[7]

In their short statement, the feminists from Frankfurt emphasized that it was not enough to support victims of domestic abuse and sexual violence. As the title of the flyer, which was borrowed from one of Berthold Brecht's late poems, illustrates, the authors wanted to fight back: 'Surely, you will see that you will go under if you don't defend yourself.' The women expressed delight at the fact that there had 'finally' been attacks against sex shops and cinemas that were showing *The Story of O* and other erotic films in Frankfurt, and they called for further attacks: 'The actions against sex shops and cinemas are an expression of our rage. We are fighting against an image of women that turns us into toys for our men, an image that is reinforced on a daily basis in the media. We need to fight back, and will learn to fight back: sex shops and cinemas are just the beginning. Women, rise up, and the world will see you. Women together are strong.'[8] The quoted statement is interesting for a number of reasons. Firstly, it shows that already by 1974 feminist activists in West Germany had developed a broad definition of violence against women, which included compulsory heterosexuality, the commodification of women's bodies in advertising and a range of structural disadvantages that women faced in West Germany, and which emphasized the interrelatedness of these phenomena. Secondly, the statement illustrates that violence against women was no longer seen as a violation of the existing laws and norms affecting individual women but as a structural problem that affected *all* women.

The authors further emphasized this common ground by quoting popular feminist slogans, such as the previously mentioned, 'Women rise up, and the world will see you.'[9] Although attacks against sex shops and erotic cinemas have certainly not been met with unanimous approval in the New Women's Movement, many feminists could identify with the 'rage' against male violence that the women from Frankfurt expressed. In the course of the 1970s, feminist activists in West Germany created a range of feminist initiatives against gender-based violence including support networks for battered women and survivors of sexual violence, street protests, educational programmes, court actions and self-defence courses. As this chapter illustrates, there were also some women who took the law into their own hands and tried to punish alleged rapists or their lawyers.

Tackling Domestic Violence and Rape

One of the key principles of the New Women's Movement was that the personal was political. In the Western tradition, women have been associated with, and often limited to, the domestic sphere. In contrast to the male-dominated public domain, the domestic sphere has long been seen as a private space 'outside' of politics. West German law reflected this bias. The definition of rape in the Federal Republic was based on that in the Reich Penal Code from 1871. According to this definition, rape was limited to coerced extra-marital sex, and it was socially expected that married women have sexual intercourse with their husband. While attacks by strangers and acts of physical aggression in the public sphere were punishable under criminal law, domestic violence and sexual abuse in the family received little attention, and marital rape was not considered a crime. Feminist activists in West Germany tried to change this situation. In the early 1970s, they created networks and infrastructures with the aim of creating awareness for domestic violence and of supporting women who had experienced violence and sexual abuse.

Although the feminist movement against violence towards women in West Germany attracted considerable media attention and stimulated a broader public debate, the legal situation of survivors remained difficult.[10] It was only in 1997 that marital rape was considered as a crime in the FRG, and it took another five years before the Protection against Violence Act granted survivors of domestic violence and marital rape the right to stay in their home even if they had previously shared it with their abuser. Since they had little trust in Germany's 'male justice' (*Männerjustiz*), many activists in the New Women's Movement reached the conclusion that they had to take matters into their own hands. They set up support networks for survivors of domestic violence and sexual abuse, encouraged women to fight off attackers with whistles and self-defence skills, and started a range of initiatives to tackle the power structures that they associated with violence against women. One of the most successful initiatives in this area was the creation of radical feminist women's shelters (*Frauenhäuser*).

While women in the GDR and other socialist countries were well integrated into the labour market, less than half of the women in the FRG were gainfully employed until the late 1970s.[11] This resulted in the problem that many survivors of domestic violence simply did not know where to go, because they lived under the same roof as their abusers and were financially dependent on them.[12] In response to this problem, the world's first shelter for battered women opened its doors in Chiswick, London, in 1971. It was founded by feminist activist and author Erin Pizzey, whose 1974 book *Scream Quietly or the Neighbours Will Hear* became an important inspiration for feminist activists in West Germany and many other countries. By the time that Pizzey's book was published, the number of women's shelters in the United Kingdom had already grown to twenty, and feminist activists had set up similar projects in the United States, the Netherlands, Australia and Scotland.[13] The first German women's shelter opened its doors in West Berlin in 1976. Within a few months, similar projects were set up in Frankfurt, Cologne and Bielefeld. By the mid-1980s, there were more than one hundred women's shelters across Germany.[14]

Marx Ferree rightly emphasizes that 'although the idea of creating a place for women to escape their batterers was international, the feminist framework of autonomy turned it into a distinctive form of practice in West Germany'.[15] Rather than distinguishing between clients and service providers, political activists and ordinary women, or between victims and helpers, feminist activists in West Germany wanted to create non-hierarchical autonomous spaces for the collective empowerment of women. Many of the women involved in setting up the first women's shelters in West Germany had participated in the International Tribunal on Crimes against Women in Brussels, where violence against women had been discussed as a way in which men 'maintain, advance, or protest a setback in their power relations vis à vis women'.[16] In this spirit, activists in the women's shelter movement in West Germany did not merely want to support survivors of domestic violence and sexual abuse, but saw their activities as part of a broader struggle against patriarchal power relations. This political agenda distinguished radical feminist women's shelters from women's refuges run by the Church and other charitable organizations, with which feminist women's shelters in some cities competed for funding.[17] The question of whether it was legitimate or necessary to use public money to fund radical feminist women's shelters has been the subject of great controversy in the New Women's Movement. Despite tight financing conditions, women's shelters could establish themselves across the Federal Republic. According to a report by the Association of Women's Shelters in Germany, the 340 women's shelters across the country opened their doors in 2007 to 40,000 women and children.[18]

Feminist initiatives to create safe spaces for women in West Germany went hand in hand with attempts to reclaim and redefine the public sphere. Unlike marital rape, sexual attacks by strangers in public spaces were criminally prosecutable acts. Yet very few perpetrators were caught and convicted, and there was a high number of unrecorded cases. If alleged rapists had to defend themselves in court, the testimonies of survivors were not necessarily taken seriously, and many defendants claimed that their victims had provoked them by walking alone through dark streets or by wearing sexy clothes. Feminist activists across the world rejected such justifications as victim blaming. Inspired by Susan Brownmiller's book *Against Our Will: Men, Women and Rape* from 1975 and other radical feminist texts, West German feminists saw sexual harassment and rape in public spaces not merely as tragic incidents involving individual men and women, but as part of a systematic effort to intimidate *all* women and to reinforce male supremacy. From this point of view, it was not only legitimate but also necessary for women to fight back against sexual violence. In this context, 'fighting back' could quite literally mean violent self-defence, but it was by no means limited to that. As this chapter illustrates, feminist activists have staged creative and provocative protests to 'reclaim' public spaces, supported survivors of violence and abuse in court, and some groups even went so far as to carry out acts of vigilante justice. Although such tactics were met with vocal criticism in the New Women's Movement, it is important to note that there was no other feminist struggle in West Germany in which the use of counter-violence was discussed more openly and candidly as in the movement against gender-based violence.

In 1973, a group of lesbian and feminist activists in West Berlin began to practice martial arts, and set up a karate school for women. According to a former member, the participants wanted to use the newly gained fighting skills to protect themselves and other women. 'When women find themselves in conflicts with men, they tend to back down until it's too late', claimed the activist, 'resolute resistance by women, by contrast, hits male opponents by surprise and can create an opportunity to escape.'[19] In 1974, the group released a statement entitled 'Disarm Rapists', in which they encouraged other women to follow their example and to practice self-defence.[20] Soon, there were self-defence classes for women in cities across the country (mostly karate and Wen-Do, a form of self-defence specifically for women). The first issues of the feminist magazine *Courage: Berliner Frauenzeitung* from 1976 included detailed instructions on how to incapacitate male attackers, and in the following years leading German newspapers and magazines like *Der Spiegel* and *Bild* published illustrated reports on self-defence techniques.

Discussions about feminist counter-violence against rape and other forms of violence against women have continued well beyond the German Autumn in 1977. In 1990, the Swiss magazine *Fruezitig* published an interview with two feminist activists who claimed that they carried weapons with them at all times, because they saw every man as a potential rapist.[21] 'If a guy seriously threatens me, I would have no qualms about killing him', claimed one of the two women when asked how she would use her 20-cm-long dagger in case of an attack.[22] Although it would be wrong to conclude that all feminists armed themselves to fight off potential rapists, the Swiss article illustrates that violent self-defence has remained an important topic in feminist circles. In 1992, an article in the feminist magazine *Emma* gave an overview of brutal sex crimes documented by feminist activists from across the country.[23] The article called for more solidarity and resistance. Drawing on statistics from the United States, the author claimed that thousands of rapes could be prevented if more women would dare to fight back. The article featured a list of successful examples of self-defence: women who had kicked their attackers in the lower abdomen, bitten them, hit them with rocks or who had given warning shots with alarm guns or defended themselves by other means. Tellingly, one of the few advertisements in the article promoted a defence spray that would fit in any handbag. Although they were convinced that pepper sprays and other forms of self-defence could save lives, activists in the New Women's Movement insisted that the struggle against violence against women required collective action. One of the first occasions when feminist activists in the FRG called for a joint fight against sexism and violence against women was a demonstration in West Berlin in February 1977. It provided the impetus for the feminist Walpurgisnight, which women's groups in the FRG have marked with colourful protest marches and feminist gatherings since.

The Walpurgisnight Marches: Feminists Reclaim the Night

After the rape and murder of the 26-year-old feminist activist Susanne Schmidtke in Berlin Charlottenburg in February 1977, approximately 1500 women staged a demonstration to commemorate her death. On this occasion, feminist artist and activist Sarah Haffner gave a passionate speech, in which she claimed that rape and abuse could not be tackled with the existing legal instruments, because they reinforced the existing social order. 'Susanne', claimed Haffner, 'is the victim of a political crime, and each of us could be the next victim. We are all frightened, and we are supposed to be frightened.'[24] Haffner insisted that women had to free themselves from the oppressive gender norms that confined them to the status of passive victims and 'fight for their liberation' (*für unsere Freiheit kämpfen*). This view was shared by many radical feminists in West Germany. A few weeks after the protest in Berlin, women's groups from across the country began to plan the first feminist Walpurgisnight on 30 April 1977 – a night of creative and provocative protests against sexual violence. While the theme was borrowed from the women's movement in the United States, Marx Ferree points out that 'the choice of Walpurgis Night, the historical gathering time of Goddess worshippers, invoked not only women's potential power but also the European history of gendered political repression by church and state'.[25]

Although there was a broad consensus among radical feminist activists in West Germany on the need to fight back against violence and sexual abuse, debates surrounding the first Walpurgisnight demonstrations illustrate that there were different views on the question of legitimate and necessary protest forms in this struggle. The national women's conference in Munich in March 1977 became a central platform for the planning of the first feminist Walpurgisnight. Here, participants agreed that protests on 30 April should involve street theatre performances, torches, witch costumes and dramatic makeup. They also discussed slogans for banners, songs and flyers, and discussed possible locations for rallies (e.g. town centres and red-light districts). Controversy erupted when some participants suggested that protesters should take direct action against sex shops, sexist newspapers and brothel-visitors. Although many women endorsed go-ins in sex shops and in red-light districts, they did not want to denounce or attack individual men who used these services. When it came to the question of violent tactics, many feminists distinguished between legitimate '*Selbstverteidigung*' (self-defence) and illegitimate '*Selbstjustiz*' (vigilante justice). A women's group from Munich rejected this distinction and called for the development of a 'distinctively female form of counter-violence' – an idea that met with strong opposition from other participants.[26]

According to a report in the leftist magazine *analyse & kritik*, the biggest Walpurgisnight demonstrations in 1977 took place in West Berlin (3000–4000 participants), Frankfurt (2000) and Munich (1000), but there were protests in at least eight other cities.[27] The feminist Walpurgisnight in 1977 was beyond doubt the biggest transregional demonstration in the New Women's Movement since women from across the country had taken to the streets to protest against the abortion ban in the early 1970s. *Emma* journalist Sabine Schruff reported enthusiastically about the protests: 'The witches are out: they flock to the streets in flowing colourful frocks, their faces painted in white or hidden behind scary masks.'[28] While many participants in these protests deliberately avoided protest tactics that could be perceived as violent, some protesters have clearly embraced the idea of feminist counter-violence. Participants in the protest in Frankfurt chanted: 'If men attack us, we attack them back – if men hit us, we hit them back.'[29] Some women took up the suggestion that was made at the conference in Munich and staged disruptive protests in sex shops and tried to harass and intimidate customers (see figure 4.1).

Although few protesters engaged in protest actions with such a high degree of confrontation, there was a strong sense of solidarity among the demonstrators.

Figure 4.1 Walpurgisnight demonstration in Frankfurt, 1978. Photographer: Barbara Klemm.

The first Walpurgisnight march in Frankfurt resulted in a court case against one of the organizers. According to police reports, protesters had deviated from the protest route, had made terrible noise, had attacked sex shops and male customers with flour bags, and some property had been damaged with graffiti and stickers. In June 1978, three former participants reported on the ongoing trial against the alleged 'ringleader' of the protest, which had to be postponed because more than one hundred 'witches' disturbed the court proceedings with loud protest.[30] The three women insisted that protesters had no other option but to use violence to defend themselves against violent attacks by men who felt provoked by their presence and behaviour.

Personal accounts by participants in Walpurgisnight protests in the late 1970s and early 1980s paint a mixed picture of the role of confrontational and violent tactics in the demonstrations. A militant feminist from Heidelberg wrote in a local magazine that she found it liberating to be part of a protest that allowed her to 'scream and shout' back at men, and that she had been thrilled to see feminist graffiti on vehicles. She expressed anger at the fact that some participants in the first Walpurgisnight protest in Heidelberg had been chatting and laughing with police officers.[31] Similar scenarios unfolded at protests in other cities. Many participants in the demonstrations were shocked about the confrontational attitude of some of their fellow protesters. A feminist activist from Cologne reported in *Courage* that she had been subjected to harsh criticism by a group of young women at a Walpurgisnight protest in 1978, because she had had a friendly conversation with a police officer. Apparently, they had scolded her that 'this is a cop, and cops are pigs'.[32] Other points of controversy included the use of torches, which created an atmosphere that reminded some women of National Socialist torchlight processions, and the symbolic nature of the protest. Some activists rejected the idea of a feminist Walpurgisnight all together, because they felt that a night of angry chants and witch costumes reinforced prevailing stereotypes about irrational and emotional women rather than tackling gender-based violence.[33]

Despite all tactical and ideological disagreements among participants in the first Walpurgisnight protests in West Germany, they shared a sense of anger at the media response to the event. Similar to newspaper articles about student protests in the 1960s, press reports about the first Walpurgisnight marches depicted protesters as a wild and excessively violent crowd. Articles in leading newspapers did not only ignore the fact that protesting women in many cities had faced brutal attacks by police and bystanders (e.g. when a woman in Frankfurt was hit by a flower pot that a man on a balcony had thrown at the protesters), they also accused participants of vicious and indiscriminate attacks against men. According to a report in the newspaper *Hamburger Morgenpost*, two police officers had to be rushed to a hospital after they had been attacked by women. The tabloid *BZ* claimed that several men in Berlin who had been brutally assaulted by women without defending themselves had shown no resistance, because they had learned that 'real men don't hit women'.[34] In July 1978, the news magazine *Spiegel* reported that 'feminists dressed up as witches had beaten up police officers' at a Walpurgisnight march in Hamburg.[35] This excess of feminist violence, argued the author, was indicative of a broader cultural change: while claiming to be innocent victims of male violence, women were abusing, attacking and humiliating men.[36] What received little attention in the West German media debate about the first Walpurgisnight marches was the fact that dozens of women were arrested, a protester was threatened with a gun and police officers attacked protesters with dogs and water cannons. Activists reported that the second Walpurgisnight protest in Hamburg resulted in eleven arrests, and that five women had to be hospitalized, because of concussions, deep cuts and bite wounds, and there were similar reports from other cities.[37]

There can be no doubt that the feminist Walpurgisnight protests in West Germany were perceived as a violent transgression of the prevailing gender norms. While the previously mentioned testimonies from Frankfurt and Heidelberg show that some activists found it liberating and empowering to 'reclaim the night' even if that involved violent clashes with police and bystanders, other feminists distanced themselves from the use of physical force against objects and people, from behaviour that could be perceived as threatening or intimidating and from other confrontational tactics. In June 1978, the feminist journalist Sabine Rosenbladt observed that there was a growing unease among feminists 'about slogans and forms of action which continue the dull tradition of worn-out leftist protest and which have become far removed from the ideas and forms of action that feminists have introduced because they felt personally affected by them as women'.³⁸

Against the background of the German Autumn and the growing isolation of the radical Left, many groups and individuals in the New Women's Movement felt the need to distance themselves from left-wing militancy. Yet, Walpurgisnight protests in the following years illustrate that there were also feminists who remained committed to the ideas and tactics that Rosenbladt associated with 'the dull tradition of worn-out leftist protest' and who tried to use them in the struggle against sexist oppression and sexual violence. In 1982, the liberal newspaper *Frankfurter Rundschau* reported that several hundred 'witches' had attacked men in the red-light district in Frankfurt with flour bags and tried to stage a go-in at a sex shop in Frankfurt. Like in previous years, police authorities responded to the unconventional protest with truncheons and water cannons.³⁹ Against the background of police brutality against feminist protesters and a perceived lack of support for female victims of domestic violence and rape, many feminists took the view that it would be foolish if female victims of violence and abuse hoped for help from public authorities. Some activists concluded that women had to take the law into their own hands if they wanted to see justice. Although this was not a common position in the New Women's Movement, it deserves attention because it resulted in actions that sparked important debates about feminism and violence.

Feminist Attacks against Alleged Rapists and their Lawyers

The question of whether the use of violent tactics was legitimate and necessary in the struggle against violence against women was the subject of great controversy in the New Women's Movement. As highlighted in chapter 1, already in 1976 the second edition of the *Frauenjahrbuch* included a collection of short essays written by a feminist collective whose members claimed that they had taken revenge for the brutal rape of two women by physically attacking and publicly denouncing the rapist. Although it remains unclear whether these attacks were fact or fiction, it is telling that they found their way into the volume. There are no statistics on feminist attacks against alleged rapists and their supporters, but there are some well-documented cases, which I want to discuss in some more detail.

One of the first documented feminist attacks against an alleged rape apologist took place in 1979 in West Berlin. On 12 June 1979, a group of fifty feminist activists visited left-wing lawyer Nicolas Becker in his office in West Berlin. It soon became clear that this was no friendly visit: the women started to spray sweet perfume into the office, threw saucy lingerie into file folders and disturbed a phone call that Becker had with a client. They then forced Becker to pose with a poster for a photograph (see figure 4.2). The image was strikingly similar to the photograph that members of the militant leftist group Movement of June 2nd took of their hostage Peter Lorenz in West Berlin in 1975. Together with a short

Figure 4.2 'Kidnapping' of Nicolas Becker by the 'Movement of 12 June'.

statement, the women sent the image to the leftist newspaper *die tageszeitung (taz)*, where both were published on 15 June. The authors of the text claimed that Becker had defended a notorious pimp who had raped and severely abused the plaintiff and other women. Allegedly, Becker had tried to undermine the credibility of the claimant, who worked as a prostitute and had a sexual relationship with the alleged perpetrator.

According to Becker's feminist critics, he and other left-wing lawyers identified as part of the leftist opposition, but made common cause with the state when it came to the issue of violence against women.[40] Becker and his colleagues Reiner Geulen and Otto Schily considered these allegations to be without merit. They tried to prevent the publication of the statement and photograph, and when that failed, published statements in which they strongly condemned the action. On 18 June, the *taz* editors published a short statement by Becker, in which he presented his side of the story, and emphasized that he found it legitimate and necessary to defend his client against the rape allegations by the alleged victim.[41] A statement by Geulen and Schily a few days later echoed this view. They claimed that it would be 'wrong and dangerous' if alleged rapists would be declared guilty without a fair trial.[42]

The attack against Becker sparked heated debates among the radical Left and in the New Women's Movement. When some of the women involved asked the *taz* editors to publish a statement and a photograph that they took during their protest in Becker's office, some men on the editorial board tried to block this move because they felt that it discredited a politically engaged lawyer on the basis of scandalously poor evidence. Many *taz* readers shared this view, and some went as far as to accuse the actors involved of using 'fascist' methods. In light of the fact that the intruders did not cause physical harm to Becker and that the attack did not result in damage to property, it is striking that the group was compared to Nazi thugs.

In a letter to the editors, reader Angelika Rohrwasser claimed that the attack reminded her of Gestapo raids during the Third Reich. 'It must be recalled here', emphasized Rohrwasser, 'that there have been a number of progressive, leftist, even revolutionary movements that have developed fascistic tendencies and thus belied their ideals. Will the women's movement be the next movement to go down this route?'[43]

While some readers used the opportunity to complain about everything that they found wrong about feminism (e.g. presumptuousness, hostility towards men and a lack of rationality), others critiqued the attack against Becker from a radical feminist perspective. *Taz* reader Stefanie Heimberger, for instance, criticized that the action would bring the entire women's movement into disrepute. She accused the women involved of using methods that constituted themselves a form of 'rape' (*vergewaltigende Methoden*). This criticism is interesting, because while sharing their radical opposition to the existing political structures, Heimberger and others disagreed with the tactics used by the group. Although the women involved had not used physical force against Becker, Heimberger understood their action as rape – a form of patriarchal violence, which reinforced rather than challenged the prevailing power structures. Although other feminist critics did not put the attack against Becker on the same footing as rape, they shared Heimberger's reasoning: if violence against women expressed and reinforced unequal power relations, as radical feminists asserted, they had to be very careful not to use the methods that maintained the status quo. In their eyes, there was no such thing as feminist counter-violence because the use of force and intimidation was inherently and necessarily patriarchal.

The debate over the legitimacy of the attack against Becker continued for several months. In July 1979, the editors of *Courage* published a statement by some of the women involved in the attack. The authors expressed incomprehension at the fact that they were accused of acting like fascists, simply because they had stood up for a woman who had experienced violence and abuse.[44] Although the editors of the magazine expressed sympathy for the cause, they emphasized that it was vital that feminists not abuse their power over men on the rare occasions when they were in the position to do so. Heimberger and other feminist critics were concerned that the action could be read as an open call for vigilante justice. She asked the women involved: 'What gives you the right to play police officers and judges, and to charge, sentence and punish people in the manner of the Wild West?'[45] Feminist activists who had attended the trial against the alleged rapist dismissed this critique as naïve, because they felt that Becker and other men involved in the case had defended and reinforced violent structures.[46]

After consulting feminist observers of the trial and speaking to the lawyer of the alleged rape victim, *taz* editor Gitti Hentschel reached the conclusion that it was imperative to publish the feminist claim of responsibility (although she had issues with some of the terminology used in the statement).[47] She and other women on the editorial team were shocked to see how many of their male colleagues and comrades refused to admit that sexism existed on the radical Left. A few days later, all women working for *taz* published a joint statement in which they argued that leftist solidarity seemed to be limited to solidarity among men, and emphasized that 'physical rape was just the tip of the iceberg of patriarchal violence'.[48] A number of grassroots organizations, leftist lawyers and radical feminists expressed similar views, and some openly supported the attack. 'I hope that the action against Becker won't be the last of this kind', wrote one woman; she then went on to congratulate the 'courageous women' involved for their subversive humour.[49]

Although no feminist attack against alleged rapists or their male supporters attracted as much media attention as the action against Becker, there are reports of a few similar attacks in the 1980s. According to one report from 1982, a man lured a young woman into his flat in Bremen and raped her. On the following day, she paid him a visit with twenty of her friends. The man reported the raid to the police and claimed that the intruders had threatened him with castration, demolished his kitchen and sprayed Venus-symbols on his walls. When the woman was charged with trespass and sexual assault, radical leftist and feminist activists publicized the name and address of the man and circulated flyers that ridiculed him. 'Poor Dieter, you didn't expect that women fight back, did you?' asked the authors of one flyer, mimicking the gleeful tone of newspaper articles about the court case.[50] Unlike many groups and individuals who had condemned the attack against Becker in Berlin, activists in Bremen considered the use of force and intimidation against an alleged rapist legitimate, and they did not shy away from humiliating him in public.

A few months after the attack in Bremen, a similar case occurred in Hamburg, where a young woman was charged with deprivation of liberty, robbery by blackmail and criminal assault after she and three of her friends had threatened and attacked a man who had raped her. In the first instance, the woman was sentenced to a fine of 3500 DM. Although the judgement was overturned on appeal, the court cautioned the woman and emphasized that 'there is no right to vigilante justice, even if the administrative processes involved in a legal challenge might seem arduous'.[51] The court cases in Bremen and Hamburg show that some women considered the use of highly confrontational tactics in the struggle against male violence legitimate and necessary. The two women did not want to be reduced to helpless victims of male violence. Since both used force and intimidation to fight back against their alleged rapists, their actions were widely understood as violent. As a result, they have challenged the gendered victim/perpetrator dichotomy, and there was a role reversal in court: the two rape victims faced charges, while the alleged rapists claimed to be victims of their violence. Only one judge was willing to consider that the defendant had taken justice into her own hands, because she was convinced that a trial against an alleged rapist would lead to nothing. This opinion was widely shared among feminists in West Germany, and a few took similar action against alleged rapists.

Feminist activists in the Autonomen movement tried to tackle sexual violence in their groups by addressing the problem in plenary sessions and by taking collective action against alleged rapists (e.g. by naming and shaming them in internal movement publications, or by excluding them from squats and other shared spaces).[52] The 1980s also saw further attacks against alleged rapists and their supporters. On 2 June 1986, a group of feminist activists carried out an action against a lawyer in Dortmund. The women dropped flyers into mailboxes in the neighbourhood, in which they claimed that he would support rapists and sex murderers, and they sprayed feminist graffiti on his garage door.[53] Reporting from the trial against some of the alleged perpetrators, *taz* journalist Corinna Kawaters complained that the defendants were found guilty of criminal damage and slander despite a lack of evidence. The trial was attended by 120 women who were expelled from the courtroom because they disrupted the court proceedings with angry protest.[54] Meanwhile in West Berlin, a professor at the gynaecological hospital Pulsstraße gave his lectures under police protection, because he feared angry feminist protests in the lecture theatre. For several months, feminist activists had caused disruption in his courses because the professor had paid the bail for two male colleagues who had stood trial for raping a female colleague in his clinic.[55]

In one case, journalists claimed that militant feminist protest had driven a convicted rapist into suicide. In October 1986, a sociology professor in Braunschweig killed himself. For the tabloid *Bild*, there was no doubt that the suicide was the consequence of a feminist 'witch hunt' against the professor, which had started after he had been convicted for rape.[56] As in the case of the attack against Becker, it is interesting to consider the language that was used to describe the violent nature of the feminist campaign against the man. By comparing feminist protest against a male university professor who had been found guilty of rape to the denunciation and brutal murder of thousands of innocent women in Germany and other European countries, *Bild* suggested that feminism had turned women from victims into perpetrators of violence.

There can be no doubt that feminist attacks against alleged rapists were the exception rather than the rule. Yet, some feminists felt that feminist efforts to fight back against violence and abuse had to become more organized. One of these activists was the journalist who reported on the feminist attack against the lawyer in Dortmund. Born in 1953, Corinna Kawaters grew up in Cologne. After studying sociology in Bochum, she worked as a journalist for *die tageszeitung* in Bochum, and published the detective novel *Zora Zobel findet die Leiche* (Zora Zobel Finds the Dead Body).[57] Kawaters was actively involved in the women's movement, and decided at some point to join the militant feminist group Red Zora. In December 1987, she had to go into hiding because she was on a list of suspected terrorists assembled by the Federal Criminal Police Office. As highlighted previously, the Red Zora had the aim to defend women against legal and illegal forms violence and oppression. In 1984, two members stated that the group's objective was to utilize confrontational and violent tactics in the women's movement so that every 'rapist, trafficker of women, wife batterer, porn dealer, creepy gynaecologist must fear that a gang of women finds him, attacks him and humiliates him in public'.[58] A significant facet of the attacks that the Red Zora carried out in the 1980s and late 1970s, including those discussed in the following section, centred on the issue of the sexual objectification of women in media and in the sex industry.

Pornography and Sexism in the Media

In April 1977, the editors of the leftist magazine *konkret* ran a headline suggesting that feminism 'had a weak chest' and illustrated this claim with the image of a male hand grabbing the naked breast of a woman (see figure 4.3).

'Never before', noted editors in the May issue, 'has a *konkret* article provoked such strong and controversial reactions.'[59] Feminist responses to the cover image and lead article by Hartmut Schulze ranged from critical statements to acts of vandalism. A first wave of feminist protest was directed against the author of the lead article. According to the *konkret* editors, Schulze received threatening phone calls and anonymous letters in which he was described as a stupid and sexually frustrated chauvinist. He also found the entrance door to his flat covered in 'misogynist' (*frauenfeindlich*) stickers.[60] The protests did not spare the *konkret* editorial office, either. Shortly after the article was published, in the night a group of people entered the building in central Hamburg where the office was located. They blocked the entrance with a brick wall covered with feminist graffiti (see figure 4.4), and sprayed the slogan 'Konkret '77 – a weak cock' on the walls in the staircase.[61] In a short letter to the German Press Agency, the feminist group 'Militant Panther Aunties' (*Militante Panthertanten*) claimed responsibility. Some readers found the protest 'idiotic', and insisted that *konkret* should

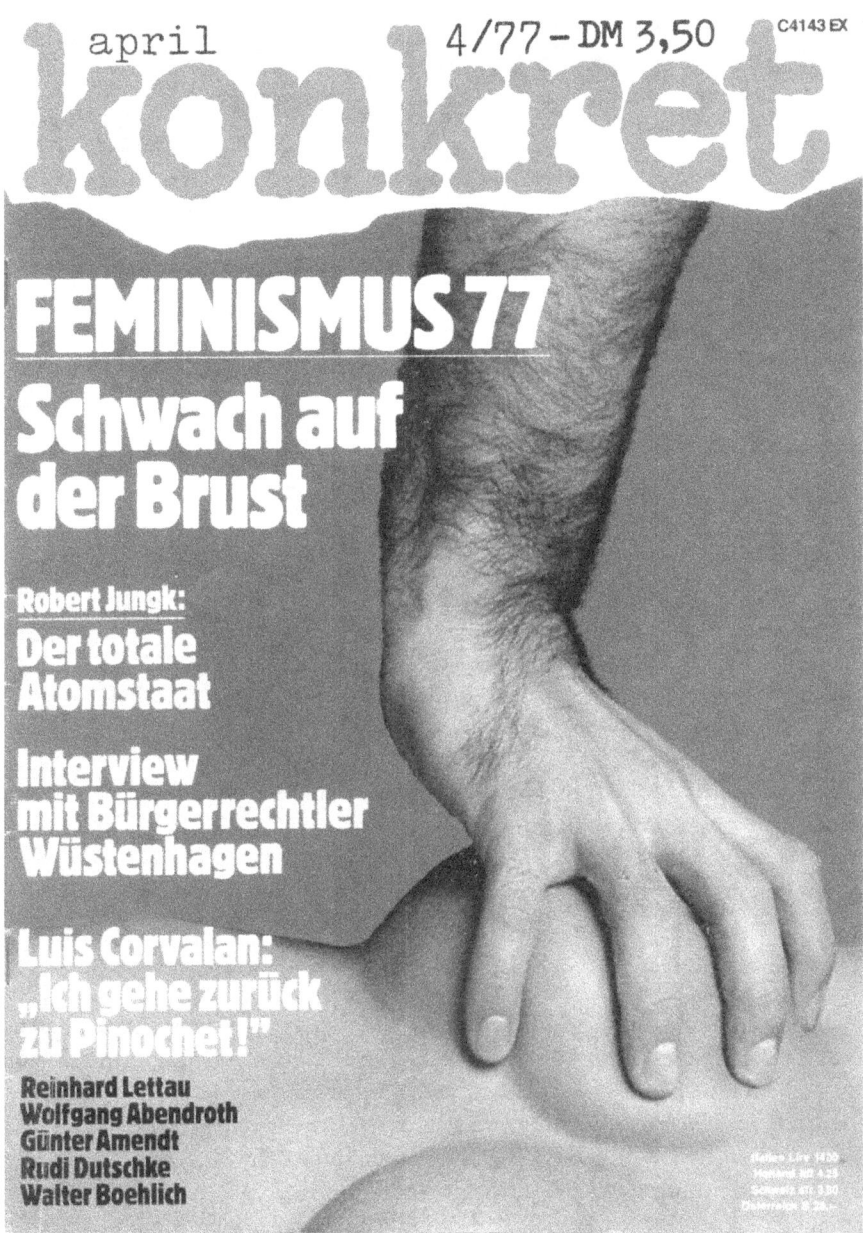

Figure 4.3 *konkret* cover, April 1977. Courtesy FrauenMediaTurm, Cologne (FB).

continue as before. Others, however, criticized Schulze's article as 'disgusting, arrogant and contemptuous drivel' and saw the cover image as an act of male violence against women.[62] The May issue of *konkret* featured critical responses by the prominent feminist journalists Ingrid Kolb and Sibylle Plogstedt and a

Figure 4.4 Brick wall with feminist graffiti. From *konkret*, May 1977, 4. Courtesy Hamburg Institute for Social Research Archives.

follow-up article by Hartmut Schulze, in which he defended his position. He considered it a wicked thought that the *konkret* editors enjoyed the image of a 'repressive male hand' (*repressive Männerhand*) on such a weak chest.[63]

In the eyes of many feminists, degrading images of women in the media were only the tip of the iceberg of sexual objectification and degradation. Feminists were angry about the ways in which the sex industry commodified women, and staged protests in red-light districts and porn cinemas. Some expressed their anger through physical attacks against sex shops. One of the first documented attacks took place in Koblenz in February 1978. According to a police report in the Federal Archives, a small incendiary device exploded under the shop desk of a local sex shop in the early hours of 2 February. Although one shop assistant and two customers were present at the time of the explosion, nobody suffered any injuries, and the fire was quickly brought under control. The incendiary device was composed of a cigarette box, pegs and a number of other components, all of which were available in supermarkets and do-it-yourself stores. One day after the attack, the shop owner found a small ampoule with a yellowish liquid. A chemical analysis in a police laboratory revealed that the ampoule contained ammonium sulphide, a substance that due to its stench is a common ingredient in stink bombs.[64]

Shortly after the incident, a local newspaper received a letter, in which the Red Zora claimed responsibility for the attack in Koblenz. Here, the group declared that it was no longer willing to accept women being reduced to their bodies and degraded to 'sex-machines' (*Sexmaschinen*) at the disposal of male consumers.[65] Like the claim of responsibility for the first RZ attack in 1977, the statement concluded with a short poem. Once more, the RZ encouraged other women to form their own gangs and to draw on creative and militant forms of protest to assert their dignity and physical autonomy. 'In their greed for profit, these men have failed to take into account our growing confidence, our will to resist and to track women's oppression down at every corner, and to fight with creativity. Everything that we have created and that we want to build – love, solidarity and a new culture – can only be maintained and come into being if we destroy what destroys us.'[66] The claim of responsibility concluded with concrete suggestions that ranged from bricking up sex shops to small acts of sabotage, including clogging toilets.

A few days before the attack in Koblenz, the Red Zora targeted six stores in Cologne that belonged to the same chain of sex shops. According to newspaper reports, these attacks caused damage worth 200,000 DM.[67] By using everyday weapons and choosing local targets, the Red Zora hoped to encourage other women to form their own gangs and carry out similar attacks. With its campaign against sex shops and pornography, the group sided with anti-porn feminists in the 'sex wars' of the late 1970s and early 1980s.[68] Feminists who took this stance denounced the porn and sex industries, because they reasoned that they were central to the degradation and objectification of women. An article published a few weeks after the attacks in Cologne indicates that other feminists in West Germany shared this stance. The March issue of *Emma* included a portion of the claim of responsibility for the attacks. A little cartoon figure next to the text, which bore a striking similarity to the magazine's chief editor, Alice Schwarzer, said: 'Help! – I feel overwhelmed with clandestine joy' (see figure 4.5). The phrase 'clandestine joy' hints at an incident in 1977, when the author of an article in a student magazine in Göttingen expressed 'clandestine joy' over the assassination of Germany's attorney general, Siegfried Buback, by members of the Red Army Faction. This statement is remarkable, because it suggests that while taking an explicitly nonviolent approach in the campaign against pornography and sexism in the media, Schwarzer was still pleased to see that the protests of other feminists were characterized by a more confrontational approach.

Schwarzer's own efforts in the late 1970s were focused on taking legal action against the sexual objectification of women in the media. At the time it was common practice for West German magazines across the political spectrum to try to increase sales figures with images of half-naked and naked women. She and many other feminists condemned such images as a form of violence against women. In 1977, *Emma*'s chief editor made her first attempt to stop this practice: she filed a complaint with the German Press Council. The subject of the complaint was not the *konkret* cover but an issue of *Spiegel*, which promoted a report about children in the sex industry with a highly sexualized image of a naked girl on the cover.[69] The Press Council cautioned the *Spiegel* editors, but no further action was taken, and sexualized images of female bodies remained common in the West German press.

Figure 4.5 Die Rote Zora: 'Clandestine Joy'. From *Emma*, no. 3, 1978, 49. Used with permission. www.emma.de.

After the newsmagazine *Stern* had published another particularly controversial image in June 1978, Schwarzer and other feminists decided to take legal action. On 23 June 1978, Gisela Wild, a prominent lawyer, filed a complaint against *Stern* chief editor Henri Nannen. Drawing on paragraph 823 of the German Civil Code, the plaintiffs argued that the sexualized images of women in *Stern* and other West German magazines constituted an offence against the freedom and dignity of all women. Psychoanalyst Margarete Mitscherlich-Nielsen, writer Luise Rinser, film-maker Margarethe von Trotta, actor Inge Meysel and other prominent women supported the lawsuit, and appeared as joint plaintiffs at the Regional Court of Hamburg. The judges dismissed the case based on the argument that Schwarzer and her fellow campaigners constituted a 'particular' group of women who could not claim to speak on behalf of all women.[70]

Despite the defeat in court, Schwarzer's campaign was successful in so far as it attracted widespread attention and support. The German Women's Council, an umbrella organization of more than fifty German women's groups with 10 million members, expressed support for the *Emma* campaign, and the magazine's editors reported that support letters were piling up on their desks. Angry reactions and personal attacks in the media in the weeks after the trial can be interpreted as further evidence that the campaign had hit a nerve. In the first *Stern* issue after the court claim, chief editor Henri Nannen provoked feminist critics with yet another image of a half-naked woman on the cover, and dismissed the plaintiffs as 'cheerless bluestockings' (*freudlose Grauröcke*).⁷¹ In a similar tone, *Spiegel* editor Rudolf Augstein discounted the legal complaint as 'hypocritical nonsense' (*zweischneidiger Unfug*).⁷² Although many feminist groups and conservative women's organizations in West Germany supported Schwarzer's campaign, it is important to highlight that there were also feminists who did not share her negative view of pornography.

Cultural anthropologist and sex-positive feminist activist Gayle Rubin was one of the first vocal critics of the feminist anti-porn discourse in the United States. According to Rubin, feminist activists have attributed 'a wildly exaggerated role . . . to pornography in the creation, maintenance and representation of women's subordination' since the equation of pornography and violence had become a 'coercive dogma and a premature orthodoxy' in the women's movement in the late 1970s.⁷³ Rubin was critical of anti-porn activists for claiming to protect women in (and from) the sex industry, while ignoring the fact that these women were not merely victims. Rather than supporting these women, argued Rubin, anti-porn feminists 'played into the hands of the right wing and its reactionary agenda' by further stigmatizing them.⁷⁴ As a lesbian feminist activist with an active interest in sadomasochism (SM), Rubin knew from her own experience that many men and women were 'not only willing but eager participants in SM activity'.⁷⁵ She and other sex-positive feminists criticized feminists for tending to reduce women in the sex industry to mere victims of patriarchy.

The feminist sex-wars in the United States had a profound impact on feminist debates surrounding violence and pornography in West Germany. Some activists reconsidered their position on the sex industry in light of the critical contributions of sex-positive feminists, sex workers and feminist activists from the so-called Third World. Retrospectively, members of the Red Zora admitted that their rage against sex shops was at least in part the result of an 'unquestioned bourgeois-Christian' (*bürgerlich-christliche*) distinction between 'good' and 'bad' sexuality.⁷⁶ In 1993, the women declared that there were still good reasons to attack sex shops, but they confessed that their protest in the 1970s had failed to consider the views of women who worked in the sex industry, and that they had not paid enough attention to less visible forms of sexism and abuse.⁷⁷ Most feminist activists in the FRG, however, remained fundamentally opposed to pornography, and engaged with the sex wars in a very selective way. It is therefore not surprising that texts by Andrea Dworkin, Catherine MacKinnon and other feminists in the anti-pornography movement in the United States were translated and published by feminist activists in West Germany in the 1980s, while the arguments of sex-positive activists received very little attention.⁷⁸

In the years prior to and during reunification, the FRG saw another wave of feminist protests against pornography and sexualized images of women in the media. In 1987, Schwarzer started her PorNO campaign. Inspired by similar initiatives in the United States and in other countries, she called for a law that defined pornography as a violation of women's civil rights. Although she managed to win prominent supporters for her campaign, Schwarzer's draft law was rejected. Other activities by anti-porn activists in the 1980s included feminist 'tours' through red-light districts, 'walk-in' protests in sex shops and feminist graffiti on sexist billboards.[79]

Discussions about confrontational tactics in the struggle against pornography and sexism in the media continued into the 1990s. In March 1990, *Stern* featured a lead story about Sina-Aline Geißler's book *Lust an der Unterwerfung. Frauen bekennen sich zum Masochismus* (Desire for Submission: Women Commit to Masochism) and female masochism. In response to this report, a group of approximately sixty participants in a feminist gathering in Hamburg staged a spontaneous protest in *Stern*'s editorial offices. According to one of the activists involved, the crowd of whistling, shouting and singing feminists demanded to speak to the chief editors, but the discussion quickly escalated. The women explained the motivation behind the protest as follows: 'If a woman describes herself as a masochist, and wants to act on her masochism, that's up to her. If a *Stern* article reports about this in the usual sexist manner along the lines of "As a matter of fact, every woman likes brutal sex" – I am directly affected.'[80] Once again, the *Emma* editors openly expressed joy and '*Schadenfreude*' about a highly confrontational protest action.[81]

As the protest in Hamburg and other events discussed in this chapter illustrate, many women felt offended and affected by sexualized images of women in the media and by reports about rape and other forms of violence against individual women. While this created a bond of solidarity between women, it risked neglecting important differences among women. Due to differences in age, class, physical ability, sexual orientation, ethnicity and nationality, women were and are affected in different ways by sexism and violence. Due to the influence of the proletarian women's movement in the early twentieth century and of the New Left, there was a strong awareness of class-based differences in the New Women's Movement. Other differences, however, have initially received less attention. Although there is a long tradition of internationalism in feminist activism, it has been a long and difficult process to identify and tackle racism in the New Women's Movement and to work towards a notion of transnational solidarity that does not reduce Third World women to passive victims. Based on a discussion of key events and developments, the next chapter shows that this process has had a significant impact on the limit and scope of feminist protest.

Notes

1. Bundesministerium für Familie, Senioren, Frauen und Jugend (ed.) (2012), 'Lebenssituation, Sicherheit und Gesundheit von Frauen in Deutschland', Rostock. Retrieved 21 November 2015 from http://www.bmfsfj.de/BMFSFJ/Service/Publikationen/publikationen,did=20560.html, 9. The same study finds that about half of violent attacks against women are carried out by male partners and ex-partners; ibid., 13.

2. Elizabeth Heinemann illustrates this development based on a detailed analysis of the career of leftist publisher and 'king of porn' Jörg Schröter. E. Heinemann (2010), 'Jörg Schröter, linkes Verlagwesen und Pornografie', in S. Reichardt and D. Siegfried (eds), *Das Alternative Milieu: antibürgerlicher Lebensstil und linke Politik in der Bundesrepublik Deutschland und Europa 1968–1983*, Göttingen: Wallstein, 290–312.
3. M. Lee (2014), 'Political Pornography in the West German Underground Press', *History Workshop Journal* (1)78, 186–203, 200.
4. 'Top 25 Deutschland 1975'. Retrieved 18 October 2015 from http://www.insidekino.com/DJahr/D1975.htm.
5. S. Volk (2015), 'Mit Hundehalsband, ohne Höschen', *Spiegel Online*. Retrieved 17 October 2015 from http://www.spiegel.de/einestages/sadomaso-film-die-geschichte-der-o-mit-hunde halsband-ohne-hoeschen-a-1017550.html.
6. Morgan first set out this position in writing in her contribution to Laura Lederer's anthology *Take Back the Night: Women on Pornography*, which was first published in 1980.
7. 'Daß Du untergehst, wenn Du Dich nicht wehrst, wirst Du doch einsehen!', FMT, PD-FB 01, 1974.
8. 'Die Aktionen gegen Sex Shops und Kinos sind Ausdruck unserer Wut: Wir wehren uns gegen ein Frauenbild, das uns zum Spielzeug unserer Männer macht, ein Bild was uns tagtäglich durch sämtliche Medien in den Kopf gehämmert werden soll. Wir müssen und werden es lernen, uns zu wehren: Sex- Shops und Kinos sind nur der Anfang. Frauen erhebt euch und die Welt erlebt euch. Frauen gemeinsam sind stark'; ibid.
9. 'Frauen erhebt euch und die Welt erlebt euch.'
10. According to Elisabeth Zellmer, the weekly newspapers *Stern*, *Der Spiegel*, and *Die Zeit* published the first detailed reports and surveys about violence against women in 1976; Zellmer, *Die Töchter der Revolte*, 228.
11. According to Ilse Lenz, the percentage of women between the ages of 16 and 65 who were gainfully employed was 47.2 per cent in 1960, and rose to 50.2 per cent; Lenz, *Die Neue Frauenbewegung*, 145.
12. As the following chapter illustrates, female migrants who had moved to Germany to live with their spouses were in a particularly difficult situation: most were not allowed to work and lost their right to remain in the country in the event of divorce.
13. Ibid., 291.
14. Marx Ferree, *Varieties of Feminism*, 96.
15. Ibid., 94–95.
16. D.E.H. Russell and N. van de Ven (1990), *Crimes Against Women: Proceedings of the International Tribunal*, 3rd edition, 81. Retrieved 21 December 2015 from http://www.diana-russell.com/f/Crimes_Against_Women_Tribunal.pdf.
17. For a good overview of rivalling women's shelter projects in Munich, see Zellmer, *Die Töchter der Revolte*, 237–40.
18. Frauenhauskoordinierung e.V. (ed.), 'FrauenHäuser in Deutschland', 3. Retrieved 15 December 2015 from http://www.frauenhauskoordinierung.de/fileadmin/redakteure/pdfs/Medienpaket/RZ_frauenhaus_broschuere_ANSICHTS.pdf.
19. 'in Konflikten mit Männern geben Frauen oft nach, bis es zu spät ist, wohingegen eine entschlossene Gegenwehr den Angreifer verwirrt und so eine Flucht ermöglicht'; Perincioli, *Berlin wird feministisch*, 132–33.
20. Lenz, *Die Neue Frauenbewegung*, 284.
21. FMT PD-G8, 'Wir kriegen Euch', *Fruezitig*, no. 33, 1990.
22. 'Wenn mich einer ernsthaft bedroht, hätte ich keine Skrupel, ihn zu töten'; ibid.
23. 'Aktion Stoppt Frauenhass', *Emma*, no. 10, 1992, 36–41.
24. 'Vergewaltigungen und Misshandlung sind politische Akte durch die Macht demonstriert und Macht aufrechterhalten wird. Susanne ist das Opfer eines politischen Verbrechens. Jede von uns könnte die nächste sein. Wir alle haben Angst und sollen Angst haben';

S. Haffner (1977), 'Die Angst ist unser schlimmster Feind', *Courage: Berliner Frauenzeitung*, no. 4, 5.
25. Marx Ferree, *Varieties of Feminism*, 90.
26. Zellmer, *Töchter der Revolte*, 233.
27. '"Walpurgisnacht" gegen "Männergewalt"', *Analyse & Kritik*, no. 104, May 1977.
28. 'Die Hexen sind los: in wallenden bunten Gewändern, die Gesichter weiß bemalt oder hinter schaurigen Masken versteckt ziehen sie durch die Straßen'; S. Schruff (1977), 'Die Hexen sind los', *Emma*, no. 6, 58.
29. Ibid., 58.
30. FMT Z125: 1978 – 25, 'Walpurgisnacht in Frankfurt und ihre Konsequenzen', *Frauenzeitung Frauenzentrum Hamburg*, no. 25, 1978, 11.
31. FMT Z129: 1977 – 2, 'Walpurgisnacht', *II. Heidelberger Frauenzeitung*, June 1977.
32. 'Walpurgisnacht', *Courage: Berliner Frauenzeitung*, no. 6, 1978, 4–5.
33. FMT Z149: 1977 – 16, 'Zur Diskussion gestellt: Walpurgisnacht', *protokolle: informationsdienst für frauen*, no. 16, 1977, 30–31.
34. 'weil sie dazu erzogen wurden, daß man keine Frauen schlägt', 'Auseinandersetzungen nach der Walpurgisnacht', *Analyse & Kritik*, no. 107, June 1977.
35. 'Sie schlug mich, ohne mich anzusehen', *Der Spiegel*, no. 27, 3 July 1978.
36. Ibid.
37. S. Rosenbladt (1978), 'Walpurgisnacht', *Emma*, no. 6, 16–17.
38. 'Unbehagen über Parolen und Aktionsformen, die sich in der platten Tradition linken, längst leergelaufenen Protestes bewegen und weit von dem entfernt haben, was Feministinnen von ihrer Betroffenheit als Frauen ausgehend an Inhalten und Aktionsformen neu einbrachten'; ibid.
39. M. Weber-Nau, 'Einige "Hexen" zogen sogar in ein Eros-Center', *Frankfurter Rundschau*, 3 May 1982.
40. 'Die Frauenbewegung zu Gast bei Rechtsanwalt Becker', *die tageszeitung*, 15 June 1979.
41. 'Erklärung von Rechtsanwalt Becker', *die tageszeitung*, 18 June 1979.
42. R. Geulen and O. Schily, 'Seht ihr denn keinen Unterschied zwischen "Verteidigung von Vergewaltigung" und Verteidigung eines Angeklagten, der verdächtigt wird, eine Vergewaltigung begangen zu haben?' *die tageszeitung*, 21 June 1979.
43. 'Vielleicht ist es angebracht daran zu erinnern, daß schon öfters fortschrittliche, linke oder sogar revolutionäre Bewegungen faschistoide Tendenzen annahmen und sich dadurch selbst Lügen straften. Jetzt auch die Frauenbewegung?'; 'Männer – Frauen – Männer', *die tageszeitung*, 22 June 1979.
44. 'Frauenaktion bei Rechtsanwalt Becker', *Courage: Berliner Frauenzeitung*, no. 8, 1979, 42–43.
45. 'Woher nehmt ihr euch das Recht selbst Polizei und Gericht zu spielen, nach Wildwest-Muster jemanden anzuklagen, zu verurteilen und zu bestrafen?' ibid.
46. 'Zum "Vorfall" Frauenbewegung zu Gast bei RA Becker', *die tageszeitung*, 25 June 1979.
47. '. . . Und keiner beschmutze das eigene Nest . . .', *die tageszeitung*, 21 June 1979.
48. 'Eine körperliche Vergewaltigung ist die äußerste Spitze vom Eisberg der patriarchalen Gewalt'; 'Zum "Vorfall" "Frauenbewegung zu Gast bei RA Becker', *die tageszeitung*, 25 June 1979.
49. 'Männer – Frauen – Männer', *die tageszeitung*, 22 June 1979.
50. FMT PD – G8, 'Rabiate Frauenschar fiel über Mann her', *Bremer Fraueninfo*, no. 2, 3 December 1982.
51. 'kein Recht auf Selbstjustiz gibt, auch wenn der Weg durch staatliche Instanzen schwierig erscheint'; FMT PD – G8, Frauenzentrum Hannover, 'Solange es Männergewalt an Frauen gibt, wird es unseren Widerstand geben', 4.
52. Although rape and violence against women has been the subject of heated public debates in the Autonomen Movement since the mid-1980s, there is to date no detailed scholarly analysis of these discussions. Jan Schwarzmeier's book *Die Autonomen zwischen Subkultur und sozialer Bewegung* from 2001 includes an overview of discussions about sexual violence in the Autonomen

Movement that was rightly criticized for its profoundly anti-feminist perspective; for a critical review, see e.g. B. Hüttner, 'Die Autonomen zwischen Subkultur und sozialer Bewegung'. Retrieved 14 October 2015 from http://www.archivbremen.de/cgeschic/schwarzm.htm.
53. C. Kawaters, 'Ein lila Auto ist sehr verdächtig', *die tageszeitung*, 9 February 1987.
54. Ibid.
55. FMT PD- G8, 'Zoff in Berlin', *Emma*, no. 7, 1986.
56. 'Sex-Professor erhängte sich', *Bild*, 31 October 1986.
57. C. Kawaters (1984), *Zora Zobel findet die Leiche: Roman*, Frankfurt: Zweitausendeins.
58. 'Unser Traum ist, daß es überall kleine Frauenbanden gibt – wenn in jeder Stadt ein Vergewaltiger, ein Frauenhändler, ein prügelnder Ehemann, ein frauenfeindlicher Zeitungsverleger, ein Pornohändler, ein schweinischer Frauenarzt damit rechnen und sich davor fürchten müßte, daß eine Bande Frauen ihn aufspürt, ihn angreift, ihn öffentlich bekannt und lächerlich macht'; ID Verlag, *Die Früchte des Zorns*, 462.
59. 'Zuviel der Ehre', *konkret*, no. 5, 1977, 5.
60. 'konkret intern', *konkret*, no. 5, 1977, 4.
61. 'Konkret '77 – Schlapp auf'm Schwanz'; ibid.
62. 'widerliches, hochmütiges, menschenverachtendes Gewäsch'; 'Briefe', *konkret*, no. 5, 1977, 5–6.
63. 'Forum', *konkret*, no. 5, 1977, 13–15.
64. BAK B362/6827, 'Vermerk', 2 February 1978.
65. Ibid., 'Bekennerschreiben', 5 February 1978.
66. 'Was die Herren bei ihrer unersättlichen Profitgier aber nicht mit einkalkuliert haben ist unser wachsendes Selbstbewusstsein, unser Wille Widerstand zu leisten und Frauenunterdrückung an jeder Ecke aufzuspüren und mit Phantasie zu bekämpfen. Was wir uns an neuem aufgebaut haben und aufbauen wollen – Liebe, Solidarität, Menschlichkeit unsere eigene Kultur – können wir nur dann erhalten und schaffen, wenn wir all das zerstören, was uns kaputt macht'; ibid.
67. G. Elendt, 'Das hält die Polizei für möglich: Frauentrupps räumen Kölner Sex Shops aus', *Express*, 4 February 1978.
68. An in-depth discussion of the feminist sex wars goes beyond the scope of this chapter and has been provided by other scholars; see e.g. L. Duggan and N.D. Hunter (2006), *Sex Wars: Sexual Dissent and Political Culture*, New York: Routledge.
69. *Der Spiegel*, no. 22, 23 May 1977.
70. 'Frauen klagen gegen den Stern', *Emma*, no. 8, 1978, 6–15, 6.
71. A. Schwarzer (1978), 'Antwort an Nannen & Co', *Emma*, no. 8, 5.
72. R. Augstein (1978), 'Die Frauen schlagen zurück', *Der Spiegel*, no. 27, 76.
73. G. Rubin (1993), 'Misguided, Dangerous and Wrong: An Analysis of Anti-Pornography Politics', in A. Assiter and A. Carol (eds), *Bad Girls & Dirty Pictures*, London: Pluto Press, 18–40, 20, 19.
74. Ibid., 33.
75. Ibid, 32.
76. Die Rote Zora, 'Mili's Tanz auf dem Eis'.
77. Ibid.
78. The only reference to Gayle Rubin's work in *Emma* in the 1980s was made in a translation of a text by an American anti-porn activist in 1988; J. Raymond, 'S & M', *Emma*, no. 9, 23–25, 24.
79. 'Magazin', *Emma*, no. 9, 1987, 7.
80. 'Wenn eine Frau sich als Masochistin bezeichnet, und diesen Masochismus ausleben will, ist das erst mal ihre Sache und geht mich nix an. Wenn diese Frau aber zum STERN geht und dieses Wichsblatt das in einem Artikel auf die übliche sexistische Art und Weise ausschlachtet – nach dem Motto; "Jede Frau will eigentlich hart rangenommen werden" (Zitat) – geht mich das sehr wohl was an'; FMT PD- G8, 'Beim STERN zu Besuch – Bericht über eine kleine Aktion', *Else Wohin*, no. 6, 1990.
81. 'Es reicht', *Emma*, no. 4, 1990, 11.

Chapter 5

SISTERS IN ARMS?
MILITANT FEMINIST PROTEST AND TRANSNATIONAL SOLIDARITY

Campaigns in the New Women's Movement were, as Brown highlights, 'fundamentally transnational in both makeup and genesis'.[1] In part, this was the result of new alliances and networks, while also part of a long tradition of feminist internationalism. Even in times of great turmoil and war, women's organizations have forged links across national borders and campaigned for women on an international scale. 'It is hard to imagine', wrote feminist historian Leila J. Rupp in the late 1990s, 'the women of warring countries crossing enemy lines, gathering to try to end bloodshed and bring about peace. Yet this, in broad strokes, is what women from Europe and North America did in 1915.'[2] Indeed, amidst the chaos of the First World War, approximately 1200 women from twelve countries, including Germany, attended the International Congress of Women in The Hague, and many more sent messages of solidarity and support.[3]

Rupp rightly emphasizes that the gathering in the Netherlands, which has become one of the most celebrated expressions of internationalism in the history of European women's movements, was not the first international gathering. Already in the nineteenth century, abolitionism, socialism, temperance, peace and other issues had brought together women from Europe and the United States in mixed-gender conferences, and 1878 saw the first international congress on women's rights in Paris.[4] The International Socialist Women's Conferences in 1907, 1910 and 1915 were attended by delegates from a range of countries focused on women's suffrage, the situation of women workers and other issues that affected women across Europe and in the United States. Participants in the Second International Socialist Women's Conference

---

Notes for this section begin on page 130.

voted in favour of the establishment of an annual 'International Women's Day' to mobilize against the social and legal discrimination of women around the globe. In March 1911, more than one million women took to the streets to demand social and political equality for women.[5] To this day, women from many countries use the annual event to campaign for women's rights, celebrate women's contributions to society, and initiate and develop campaigns on a local and global scope.

Although the rise of fascism and totalitarianism in the twentieth century had a detrimental effect on the international women's networks and feminist alliances, some survived the Second World War, and internationalism enjoyed a revival in the 1960s and 1970s. Personal connections and joint struggles with women in other countries were of central importance to the formation of the New Women's Movement and feminist activism in West Germany. Alice Schwarzer's media campaign against the abortion ban, the women's shelter movement in West Germany, feminist protests against pornography and other campaigns discussed in this book were inspired by similar movements in other countries and have contributed to the formation of transnational feminist networks. A number of events in the 1970s strengthened social cohesion within and beyond these transnational networks. In November 1974, approximately six hundred women from eighteen countries took part in the first International Women's Conference in West Germany.[6] Among other issues, the attendees discussed possible actions for 1975, which the United Nations (UN) had declared 'international women's year'. The year marked the beginning of the UN 'decade for women' and saw a major international conference in Mexico City: the '1st World Conference on Women'.[7] The conference was attended by delegates from 133 countries, including representatives from both West and East Germany. Radical feminists in Western Europe and in the United States viewed the UN's 'sudden interest' in gender equality with deep distrust, and considered the vote on the international women's year by a male-dominated institution like the UN a 'hypocritical and token gesture'.[8]

One of the outcomes of the Women's Conference in Frankfurt was that the participants decided to engage in 'radical and constructive counteractions' against the international women's year. Some began to organize a major international conference with a radical feminist agenda: the Tribunal on Crimes Against Women in Brussels.[9] The tribunal took place from 4 to 8 March 1976, ending on International Women's Day. Its structure and form were inspired by the International War Crimes Tribunal in 1967, which had investigated atrocities during the Vietnam War. According to co-organizer Diana E.H. Russell, the Tribunal on Crimes Against Women in Brussels was attended by two thousand women from forty countries. The testimonies and reports discussed were chosen on the basis that they were documenting different forms of violence against women and that they represented cases from a range of countries. The organizers highlighted that Third World Women and immigrant women had to carry a double or triple burden: they were women, they were not citizens of a welfare state and they were often forced into poverty. The notion of sexist oppression that the conference organizers endorsed, however, flattened out these and other differences among women in favour of a universalist notion of patriarchal violence: 'It is important to show that the oppression of women is the same everywhere, only different in degree; and that each case is not an isolated case, but typical of what happens in the particular country. The aims are to reach women everywhere, to reinforce solidarity between women, and to discover ways to combat crimes against women.'[10]

The notion of global sisterhood, a central concept in feminist discussions in the FRG and other Western countries in the 1970s and 1980s,[11] has become the subject of growing criticism since.[12] The feminist author and theorist bell hooks traces the concept of universal sisterhood back to a problematic idea of common oppression, evoked mainly by 'bourgeois white women, both liberal and radical in perspective'.[13] Chandra Talpade Mohanty makes a similar criticism. She argues that the notion of sisterhood 'erases material and ideological power differences within and among groups of women, especially between First and Third World women'.[14] Unlike Mohanty, hooks does not dismiss the notion of sisterhood. Instead, she encourages women to understand it as the achievement of a common and constant struggle rather than taking it as a given. According to hooks, the feminist struggle against sexism can only succeed if it is also a fight against racism and classism.[15] Women, according to hooks, should bond 'on the basis of our political commitment to a feminist movement that aims to end sexist oppression'.[16] Mohanty proposes a notion of solidarity that is remarkably similar to hooks's conception of sisterhood. She suggests thinking of solidarity 'in terms of mutuality, accountability and the recognition of common interests as the basis for relationships among diverse communities. Rather than assuming an enforced commonality of oppression, the practice of solidarity foregrounds communities of people who have chosen to work and fight together.'[17] The critical contributions of Mohanty and other feminist thinkers, who have discussed women's movements and feminist solidarity in the context of colonialism, imperialism and global capitalism, have inspired a 'transnational turn' in feminist theory.

Unlike internationalism, transnationalism is a fairly new concept in feminist theory and activism. Coined in the 1920s, the term gained popularity among scholars in the humanities and social sciences in the late 1990s and early 2000s. Leila Rupp was, as Oliver Janz and Daniel Schönpflug highlight, 'among the first to consider the work she did on the first wave of and international women's movements "as part of a transnational history that we are only beginning to write"'.[18] What distinguishes Rupp's book *Worlds of Women* from other studies on the subject is that she viewed unity and division in international women's organizations from a perspective that emphasizes the interconnectedness of identities and political networks across national borders. Although there is no shared definition of transnationalism, most scholars would probably agree that a transnationalist perspective emphasizes 'the ongoing interconnection or flow of people, ideas, objects and capital across the borders of nation-states, in contexts in which the state shapes but does not contain such linkages and movements'.[19] Transnationalism has had a profound impact on feminist theory and practice in the FRG. 'Facilitated, but not caused by improved transportation, technology and telecommunications', many feminist activists in Germany are now are now using the theoretical framework of intersectionality[20] to analyse the complex interplay of multiple forms of oppression on a local and global scale.[21] Yet it should be added that although German feminists might have been more sceptical of the idea that 'gender and race are naturally similar' than their American counterparts, it would be wrong to assume that there were no discussions about racism in the New Women's Movement prior to the rise of intersectionality as a paradigm in feminist theory in the 1990s.[22]

Feminism and Racism in West Germany

While groups in the New Women's Movement in the FRG quickly and enthusiastically embraced the notion of global sisterhood, it was a long and difficult process to identify and tackle racism. Critical contributions by women's groups from different migrant communities, Afro-German activists and Jewish women in West Germany have played a central role in this process. In many projects, migrant women and German citizens worked side by side to support women and girls with a migration background and to make their voices heard. One of the first projects of this kind was the Meeting and Information Centre for Turkish Women in West Berlin (*Treff- und Informationsort für türkische Frauen e.V.*). Founded in 1978, the project made headlines in 1984, when an armed intruder killed two women in the centre. The organizers did not let themselves be intimidated by this attack, and the centre has remained a hub of activity to this day. One of the first events that brought together women from different countries took place in September 1977, when forty women from Turkey, Greece, Spain, Yugoslavia, the Netherlands and West Germany organized a conference to identify and tackle problems that female immigrants faced in West Germany.[23] Most of the participants had moved to the FRG in the 1960s, when the unemployment rate had been historically low, and when the government had made a deliberate effort to recruit foreign workers. When the number of unemployed people rose significantly in the 1970s, the visas of many migrant workers were not renewed, and they were expected to go back to their countries of origin. This decision met with strong opposition in migrant communities.

Korean women were among the first migrants to publicly protest against the U-turn in West German immigration policy. Many of them had come to West Germany in the 1960s and 1970s to work as nurses in hospitals and care homes. When thousands of nurses were sent back to Korea in 1977, the remaining women collected 11,000 signatures against their expulsion, and urged the government to reconsider its decision.[24] To connect and support Korean women in West Germany and in their country of origin, some of the participants involved in the petition started the Korean Women's Group in Germany (*Koreanische Frauengruppe in Deutschland*). As the second part of this chapter illustrates, this organization played a pivotal role in a transnational campaign for women workers in South Korea in the 1980s.

In March 1984, women migrants and West German supporters organized the First Joint Women's Congress Against the Particular Oppression of Migrant Girls and Women (*Erster Gemeinsamer Kongress gegen die besondere Unterdrückung von ausländischen Mädchen und Frauen*). Although migrant workers from Turkey, Southern Europe and South Korea, refugees from Chile, Iran and Vietnam, and/ or spouses of German citizens from Southeast Asia, had different lives, political views and backgrounds, they and other groups of migrant women experienced forms of discrimination that many German women could not even imagine. They were, as the organizers criticized, 'not treated as second but as third-class people – as the slaves of slaves'.[25]

In the 1980s, two thirds of the migrant women in West Germany were not gainfully employed, for the most part not by their own choice, but because they were legally prohibited from working. More than half of those migrant women who were employed worked as unskilled labourers in industry, earning 20 per cent less than male migrants, and less than women with a German passport.[26] Others worked in poorly paid part-time jobs as nurses, cleaners and in catering. According to immigration law, work permits for migrants could be withdrawn if it was felt that their jobs could and should be done by German citizens. The situation of female migrants who had moved to Germany to live with their spouses was even worse: most were not allowed to work and lost their right to remain in the event of divorce. If they were abused by their husbands, they could not seek refuge in women's shelters, because they were not entitled to benefits, and they risked deportation. At the Frankfurt Women's Congress, more than one thousand women discussed these and other problems faced by migrant women in West Germany.

At the final meeting at the Frankfurt Women's Congress, participants emphasized that they did not want to be seen as helpless victims. They presented a catalogue of demands concerning the social and legal status of migrant women, including equal rights for German women and migrant women, equal rights for immigrants and German citizens and a complete halt to deportations.[27] In this context, the participants made clear what they expected from feminist activists from the FRG: 'practical solidarity and new initiatives, which allow foreign and German women to meet each other, foster real exchange and to make sure that equal and joint collaborations between them are no longer the exception but the rule'.[28] The Frankfurt Women's Congress itself can be seen as an example that such collaborations between German women and female migrants were possible. In the organizing team, women from different migrant communities worked side by side with German women who supported their cause. In their concluding remarks, the organizers emphasized that there were many open questions and unresolved issues regarding everyday racism and sexism. Yet, they saw the gathering in Frankfurt as a first step in a joint struggle against sexist and racist discrimination.

Sociologist Dagmar Schultz was one of the first feminist activists in West Germany to publicly demand more critical self-reflection on racism in the New Women's Movement. Schultz had lived and worked in the United States for several years, and felt that she had learned a lot from discussions about race, class and sex in the US women's movement. In 1981, she asserted self-critically in the feminist magazine *Courage*: 'Until now, we have dealt with racism and anti-Semitism to a much smaller degree than our American sisters.'[29] Schultz tried to stimulate feminist debates in West Germany by bringing feminist activists and scholars from the United States to West Berlin. In 1984, she invited the feminist icons Gloria Joseph and Audre Lorde as visiting lecturers to the Free University. The feminist historian Katharina Oguntoye attended one of the events with Lorde and Joseph, and described their visit as 'incredibly important' (*von überwältigender Bedeutung*) for her personal development and for the German women's movement.[30] Since Oguntoye and other Afro-German women had experienced the disappointment of having white feminists reject their voices, they began to set up their own networks and discussion platforms.[31] Oguntoye became a regular contributor to the Afro-German magazine *Afrekete*, and co-edited the book *Farbe bekennen. Afro-deutsche Frauen auf den Spuren ihrer Geschichte* (Showing Our Colours: Afro-German Women Retrace their History) with Dagmar Schultz and May Ayim, the Afro-German poet and activist.

A leading voice in the Afro-German women's movement and a pioneer in critical whiteness studies in West Germany, Ayim pointedly criticized German reunification as a '*Sch-einheit*' (sham-unity), because it reinforced a notion of white Germanness that can be traced back to Germany's colonial past.[32] According to literary scholar and critical race theorist Peggy Piesche, ethnic difference and racism were officially 'non-issues' in the GDR.[33] Yet, Piesche also highlights that foreign workers and black GDR citizens saw themselves confronted with similar racial stereotypes as '*Gastarbeiter*', refugees and black citizens in West Germany. Although the number of foreign workers in the GDR was considerably smaller than in West Germany, both countries responded to staff shortages in heavy industry and other sectors by recruiting migrant workers. Yet there were also differences. In contrast to the FRG, foreign workers in the GDR were not allowed to bring spouses. Marriages between migrant workers and GDR citizens were rare, and if women workers got pregnant, they were left with the choice between an abortion in the GDR and deportation to their home countries.[34] While the 1980s in West Germany saw a growing number of media reports on women trafficking and forced prostitution, there were no such accounts in the GDR.[35]

Trafficking and Forced Prostitution

The late 1970s saw a boom in male sex tourism to Africa and Southeast Asia, and there was a growing interest in 'exotic' prostitutes and wives in the FRG and other Western European countries. Marriage agencies, strip bars, travel agencies and brothel owners in Switzerland and West Germany earned good money with 'Asian girls' that they promoted as 'sweet', 'loyal' and 'cheap' sex objects in newspaper and magazines.[36] In 1981, a Philippine go-go dancer took court action against her Swiss employer and drew public attention to the unbearable conditions in which she and up to nine hundred other Philippine women had to work in Swiss brothels.[37] In 1979, the Regional Court Hannover had to decide on a similar case: two brothel owners were charged with enticing thirteen Thai women to West Germany with false promises, and then forcing them to work as prostitutes.[38] Like marriage agencies 'specializing' in Asian women, brothel owners operated in a legal grey zone. Asked to comment on this issue, a government spokesman explained that 'due to a lack of evidence' there was nothing they could do to stop this practice.[39]

In the 1980s, the boom in sex tourism to and trafficking from Asia continued – despite growing fear of aids and other sexually transmitted diseases. According to feminist journalists, 700,000 men, including 30,000 German citizens, travelled to the Philippines in 1980 for sex.[40] A few years later, journalists reported that 100,000 West German sex tourists travelled to Thailand in 1987 alone, and predicted that this number would continue to increase.[41] According to Thai law, prostitution was a crime, but many politicians and police authorities turned a blind eye to sex tourism, because they were bribed by local brothel owners and their business partners in Europe.[42] West German marriage broker Günther Menger told the newsmagazine *Spiegel* that his business was one of at least two hundred agencies across the country 'specializing in exotic women', and that he arranged four hundred marriages between German men and Asian women each year. Menger emphasized that his clients had a range of social backgrounds, and they included construction workers, police officers and professors.[43]

A commonly held view among West German sex tourists and men who wanted to marry Asian women was that German women had become too emancipated to be good lovers or submissive wives. An essay by Bodo Kirchhoff in the sixty-eighth issue of the left-wing intellectual magazine *Kursbuch* illustrates that this view had prominent advocates in the New Left. Here, Kirchhoff presented a character who turned to women in Thailand, because he felt that they had kept their 'natural character' (*natürliches Wesen*), whereas German women had been ruined by feminism.[44] The article featured graphic descriptions of violence against women (e.g. when Kirchhoff's friend recommends that he should examine Thai girls for sexually transmitted diseases by putting cigarette ashes into their vagina), and was heavily criticized by feminist activists. In a response in *Emma*, the feminist journalist Ingrid Strobl expressed her shock at the fact that 'it had once again become good form in progressive circles to publicly masturbate about rape'.[45]

The 1980s in West Germany saw a number of feminist initiatives to tackle trafficking, forced prostitution and racist and sexist news reports about Asian women. In September 1983, a group of feminist journalists and other women filed a complaint against the publisher Axel Springer.[46] The claimants argued that a series of reports with the telling title 'I bought my wife' (Ich habe mir eine Frau gekauft) featured in Springer's tabloid *Bild* in June 1983 incited hatred against women and was harmful to young people. According to the charges, the newspaper presented Asian women as submissive sex slaves who could be purchased like commodities and replaced if they failed to meet the expectations of the consumer. The charges, however, had no legal consequences for Axel Springer. Since they felt that court proceedings would not put a stop to the thriving business with Asian women, some feminists adopted more confrontational tactics to fight against trafficking and forced prostitution.

In the course of the 1980s, radical women's groups in West Germany carried out a number of attacks against alleged women traffickers and their supporters. In 1983, the Red Zora planted a bomb at the Philippine consulate in Bonn. They claimed that corrupt politicians in the Philippines and in other Asian countries profited from sex tourism, trafficking and prostitution. With their attacks against the Philippine consulate and their German business partners, the RZ sought to protest against the exploitation and oppression of Philippine women. 'The possibility to advertise and sell Philippine women here like commodities', they argued, 'is an aggravated expression of social power relationships, and of violent and exploitative relations between men and women.'[47] According to the authors of the short statement, the exploitation of women in the Philippines and in other Third World countries constituted an offence against all women, including themselves. They declared that they wanted to express their solidarity with Philippine women, 'because, as women, we feel offended by this practice'.[48]

The RZ statement forces us to consider to what extent a group of white German women can and should feel offended by a practice affecting women from different countries, ethnic backgrounds and social classes. In 1993, some members of the Red Zora released a statement in which they critically examined the position that they had held in the early 1980s. They acknowledged that the notion of sexism as a primary and universal form of oppression that they promoted in this period did not take account of their privileged position as white German women.[49] In the early 1990s, the group emphasized that it was wrong to think of sex workers from the Third World as passive victims of sexism and imperialism. They recognized that many women 'decide – even though under an existential pressure – that they "prefer" a life as a sex worker or wife in Germany to the struggles for survival or hard graft in factories in their own countries (which allows them to send urgently needed money back home)'.[50]

Considering the public interest in trafficking and forced prostitution in the 1980s, it is striking that the bomb at the Philippine consulate and other attacks by militant feminists received virtually no attention in the West German media. The only exception was an article in *Der Spiegel*, which pointedly remarked that women traffickers in the FRG had nothing to fear from politicians or prosecuting authorities, but they had every reason to be scared of the Red Zora.[51] In addition to the bombing at the Philippine consulate, the article listed three other RZ attacks against trafficking and forced prostitution: an attack against a sex shop in

Koblenz and arson attacks against the private property of a marriage broker in Cologne and in Münster.

Although the attack in Koblenz was not part of the RZ campaign against alleged women traffickers, the fact that it was mentioned in this context suggests that the author of the *Spiegel* article was aware of the fact that the RZ tried to fight against the objectification and sexual expoitation of women in a range of contexts.[52] In the claims of responsibility for the attacks against trafficking and forced prostitution, the RZ drew on facts and quotes from feminist publications, media reports and other sources to explain why they considered it necessary to express solidarity with Philippine women by attacking 'representatives of the patriarchal order' in West Germany.[53] On International Women's Day on 8 March 1983, the group carried out attacks against the Philippine consular in Bonn and against the car of a marriage broker in Cologne. And the RZ did not stop there. Five months later, the group torched the van of marriage broker Günther Menger to protest against the smugness with which he and his colleagues promoted Asian women in *Bild* and other newspapers. According to *Der Spiegel*, Menger was very lucky: the only reason the fire did not spread to his villa was that the fire brigade was quick to respond to his call for help.[54]

While the *Spiegel* article focused almost exclusively on the Red Zora, it is important to note that there were also other groups who carried out attacks against alleged women traffickers and their property. In 1986, members of the Revolutionary Cells planted a bomb at the headquarters of the German airline Lufthansa in Cologne. The group claimed that it had attacked the airline, because it was responsible for the deportation of thousands of refugees, and because it benefitted financially from sex tourism to Bangkok and Manila.[55] While the Lufthansa bombing is well documented, there is virtually no information about other attacks in this period. While collecting data for this book, I found a copy of one claim of responsibility in the Stasi archive in Berlin. The statement includes one of the few records documenting the use of physical force and intimidation in the history of the New Women's Movement. A group of women forced a man, who was – according to them – a notorious trafficker in women from Hamburg, to pose naked with a sign around his neck which read, mimicking the style of his own newspaper advertisements, 'woman trafficker – sweet, affectionate – to be used at any time, with toad-prick'.[56] The claim of responsibility, which featured a photograph of the scene, concluded as follows: 'We will put up resistance against all woman traffickers, rapists, and shitty machos and against the imperialist, misogynist system for as long as we can think and feel!!'[57]

At first sight, the attack against the alleged trafficker in Hamburg seems very similar to the feminist action against the lawyer Becker in Berlin discussed in the previous chapter: a group of feminist activists drew on highly confrontational tactics to protest against institutionalized sexism and violence against women. In both cases, feminist activists have attacked and humiliated a man in public. Yet, there were important differences. Although Becker was clearly irritated by the attack, he was at no point in fear of violence and took no legal action against the intruders. The attack against the alleged trafficker from Hamburg, by contrast, has probably involved the use of force or threats of violence, because it is extremely unlikely that the man posed naked voluntarily for the photograph. It is not known whether the man filed a criminal complaint.

Since the statement was signed 'raging/racing Zora',[58] it is tempting to assume that the attack was carried out by the Red Zora. However, since it is not mentioned in any statement by the group, and the former group members that I have interviewed for this book told me that they had never heard of it before, it is more likely that the attack was carried out by 'copycats'. Like in the case of most feminist attacks against trafficking and forced prostitution in the 1980s, there have been no media reports about the action of the raging Zora. The only context in which the media reported extensively about militant feminist protest by the Red Zora and other women's groups in this period was a transnational solidarity campaign for women workers in South Korea, which gathered momentum in 1986.

Adler I: A Transnational Solidarity Campaign for Korean Women Workers

On 4 May 1986, the Korean Women's Group in West Berlin received a letter that caused great concern among its members. It included a report in which trade unionists described the poor working conditions in the garment factory Flair Fashion, in Iri, South Korea (a Free Trade Zone 250 km from Seoul).[59] The factory produced clothes that the German company Adler sold at cheap prices to customers in West Germany and other European countries. In 1988, the company ran thirty-eight stores with a selling space of more than 100,000 m² and aimed for a turnover of 1,000,000 DM.[60] By August 2012, the number of local stores had grown to 166. According to a recent report, the turnover in the first six months of 2012 was 263.2 million euros.[61] Founded in 1959, Adler had initially produced its entire stock in Germany, but then outsourced a growing part of its production to Asia. In 1978, Adler opened a garment factory in Iri to benefit from the relatively low labour costs and the financial benefits of the South Korean Free Trade Zone. By 1986, 60–80 per cent of the clothes that Adler sold in its European stores were 'made in Korea'.[62] According to the German management, Flair Fashion was a 'model factory'.[63] Trade unionists, by contrast, criticized the working conditions at Flair Fashion as 'inhumane'.

In their letter to the Korean Women's Group in Berlin, workers reported that they were expected to do at least one hour of overtime per day while receiving salaries below minimum wage.[64] Apparently, the management constantly monitored the employees and punished them for mistakes. According to the authors of the letter, many workers could meet the required output only by foregoing breaks and exhausting themselves beyond their limits.[65] They added that the German management at Flair Fashion treated the Korean workers with disrespect.[66] The authors were particularly concerned about the situation of female employees at Flair Fashion. Since the 1960s, women's involvement in the South Korean labour market had grown constantly. By the late 1980s, women made up almost 50 per cent of the work force,[67] and more than 70 per cent of the workers at South Korean clothing manufacturers.[68] At Flair Fashion, the ratio of female employees was even higher than in other garment factories: 85 per cent of 1600 employees were women.[69]

For the most part, female employees at Flair Fashion were unskilled workers between the ages of seventeen and twenty-five. As in other garment factories, women's wages at Flair Fashion were considerably lower than those of their male colleagues. On average, female workers earned 40–50 per cent less than men in the same positions.[70] And, unlike male employees, not all women workers were insured against industrial accidents: female employees could claim compensation from the Korean insurance system only if they were under twenty-five. At twenty-five, they were expected to leave the workforce to dedicate themselves fully to marriage and motherhood.[71]

Confucian gender norms imposed a strongly subordinate position on women in Korea under which girls and unmarried women were under the authority of male relatives, while married women must submit to their husbands.[72] Adler and other foreign investors benefited from the low wages and docile demeanour of female workers. Fürchtegott Adler, the head of Flair Fashion, openly admitted to this in an internal publication in 1984: 'The rapid rise of the ADLER company', he declared, 'was possible only because of the black-haired, almond-eyed Korean women.'[73] He added that, to his regret, he lost most of his employees at the age of twenty-five, because the Flair Fashion 'girls' wanted to 'spoil their men and dedicate themselves fully to family and household'.[74]

Trade unionists claimed that sexual assault by management was commonplace at the Adler factory. 'When a German manager likes a worker', explained the authors of the letter to the Korean women in Berlin, 'she has to meet his desires, or she risks being moved to a worse position or being fired.'[75] They did not refer to concrete cases, but they left no doubt that a sexual relationship with a German manager was the only way for women to be promoted to overseer or shift leader.[76] The workers saw no way to solve their problems internally, as German management prohibited general assemblies and refused to discuss employment issues with trade union activists. In view of these circumstances, a group of trade unionists decided to go public. In their letter to the Korean Women's Group in West Berlin, the women described the problems at Flair Fashion and appealed for 'sisterly help' from Germany.[77]

The plea for help from South Korea sparked a thriving solidarity campaign in West Germany that involved groups across the political spectrum. The Korean Women's Group in Berlin and Terre des Femmes (TdF)[78] activists were the first to respond, with a public relations campaign that mobilized a number of other groups including Christian organizations, radical leftist groups, trade unions and Third World activists. According to one observer, the motives and political backgrounds of the actors involved varied considerably, but the decentralized and non-hierarchical nature of the campaign allowed them to express solidarity with the Korean workers in their own ways.[79]

Shortly after receiving the alarming report from South Korea in May 1986, members of the Korean Women's Group translated the letter and sent it to women's groups and human rights organizations in Germany. Members of the Korean Women's Group and Terre des Femmes publicized the complaints and demands of the Flair Fashion workers, and urged Adler representatives to improve the working conditions at Flair Fashion, but Adler denied all allegations. A few months later, the situation in Iri escalated. In April 1987, the Flair Fashion management fired nine women and three men, because they claimed that these workers had been 'ringleaders' in a protest for higher wages and improved working conditions at the factory.[80] Eight hundred workers went on strike to express solidarity with their twelve colleagues and to underline their demands. According to a journalist in Iri, 90 per cent of the participants in the protest were women between the ages of seventeen and twenty-five.[81] Police and security forces ended the strike with brutal force and arrested ten participants.[82] In May 1987, a Flair Fashion employee tried to kill herself in a factory bathroom. In her farewell note, the woman stated that she wanted to commit suicide to draw attention to the industrial action of the Flair Fashion workers.[83]

When news of the attempted suicide and the strike at Flair Fashion reached West Germany, the solidarity campaign entered a new stage. Members of the Korean Women's Group, Christian organizations, feminist groups and human rights organizations staged protests in front of Adler shops throughout West Germany. The actors involved wanted to create awareness of the industrial dispute at Flair Fashion and to mobilize consumers and employees in German Adler stores to express solidarity with the Korean workers. In flyers, the groups called on Adler customers to rethink their attitude towards fashion and consumption, to write protest letters to Adler management, to discuss outsourcing of production to Third World countries in unions and political organizations and to sign a petition against the company.[84] As the protest campaign gathered momentum, it attracted national media attention, and several national newspapers and TV programmes reported critically on the working conditions at Flair Fashion.[85]

Adler II: 'Playing with Fire'? Feminists Attack Adler Stores in West Germany

For the most part, participants in the solidarity campaign avoided direct confrontations with Adler management and police forces. However, there were some exceptions. During one of the first demonstrations at the Adler headquarters in Haibach, activists tried to confront the management and were assaulted by one of the co-founders of the company and his wife.[86] In May 1987, several participants in a demonstration in Sankt Georgen broke into an Adler store and were arrested.[87] In late July, armed police forces attacked protesters who had blocked the entrance of an Adler store in Bremen.[88] On 21 June, members of the Red Zora planted a bomb at the Adler headquarters in Haibach to express 'solidarity with the fighting women at Adler in South Korea' and to destroy a part of the company's 'administrative machine'.[89] The failed bombing marked the beginning of a series of feminist attacks against Adler premises in Germany.

Because the self-built bomb at the Adler headquarters failed to detonate, however, the attack received little attention in the German press.[90] A claim of responsibility, released by the Red Zora shortly after the attack, is to this day not publicly available. It does provide a detailed explanation of the Red Zora's thinking, however, so I want to briefly summarize its content here. The statement opens by describing the situation of women workers at Flair Fashion. Drawing on intelligence gathered by TdF members and other activists, the RZ presented the conditions in the factory as 'wage slavery based on sexist and racist oppression'.[91] In the second part of the statement, the authors discussed how globalization in the garment industry and other sectors of the economy affected women in Germany as workers and consumers. While acknowledging that a growing number of women with little or no income slipped below the poverty threshold, the RZ warned them not to accept consumption 'as a surrogate for [a better] life'. 'Despite the fact that living conditions in [Western] cities worsen, we musn't forget a central point: our privileges, including that of consumption, are based on the exploitation, use and destruction of people in the Third World.'[92]

A few weeks after the failed bombing in Haibach, the Red Zora struck again. On the night of Saturday, 15 August, the group tried to set fire to Adler stores in Hamburg, Bremen, Oldenburg, Isernhagen, Holzwickende, Kassel, Neuss, Aachen and Frankfurt. Initial crime scene investigations led police to conclude that the arson attacks had been carefully planned. Using electric time fuses, the RZ could synchronize the arson attacks and delay the ignition of the incendiary compositions. Between 8:30 and 9:30 PM, fires broke out in eight of the nine shops.[93] For unknown reasons, the two incendiary devices in the store in Aachen failed to catch fire. Due to the large sales floor in Adler stores, it was easy to place and almost impossible to locate incendiary devices. Only when the perpetrators informed a pastor about their location could special forces detect and destroy the incendiary devices in Aachen.[94] An extensive search for traces in and around the store revealed that the homemade incendiary devices in cigarette boxes had a similar composition to those used in the arson attack at the sex store in Koblenz discussed in the previous chapter.[95] Apparently, the incendiary devices in other stores were also homemade but constructed in a slightly different way. The two incendiary devices placed in coat pockets in a store in Frankfurt reminded a journalist of 'Molotov cocktails from the era of the department store arsonists in 1968'.[96] Incendiary devices in other stores included alarm clocks of the *Emes sonochron* type, which had been used in a number of previous RZ attacks. [97]

The fires and the sprinkler systems that they activated caused substantial property damage. According to Adler management, the loss to the company amounted to 30–35 million DM.[98] Due to the geographic focus and the range of incendiary devices used, police authorities considered it likely that the attacks were a concerted effort by women's groups across West Germany. During a press conference a few days after the attack, police officials announced that the Red Zora had claimed responsibility for the attacks. The police had to admit, however, that they knew virtually nothing about the structure and strength of this organization.[99]

On 17 August, the German Press Agency and the editorial teams of several newspapers received a letter with a claim of responsibility entitled 'Eagle flambéed'.[100] Of all recipients, only the editors of the newspaper *taz* chose to publish the full text. As in the claim of responsibility for the failed bombing in June 1987, the statement called on Adler management to meet the demands of the striking women in Iri. In the short statement, the group explained their motives, underlined the demands of the Flair Fashion workers and sent 'fiery greetings' to the Korean women. While highlighting the importance of information events and other nonviolent actions against Adler, the perpetrators presented their arson attacks as a form of solidarity with the Flair Fashion workers and as a complement to the predominantly peaceful protest campaign in West Germany.[101]

Due to its spectacular nature, the series of attacks against Adler attracted more media attention than any other activities of the Red Zora.[102] In the days after the fires, many national and numerous local newspapers reported on the attacks. It is interesting to note in what terms journalists described the perpetrators. Most articles introduced the RZ as a 'feminist terror group' (*feministische Terrorgruppe*) that consisted exclusively of women.[103] Unlike women in the RAF in the early 1970s, the members of the Red Zora were not belittled with the infantilizing label 'terror girls', but rather presented as 'angry ladies' (*wütende Damen*) and frustrated feminists.[104]

Drawing on information provided by the Federal Bureau of Criminal Investigation, journalists described the Red Zora as a feminist 'subgroup' (*Untergruppe*) or 'female offshoot' (*weiblicher Ableger*) of the Revolutionary Cells that had attacked Adler out of frustration with machismo within the militant leftist network.[105] 'With the large-scale action against Adler', suggested the news magazine *Der Spiegel*, 'the angry ladies in the Revolutionary Cells might have wanted to prove to ignorant men in their own circle what they were capable of.'[106] The *Spiegel* article claimed that the members of the Red Zora felt 'oppressed' by male comrades in the Revolutionary Cells. 'Is this', added the journalist polemically, 'why they played with fire at the Adler stores?'[107] The author here both reduced the militants' motives to a perceived oppression by male comrades, and belittled the arson attacks of the Red Zora as 'playing with fire'.[108]

While the group certainly did not attack Adler to impress their male comrades or outdo them, it is true that the months prior to the arson attacks had seen a heated debate over sexism in the radical Left. In 1987, the first comprehensive collection of RC statements circulated in leftist circles in West Germany but, apart from one contribution to the RC magazine *Revolutionary Rage*, the book included no texts by the RZ. On 21 July 1987, the newspaper *die tageszeitung* documented an appeal by a group of men and women who distributed legal and illegal leftist literature in the Ruhr area. The authors declared: 'We refuse to distribute this masculinist book . . . , because the book reinforces a one-sided, thus false, misogynist historiography of the Revolutionary Cells and the Red Zora for years to come, and it declares the guerrilla a male preserve.'[109]

Adler III: Feminist Responses to the Red Zora

The question of whether the attacks against Adler were part of a 'battle of the sexes' (*Geschlechterkampf*) in the militant Left, as the *taz* article indicated, was of little interest to most participants in the solidarity campaign with the Flair Fashion workers. Here, the militant protest provoked heated debate on a different question: did the attacks benefit or harm the campaign? In a press release from 17 August, the executive board of TdF expressed its indignation about the militant protest against Adler and 'strongly condemned' the attacks. The women declared: 'Actions of that kind discredit the nonviolent work of a women's rights organization that has been in close contact with women workers at the Adler factory Flair Fashion in South Korea.'[110]

The TdF women were concerned that the militant protest of the Red Zora could lead to an association of their organization and the women's movement as a whole with violence. Moreover, they expressed the fear that the attacks deflected attention from the situation of the Flair Fashion workers. The Korean Women's Group in Germany took a similar stance. In early September, the organization declared in a public statement: in the 'interest of effective and far-reaching educational work . . . , we distance ourselves decisively from any recourse to violence to enforce the objectives of unions'.[111]

At least initially, the response of Adler management appeared to show that these concerns were well founded. On 17 August, representatives of the company declared that they had decided to stop production in South Korea to ensure safety and health of their customers and clients in Germany.[112] A few days later, a German manager of Flair Fashion and a representative of the Adler works council visited TdF Tübingen. In a public statement, they claimed that the TdF campaign had created 'fertile ground for manifestations of violence'.[113] The Adler workers refused further contact with the women's group because they suspected 'terrorists' among its members.[114]

On 9 September 1987, representatives of German church groups and unions organized a press conference in Frankfurt. In a joint statement, the actors involved urged Adler once again to meet the demands of the workers and to re-employ the dismissed employees.[115] Evidence suggests that there were at least two further attempted attacks against Adler stores in West Germany. On 11 September, the 'Amazons', an until-then unknown group of militant feminists, followed the example of the Red Zora and set fire to an Adler store in Berlin.[116] Like the Red Zora, the Amazons used slow-burning incendiary devices to minimize the risk of injury to members of staff or customers.[117] They, too, framed their attack against Adler as a contribution to the predominantly peaceful solidarity campaign. A few weeks later, *die tageszeitung* reported that another attack was thwarted by pure chance.[118] The Adler management responded to the repeated attacks against its premises with a surprising turnaround. A representative of the company declared that there was no alternative but to 'succumb to violence'.[119] Representatives of the company promised to accept the wage increase, to re-employ the dismissed union activists and to meet other demands of their employees in order to prevent further attacks.[120]

This unexpected decision by the Adler management provoked a range of responses in the solidarity campaign, from celebratory enthusiasm to grave concern. Terre des Femmes welcomed the concessions from Adler, but at the same time published an open letter criticizing the company for making its decision for the wrong reasons. 'You are obviously not willing to recognize fundamental rights of male and female workers as such, but you ultimately give in to violence. Does Adler want to establish a precedent?'[121] An article by feminist activist and scholar Christa Wichterich argued that the militant protest against Adler imperilled the success of the broader solidarity campaign. 'Are ten fires enough to create international solidarity among women?' she asked rhetorically.[122] While endorsing tactical diversity, she criticized 'voluntaristic actions that jeopardize other forms of resistance'.[123] According to her, notwithstanding the apparent victory, the arson attacks by the Red Zora and the Amazons posed a risk to the broader aims of the solidarity campaign. 'This firework', claimed Wichterich, 'was a disservice to the attempt to use a single protest campaign to create a triangle of solidarity between workers in the Third World and consumers and workers here. Reason enough to discuss these fiery tactics in the women's movement.'[124]

In a letter to the editors of *taz*, a radical women's group from Reutlingen made a critical contribution to this debate. They argued that Wichterich's article and the TdF statement were 'naïve' and divisive. While the authors of the letter agreed that militant protest alone did not make a solidarity campaign, they argued that the Red Zora had made an important contribution to the campaign's overall success. According to this group, the arson attacks had caused economic harm to Adler and increased the pressure on the company. 'Radical resistance on all levels is necessary if we want to put our ideas of a non-hierarchical, non-sexist, non-racist society into practice.'[125]

Addressing Wichterich and other feminists, they wrote: 'It is up to you what forms of resistance you choose and how you put your ideas about change in this society into practice.'[126] But they found it unacceptable that participants in the solidarity campaign served 'dominant forces' (*den Herrschenden*) by 'denouncing some forms of resistance in the same vocabulary as the State Protection Office'.[127] Other women in the radical Left expressed similar views. One week after Wichterich had published her article, 'a group of angry women' (*Gruppe zorniger Frauen*) openly expressed their enthusiasm at Adler's climb-down in a small advertisement in the same newspaper, congratulating the 'Red Zora and her sisters' for 'the brilliant action' (*Glanzstück*).[128] The RZ was thus clearly not the only group in the women's movement and in the radical Left who believed that women should be free to choose highly confrontational tactics in expressing their solidarity with the Korean workers and supporting their struggle.

In an interview in January 1988, Christa Stolle and Ute Kosczy from TdF and Jai Sin Pak from the Korean Women's Group in West Berlin reported back from South Korea about recent developments at Flair Fashion. They acknowledged that, by and large, the management had met the demands of the workers. By the time of their visit, Flair Fashion had been placed under Korean management, a change that was a mixed blessing in the eyes of the employees. The interviewees acknowledged that the communication in the factory had improved but they expressed concerns that the oppression of workers would continue in equally extreme, albeit more subtle, forms.[129]

While defending the exclusively nonviolent politics of her organization, Christa Stolle put the TdF response to the arson attacks into perspective. 'In hindsight, it was rash and unnecessary [that we distanced ourselves] in this manner. At the time, we thought that the media would attack us and label us as terrorists.'[130] Stolle concluded with a message from the Flair Fashion employees to the Red Zora. According to Stolle, the 'fiery greetings' had not reached their destination, and the workers knew of the attacks only because the Flair Fashion management had mentioned them in an address to the employees.[131] The women said that they would like to be informed about future attacks by the activists involved, and not by the management.[132]

Among other reasons, members of TdF and other radical and liberal feminists in West Germany condemned the arson attacks against Adler because they felt that the RZ had not tried to discuss their tactics with the workers in Iri and with other participants in the solidarity campaign. Christa Wichterich, for instance, explained that she had criticized the arson attacks because she believed that a constant dialogue with women in the Third World provides the only way for feminists in Germany to find out what their 'sisters' in the other continents want, and what they could do to support them in their struggles.[133] The Red Zora, by contrast took the view that every woman should freely decide how to express her solidarity, so long as her actions drew attention to the difficulties that the women in Iri faced and supported them in their struggle. Since this dispute offers critical insights into feminist debates about militant protest and transnational solidarity, I will discuss it in more detail in the conclusion.

Notes

1. Brown, *West Germany and the Global Sixties*, 300.
2. L.J. Rupp (1997), *Worlds of Women: The Making of an International Women's Movement*, Princeton, NJ: Princeton University Press, 3.

3. C. Alihusain (2015), 'International Congress of Women of 1915'. Retrieved 20 October 2015 from http://soz-kult.hs-duesseldorf.de/.
4. Rupp, *Worlds of Women*, 14.
5. G. Notz (2104), '(Kein) Abschied von der Idee der Schwesterlichkeit? Herausforderungen für feministische Solidarität', in Y. Franke et al. (eds), *Feminismen heute. Positionen in Theorie und Praxis*. Bielefeld: transcript-Verlag, 42. Retrieved 1 November 2015 from http://www.degruyter.com/view/product/430299.
6. '1974', *Chronik der Neuen Frauenbewegung*. Retrieved 25 October 2015 from http://www.frauenmediaturm.de/themen-portraets/chronik-der-neuen-frauenbewegung/1974/.
7. '1st World Conference on Women, Mexico 1975'. Retrieved 27 October 2015 from http://www.choike.org/nuevo_eng/informes/1453.html.
8. Russell and van de Ven, *Crimes Against Women*, 151.
9. Ibid., 151–52.
10. Ibid., 154.
11. See e.g. R. Morgan (1985), *Sisterhood Is Global: The International Women's Movement Anthology*, Harmondsworth: Penguin.
12. See e.g. N.A. Hewitt (1985), 'Beyond the Search for Sisterhood: American Women's History in the 1980s', *Social History* 10, 299–321; hooks, *Feminist Theory*; C.T. Mohanty (2003), *Feminism without Borders: Decolonizing Theory, Practicing Solidarity*, Durham, NC, and London: Duke University Press; A. Henry (2004), *Not My Mother's Sister: Generational Conflict and Third-Wave Feminism*, Bloomington: Indiana University Press.
13. Hooks, *Feminist Theory*, 43.
14. Mohanty, *Feminism without Borders*, 116.
15. Hooks, *Feminist Theory*, 63.
16. Ibid., 47.
17. Mohanty, *Feminism without Borders*, 7.
18. O. Janz and D. Schönpflug (eds) (2014), *Gender History in a Transnational Perspective: Networks, Biographies, Gender Orders*, New York: Berghahn Books, 2.
19. N. Glick Schiller and P. Levitt (2006), 'Haven't We Heard This Somewhere Before? A Substantive View of Transnational Migration Studies by Way of a Reply to Waldinger and Fitzgerald', the Center for Migration and Development – Working Paper Series 2008. Retrieved 25 October 2015 from http://www.princeton.edu/cmd/working-papers/papers/wp0601.pdf.
20. The notion of intersectionality was coined by law professor Kimberlé Crenshaw in the early 1990s. Although there was nothing new about the insight that many women face multiple forms oppression, the importance of Crenshaw's work cannot be overestimated, because she provided us with an important tool for the analysis of patterns of oppression, which vary between and within societies depending on a range of factors including gender, age, class, religion and ethnicity.
21. S. Vertovec (2009), *Transnationalism*, London and New York: Routledge, 1.
22. Marx-Ferree, *Varieties of Feminism*, 29.
23. M. Schmid (1977), 'Zwischen Angst und Unsicherheit: ausländische Frauen', *Courage: Berliner Frauenzeitung*, no. 11, 25–27.
24. S. Plogstedt (1978), '2000 mussten nach Korea zurück', *Courage: Berliner Frauenzeitung*, no. 4, 27–28.
25. 'nicht behandelt als Menschen zweiter, sondern dritter Klasse – als 'Sklavinnen der Sklaven'; FFBIZ, F Rep. 10 BRD 19.5.1 a (1099), 'Aufruf Erster Gemeinsamer Frauenkongress'.
26. Ibid.
27. 'Aufruf des ersten bundesweiten Kongresses ausländischer und deutscher Frauen und Mädchen!' in Arbeitsgruppe Frauenkongreß (ed.), *Sind wir uns so fremd? Dokumentation des 1. Gemeinsamen Kongresses ausländischer und deutscher Frauen 23. – 25. März 1984*, Frankfurt am Main, 202–208.

28. 'praktische Solidarität und neue Initiativen, die dem wirklichen Austausch zwischen ausländischen und deutschen Frauen dienen, ein echtes Kennenlernen ermöglichen und die gleichberechtigte und gemeinsame Zusammenarbeit von der Ausnahme zur Regel machen'; D. Schultz (1984), 'Ausländische und deutsche . . .', *Courage: Berliner Frauenzeitung* 9, no. 15, 7.
29. 'Wir haben uns bisher in weit geringerem Maße mit Rassismus und Antisemitismus auseinandergesetzt als unsere amerikanischen Schwestern'; D. Schultz (1981), 'Dem Rassismus in sich begegnen', *Courage: Berliner Frauenzeitung*, no. 10, 17–21, 21.
30. K. Oguntoye (1989), 'Die Schwarze deutsche Bewegung und die Frauenbewegung in Deutschland', *Afrekete. Zeitung für afro-deutsche und schwarze Frauen*, no. 4, 3–5.
31. K. Kinder (2006), '20 Jahre Schwarze (Frauen-) Bewegung in Deutschland'. Retrieved 4 November 2015 from https://heimatkunde.boell.de/2006/05/01/20-jahre-schwarze-frauen-bewegung-deutschland.
32. M. Ayim (1995), 'grenzenlos und unverschämt. Ein gedicht gegen die deutsche sch-einheit', in M. Ayim, *Blues in schwarz-weiß*. Berlin: Orlanda Frauenverlag.
33. P. Piesche, 'Schwarz und deutsch? Eine ostdeutsche Jugend vor 1989 – Retrospektive auf "ein nichtexistentes" Thema in der DDR'. Retrieved 22 December 2015 from https://heimatkunde.boell.de/2006/05/01/schwarz-und-deutsch-eine-ostdeutsche-jugend-vor-1989-retrospektive-auf-ein.
34. K.J. Bade and J. Oltmer (2005), 'Migration, Ausländerbeschäftigung und Asylpolitik in der DDR'. Retrieved 4 November 2015 from http://www.bpb.de/gesellschaft/migration/dossier-migration/56368/migrationspolitik-in-der-ddr?p=all.
35. U. Falck (1998), *VEB Bordell*, Berlin: Ch. Links, 16.
36. 'Wie Vieh', *Der Spiegel*, no. 38, 19 September 1983, 77–79, 79.
37. E. Kästli, M. Brenner and A. Ernst (1982), 'Asiatinnen: Import -Export', *Emma*, no. 6, 28–31, 29.
38. 'Wie Vieh', 79.
39. 'Wir sind in Beweisnot'; ibid.
40. Kästli, Brenner and Ernst, 'Asiatinnen: Import -Export', 28.
41. 'Böse Schlieren', *Der Spiegel*, no. 2, 11 January 1988, 116–17, 116.
42. W. Scharlau, 'Die Freier sind das Problem, nicht die Mädchen', *Die Zeit*, 11 May 1984.
43. 'Wie Vieh', 79.
44. B. Kirchhoff (1982), 'Nach Abzug der Scham', *Kursbuch*, no. 68, 119–25, 120.
45. 'es gehöhrt seit einigen Jahren wieder zum guten progressive Ton, laut darüber zu onanieren, wie es wäre sie zu vergewaltigen'; I. Strobl (1982), 'Laß jucken, Genosse', *Emma Sonderband*, no. 3, 53–55, 54.
46. 'In eigener Sache', *Courage: Berliner Frauenzeitung*, no. 9, September 1983, 2.
47. 'Die Möglichkeit, hier philippinische Frauen wie Handelsware anzupreisen und zu verkaufen ist verschärfter Ausdruck der gesellschaftlichen Machtverhältnisse, der Gewalt- und Ausbeutungsverhältnisse zwischen Männern und Frauen'; ID Verlag, *Die Früchte des Zorns*, 467.
48. 'weil wir uns als Frauen durch diese Praxis angegriffen fühlen'; ibid.
49. Die Rote Zora, 'Mili's Tanz auf dem Eis'.
50. 'Damit übergingen wir die betroffenen Frauen. Viele von ihnen treffen – wenn auch aufgrund einer Zwangssituation – die Entscheidung, die Arbeit in der Sex-industrie oder als Ehefrau hier den Existenzkämpfen oder der Abschufterei in den Weltmarktfabriken in ihren Ländern 'vorzuziehen' (z.B. können sie dadurch auch dringend benötigtes Geld nachhause schicken)'; ibid.
51. 'Wie Vieh'.
52. For a detailed discussion of this attack and other militant feminist protest against sex shops, see chapter 4.
53. ID Verlag, *Die Früchte des Zorns*, 468.
54. 'Wie Vieh'.

55. ID Verlag, *Die Früchte des Zorns*, 416.
56. 'Frauenhändler – süß, anschmiegsam – jederzeit zu gebrauchen, mit Krötenpimmel'.
57. 'Wir werden Widerstand leisten gegen alle Frauenhändler, Vergewaltiger, Scheißmacker und gegen das imperialistische, frauenfeindliche System, solange wir denken und fühlen können!!'; Stasi Archiv Berlin, MfS HA XXII 5216/8, 288–89.
58. 'rasende Zora'.
59. C. Stolle, 'Freiwild in der Freihandelszone', *die tageszeitung*, 22 December 1986.
60. U. Kosczy, C. Stolle and J.S. Pak (1988), 'Die Bescheidenheit ist vorbei. Koreanische Frauen wehren sich gegen Ausbeutung und ungerechte Weltwirtschaftsstrukturen. Das Beispiel Flair Fashion/Adler', Frankfurt: Entwicklungspolitischer Informationsdienst des Evangelischen Pressedienstes, 35.
61. Adler Modemärkte AG (2012), 'Bericht über das erste Halbjahr 2012'. Retrieved 30 January 2013 from http://www.adlermode-unternehmen.com/fileadmin/2012/IR/q2-2012/bericht/de/Adler_Bericht_2_Quartal_2012_deutsch.pdf.
62. Stolle, 'Freiwild'.
63. Adler in Kosczy et al., 'Die Bescheidenheit ist vorbei', 74.
64. Kosczy et al., 'Die Bescheidenheit ist vorbei', 61.
65. Ibid.
66. Ibid.
67. S. Sung (2003), 'Women Reconciling Paid and Unpaid Work in a Confucian Welfare State: The Case of South Korea', *Social Policy & Administration* 37, 342–60, 345.
68. S. Seguino (1997), 'Gender Wage Inequality and Export-led Growth in South Korea', *Journal of Development Studies* 34, 102–32, 106.
69. B. Schwarz (1987), 'Adler in Südkorea. Ausbeutung und sexuelle Nötigung, "Die Zwänge der Marktwirtschaft"', *klenkes*, 16–17, 16.
70. Kosczy et al., 'Die Bescheidenheit ist vorbei', 6.
71. Ibid., 2.
72. Ibid., 24.
73. 'Ohne die schwarzhaarigen, mandeläugigen Koreanerinnen wäre der steile Auftieg des ADLER-Unternehmens nicht möglich gewesen'.
74. 'verwöhnen ihre Männer und widmen sich ganz ihrer Familie und ihrem Haushalt'; Kosczy et al., 'Die Bescheidenheit ist vorbei', 72.
75. 'Wenn ihnen eine Arbeiterin besonders gefällt, muß sie die Wünsche des deutschen Leiters erfüllen, oder mit einer Versetzung auf einen schlechteren Arbeitsplatz oder gar Entlassung rechnen'; ibid., 61.
76. Ibid.
77. Ibid.
78. Alarmed by a report about 'honour killings' in the Middle East, a group of women in Hamburg founded Terre des Femmes in 1981 to support 'girls and women through raising public awareness, international networking, campaigning, individual personal assistance and the promotion of self-help projects abroad'; Terre des Femmes, 'English Site'. Retrieved 30 August 2015 from http://www.terre-des-femmes.de/. To this day, the German-based NGO seeks to 'ensure that women and girls around the world are able to lead self-determined lives as well as enjoying equal and inalienable rights'; ibid. Local groups all over Germany support TdF on a voluntary basis and contribute to the periodical *Frauensolidarität* (Women's Solidarity).
79. E. Dischereit (1988), 'Absolution vom Mainzer Bischof', *vorwärts*, 2 January 1988.
80. Ibid.
81. D. Messner, 'Deutscher Multi fährt einen brutalen Kurs', *die tageszeitung*, 11 April 1987.
82. Ibid.
83. C. Wichterich, 'Südkoreanerinnen protestieren gegen deutsche Ausbeutung', *Frankfurter Rundschau*, 20 May 1987.
84. Kosczy et al., 'Die Bescheidenheit ist vorbei', 66.

85. Examples include an article in the *Frankfurter Rundschau* on 25 May, and a report in the news magazine WISO on 20 July 1987.
86. 'Unter Adlern', *Schwäbisches Tageblatt*, 18 April 1987.
87. Kosczy et al., 'Die Bescheidenheit ist vorbei', 52.
88. 'Blockade für Südkoreanerinnen', *die tageszeitung Bremen*, 22 July 1987.
89. 'In Solidarität mit den kämpfenden Frauen bei ADLER in Südkorea haben wir in der Nacht zum 21.6.87 in der Hauptverwaltung des ADLER-Konzerns in Haibach bei Aschaffenburg eine Bombe gelegt mit der Absicht einen Teil ihres Verwaltungsapparates zu zerstören'; IISH, 'Knastarchiv', Box 23, folder 104, envelope 444, 3.
90. Kosczy et al., 'Die Bescheidenheit ist vorbei', 46.
91. 'Die Lohnsklaverei basiert auf sexistischer und rassistischer Ausbeutung'; IISH, 'Knastarchiv', Box 23, folder 104, envelope 444, 3.
92. 'Obwohl sich auch in den Metropolen die Lebensbedingungen verschärfen, dürfen wir einen entscheidenden Punkt auf keinen Fall außer Acht lassen: Unsere Privilegien, wovon der Konsum eines ist, beruhen auf der Ausbeutung, Verwertung und Vernichtung der Menschen der 3 Kontinente'; ibid., 2.
93. Ibid.
94. 'Flambieren, demolieren', *Der Spiegel*, 24 August 1987.
95. Ibid.
96. 'Mollies aus der Ära der Kaufhausbrandstifter anno 1968'; ibid.
97. Ibid.
98. 'Die "Rote Zora" bezichtigt sich der Anschläge auf Adler', *Frankfurter Allgemeine Zeitung*, 18 August 1987.
99. 'Terror soll nicht mehr männliches Vorrecht sein', *Frankfurter Allgemeine Zeitung*, 18 August 1987.
100. Translated into English, the German word 'Adler' means eagle.
101. 'Flammende Grüße bei Adler', *die tageszeitung*, 18 August 1987.
102. It should be added that this attention did not come close to the public interest with which attacks by the Red Army Faction and the Movement of June 2nd were met.
103. See e.g. 'Rote Zora: Anschläge bei Adler verübt', *Süddeutsche Zeitung*, 18 August 1987; 'Terror soll nicht mehr männliches Vorrecht sein'; '"Rote Zora" bekennt sich zu Brandanschlägen', *Rheinische Post*, 18 August 1987.
104. 'Flambieren, demolieren'.
105. 'Ermittlungen gegen die Rote Zora', *Frankfurter Rundschau*, 24 October 1986; 'Terror soll nicht mehr männliches Vorrecht sein'.
106. 'mit der Großaktion bei Adler hätten die wütenden Damen der RZ es auch den ignoranten Männern in den eigenen Zirkeln einmal zeigen wollen'; ibid.
107. 'Die Frauen der "Roten Zora" fühlen sich von den Männern der 'Revolutionären Zellen' unterdrückt. Zündelten sie deshalb bei Adler?'; ibid.
108. In the German original, the author repeatedly uses minimizing verbs like '*zündeln*' and '*kokeln*' to describe the actions of the Red Zora.
109. 'Wir lehnen es ... ab, dieses männliche Buch zu verbreiten ... , weil das Buch eine einseitige, damit falsche, frauenfeindliche Geschichtsschreibung über die Revolutionären Zellen und die Rote Zora auf Jahre hinaus festschreibt und Guerilla zur Männersache erklärt'; 'Geschlechterkampf im Untergrund', *die tageszeitung*, 21 July 1987.
110. 'Derartige Aktionen diskreditieren die gewaltfreie Arbeit einer Frauenrechtorganization, die seit einem Jahr in engem Kontakt mit den Arbeiterinnen im Adler-Produktionswerk Flair-Fashion in Südkorea steht'; Kosczy et al., 'Die Bescheidenheit ist vorbei', 91.
111. 'Im Interesse einer wirksamen und möglichst weitreichenden Aufklärung ... distanzieren wir uns eindeutig von jeglicher gewalttätiger Form der Durchsetzung gewerkschaftlicher Zielsetzungen'; ibid., 95.
112. 'Rote Zora: Anschläge bei Adler'.

113. 'Den Boden fruchtbar gemacht für Gewaltakte'; Kosczy et al., 'Die Bescheidenheit ist vorbei', 48.
114. Ibid.
115. 'Widersprüchliche Informationen', *Frankfurter Rundschau*, 10 September 1987.
116. 'Neuer Anschlag auf eine Filiale von Adler in Berlin', *Neue Züricher Zeitung*, 14 September 1987.
117. Die Amazonen (1988), 'Gewisses Risiko', *konkret*, 2.
118. 'Adler- Anschlag per Feuerzeug', *die tageszeitung*, 24 September 1987.
119. The management declared: 'Adler beugt sich der Gewalt' ('Neuer Anschlag').
120. Ibid.
121. 'Sie sind offenbar nicht bereit, Grundrechte der Arbeiter/innen als solche anzuerkennen, sondern beugen sich letztlich nur der Gewalt. Will Adler damit einen Präzedenzfall schaffen . . . ?'; Kosczy et al., 'Die Bescheidenheit ist vorbei', 97.
122. 'Machen zehn Feuer schon eine internationale Solidarität von Frauen?'; C. Wichterich, 'Einen Bärendienst erwiesen', *die tageszeitung*, 21 September 1987.
123. 'voluntaristische Aktionen, die andere Widerstandsaktionen gefährden'; C. Wichterich, 'Adler', *die tageszeitung*, 15 October 1987.
124. 'Das Feuerwerk hat dem Versuch, in einer einzelnen Widerstandsaktion ein solidarisches Dreieck zwischen Arbeiterinnen in der Dritten Welt, Konsumentinnen hier und Arbeiterinnen hier aufzubauen, einen Bärendienst erwiesen. Anlaß genug, um sich mit der feurigen Taktik in der Frauenbewegung auseinanderzusetzen'; Wichterich, 'Einen Bärendienst erwiesen'.
125. 'Radikaler Widerstand auf allen Ebenen auch international ist notwendig, wenn wir unsere Ideen von einer herrschaftsfreien, nichtsexistischen, nichtrassistischen Gesellschaft ernsthaft durchsetzen wollen'; 'Bärendienst für wen?' *die tageszeitung*, 8 October 1987.
126. 'Es ist eure Sache, welche Widerstandsformen ihr als Gruppe wählt und wie ihr eure Vorstellungen von Veränderung dieser Gesellschaft umsetzen wollt'; ibid.
127. 'und wenn ihr Widerstandsformen denunziert, mit dem gleichen Vokabular wie der Staatsschutz'; ibid.
128. 'Zora', *die tageszeitung*, 30 September 1987.
129. N. Boschmann, 'Aufbruchstimmung Bei "Flair Fashion"', *die tageszeitung*, 11 January 1988.
130. 'Aus heutiger Sicht war das sicher vorschnell und in dieser Form auch nicht nötig, aber damals dachten wir, die Medien fallen über uns her und stempeln uns auch als Terroristen ab'; ibid.
131. Ibid.
132. Ibid.
133. Christa Wichterich in an email to the author, 6 September 2012.

Conclusion

The tomato throwing at the twenty-third SDS conference in September 1968 marked the beginning of a wave of spectacular protests by women on the radical Left in the FRG. No longer willing to accept that state authorities, expert panels and male comrades simply ignored their views and experiences, women disrupted professional conferences, academic lectures, court proceedings, beauty contests, socialist gatherings and other events to make their voices heard. Some of the actors involved adopted methods that can only be described as confrontational: they bombarded men with flour bags and pigs' tails, exposed their breasts in court rooms and lecture theatres, damaged property with feminist graffiti and stickers, planted stink bombs in porn shops and cinemas and engaged in other provocative forms of protest.

While Sigrid Rüger's tomato throwing has become a symbol of the provocative and anti-authoritarian spirit of the New Women's Movement in the FRG, other spectacular protest actions with a feminist agenda have received little or no attention. Focusing on four major campaigns in the New Women's Movement, this book offers the first detailed analysis of militant feminist protest in the Federal Republic of Germany. Some of this protest sparked controversial debates within and beyond feminist circles, e.g. when women's groups took justice into their own hands and tried to confront and publicly humiliate alleged rapists and their lawyers, or carried out arson attacks and bombings to advance the cause of women. Up to now, studies of the New Women's Movement have focused almost exclusively on protest that was commonly understood as peaceful.

Notes for this section begin on page 142.

Patricia Melzer critically observed that 'feminist disagreements on political violence have been flattened out in favor of a definition of feminist politics as nonviolent'.[1] Indeed, a great part of the existing literature on the New Women's Movement in the FRG suggests that it is possible and necessary to draw a clear-cut line between peaceful feminist protest on the one side and 'bad' patriarchal violence on the other side. There can be no doubt that many groups and individuals in the New Women's Movement considered feminism and violence irreconcilable, and there is good reason to assume that the escalating conflict between armed leftist groups and the West German state in the 1970s has reinforced pacifist and anti-militarist tendencies in the German women's movement. This, however, does not change the fact that some feminists have supported armed leftist groups in West Germany well beyond the German Autumn and/or engaged in highly confrontational protest to advance the cause of women. At least some of the actors involved have deliberately drawn on tactics that were perceived to be threatening or violent. Their activities deserve attention, not least because of the critical debates they sparked about the scope and limits of feminist protest. I agree with Melzer that we need new conceptual tools to document, analyse and contextualize these debates.

Melzer proposes 'feminist practices' as a new analytical category for research on women's political protest and violence in the FRG. According to her, 'all actions whose gender constellations trouble, challenge and potentially redirect existing oppressive gender regimes' constitute potential feminist practices.[2] This definition is useful, because it challenges the assumption that feminist protest is necessarily peaceful, and that it 'automatically signal[s] "good" politics exempt from moral scrutiny'.[3] Melzer challenges the assumption that the use of violent tactics is destructive and ineffective, whereas nonviolent protest is always beneficial and harmless. She argues that acts of political violence carried out by women in the RAF can and should be analysed as potential feminist practices, because they had a destabilizing effect on the prevailing gender norms.[4] Melzer's study offers critical insights into the feminist potential of female participation in leftist political violence. This study complements her findings with an analysis of provocative protest and political violence with an explicitly feminist agenda.

With the notion of feminist militancy, I have proposed a conceptual tool for the study of the role of confrontational tactics and political violence within the context of feminist campaigns. In this context, I have defined feminist militancy as historically and politically specific ideas and practices that aim to overcome sexist oppression and are based on the assumption that this objective can only be reached with a confrontational attitude. This definition has two key advantages. On the one hand, it expands and enriches our understanding of feminist activism, because it acknowledges that feminist protest can take a range of forms, including protest tactics that are commonly understood as violent. Drawing on this definition of feminist militancy, this book shows that there was a complex interplay of peaceful and violent tactics in feminist campaigns, and that there was considerable disagreement over the question of which tactics were appropriate and necessary in the feminist struggle against sexist oppression. The campaigns analysed here illustrate that the notion and limits of legitimate protest were hotly contested and developed along different lines in different political struggles.

A second advantage of the definition above is that it enables us to distinguish feminist militancy from other forms of political militancy. While Melzer rightly emphasizes that the active involvement of women in RAF attacks raises interesting questions about the subversive potential of gender transgressions, it is important to note that some but not all acts of women's political violence in West Germany were expressions of feminist militancy. In chapter 2, I have identified three different positions on feminism among women in the militant leftist network Revolutionary Cells, which existed in similar forms in other armed groups. Female militants considered gender to be irrelevant and understood themselves not primarily as women but as revolutionaries. Although the ideas and actions of female militants in the RC and other armed groups have influenced militant feminist protest in the FRG, they were not part of the feminist struggle to end sexist oppression. Feminist militants engaged with ideas and campaigns in the New Women's Movement, and carried out attacks with an explicitly feminist agenda. Their thoughts and actions had a decisive influence on feminist militancy in West Germany, even if they were sometimes at odds with the ethics and principles of activists in the New Women's Movement. Militant feminists in the RC held radical feminist views, and considered a confrontational approach essential for the success of the struggle against sexist oppression. They wanted to put feminism into practice at all levels of the armed struggle, including personal relationships, ideology, structure, tactics and targets.

Two attacks discussed in this book illustrate why it is useful and valuable to distinguish feminist militancy from other forms of militancy. In May 1970, a group of several women and one man liberated Andreas Baader by force of arms from prison in West Berlin – an event that former group members and researchers refer to as 'the birth of the RAF'. Shortly after the attack, the actors involved released a statement in which they declared that they had liberated Baader because they considered him an 'essential cadre', and because they wanted to show that their urban guerrilla group should be taken seriously.[5] According to RAF founding member Monika Berberich, the participants in Baader's rescue were chosen based on their availability on the day of the attack. When it turned out that all potential candidates were women, some in the group raised concerns that Baader's armed guards would not take a group of women seriously.[6] According to Astrid Proll – who drove the getaway car – the group decided shortly before the attack to hire Hans-Jürgen Bäcker, a 'so-called expert' with a criminal record, to minimize the risk of a violent confrontation with the guards.[7] Ironically, it was Bäcker who triggered the violent confrontation between the guards and the intruders during the raid by shooting at an employee of the Institute. Although female participation in Baader's rescue and other RAF attacks was presented as 'an excess of women's liberation', it should not be mistaken for an expression of feminist militancy. The RAF did not pursue a feminist agenda, and most women in the group were female militants who showed little interest in themes and debates in the New Women's Movement.

In contrast to the RAF, the Red Zora and a few other radical women's groups in the FRG adopted central topics and aims of the New Women's Movement and carried out attacks with a distinctively feminist agenda. One of the most spectacular manifestations of feminist militancy in West Germany was the series of arson attacks against the German clothing chain Adler in 1987 discussed in chapter 5. Since these attacks have sparked critical debates about the ethics and objectives of feminist protest, I want to discuss them here in some more detail. To support a protest by women workers in a South Korean factory that produced clothes for Adler, the RZ planted incendiary devices in nine Adler stores in the FRG. The fires and the sprinkler systems that they activated caused substantial property damage. In response to these and further attacks, the Adler management agreed to meet the demands of the employees in the South Korean factory. While some feminists congratulated the RZ for its 'brilliant actions', critics countered that the attacks were 'voluntaristic' and 'counterproductive'.

The feminist controversy over the attacks against Adler cannot be explained by disagreements about violent tactics alone. A key reason why many feminists distanced themselves from the arson attacks was that they disagreed with the way the RZ sought to practice feminist solidarity. A number of activists criticized that the RZ had not tried to discuss their plans with the workers in South Korea and with other groups in the solidarity campaign. Christa Wichterich, for example, took issue with the approach of the Red Zora because she held the view that constant dialogue provides the only way to build transnational feminist networks and solidarity campaigns.

Drawing on Jodi Dean's book *Solidarity of Strangers: Feminism after Identity Politics*, the dialogic approach to solidarity that Wichterich and other feminist critics of the RZ endorsed can be understood as a form of 'reflective solidarity'. According to Dean, 'reflective solidarity refers to a mutual expectation of a responsible orientation to relationship'.[8] Following Jürgen Habermas, Dean argues that conventional forms of solidarity are often based on an externally established 'we' – a collective identity that distinguishes the actors involved from other groups (e.g. workers, Christians or members of a political party). Reflective solidarity does not assume a collective identity. Rather it seeks to create an 'internally designated "we"' based on 'ties created by dissent', which requires a constant communicative effort by all actors involved.[9] Elsewhere, Dean explains this process in more detail:

> Through language we establish a relationship with each other, creating a common space. With our queries we challenge each other, letting our space, for a time, be one of negotiation. This internally designated, communicative 'we' stresses the possibility of feminist coalitional practices in which the strength of the bond connecting us stems from our mutual recognition of each other instead of from our exclusion of someone else.[10]

Drawing on Dean, Chandra Talpade Mohanty argues that feminist solidarity has to be the product of a constant dialogue and a political struggle that accounts for similarities and differences among women. Reflective solidarity, in other words, begins with communication and involves constant negotiations. Expressions of solidarity by individual actors are based on and constrained by the consensus reached in a communicative process involving all parties. Simply put, reflective solidarity implies that individual actions have to follow from collective dialogue.

Reflective solidarity does not imply a fixed position on violence, but it requires an amount of communication and negotiation that poses significant challenges for the planning of clandestine and illegal activities. It should therefore come as no surprise that the Red Zora and other militant feminist groups in the FRG endorsed a different approach to solidarity. In the eyes of the Red Zora a call for sisterly help and the reality of living and working conditions in South Korea and in Germany were reasons enough to act. The group expressed the position that every woman should freely decide how to express her solidarity whether in nonviolent or in militant ways, so long as her actions supported the Korean women in their struggle and did not endanger the lives of Adler workers or customers. I want to refer to this approach to solidarity as 'proactive'.

In general terms, a proactive approach can be defined as 'creating or controlling a situation rather than just responding to it after it has happened'.[11] While reflective solidarity is based on the assumption that expressions of solidarity follow from dialogue, proactive solidarity implies that expressions of solidarity can create and amplify dialogue. According to one former member, the Red Zora understood the attacks against Adler as a form of 'armed propaganda' (*bewaffnete Propaganda*) for the cause of the Korean women, acts with which the RZ wanted to spark a discussion in Germany and to intensify the dialogue between women in the FRG and in South Korea.[12] In parts of the radical Left, this approach to solidarity met (and meets) with great enthusiasm. Most groups and individuals in the New Women's Movement, however, distanced themselves from this approach. They gave priority to a notion of reflective solidarity and drew primarily or exclusively on tactics that were commonly understood as nonviolent.

Since the early 1990s, confrontational and violent protest by feminist groups has become a rare phenomenon in Germany. After a period of inactivity, the Red Zora carried out its last attack on 24 July 1995: a failed bombing at a shipyard in Hamburg, where a German company produced boats for the Turkish military. In the claim for responsibility, the RZ called for 'practical solidarity with the resistance of women in Kurdistan and of Kurdish women here'.[13] For several months, the attack received virtually no attention in feminist circles. One year after the bombing, a group of women responded to it with an article in the leftist magazine *radikal*. While expressing sympathy for the aims and principles of the Red Zora, the authors criticized the group for romanticizing life in Kurdish villages and suggested that it had to do more to communicate its politics.[14] Since then, there have been no major attacks by militant feminist groups in the Federal Republic of Germany.

A recent protest action in Russia demonstrates that feminist militancy manifests itself today in ways that are similar to and different from those in West Germany during the 1970s and 1980s. In February 2012, the feminist punk rock group Pussy Riot staged an unauthorized performance in the Cathedral of Christ the Saviour in Moscow, which resulted in the arrest and prosecution of three group members. A few days before their arrest, the group gave an interview in which they explained that they had founded Pussy Riot in 2011 when Russian President Vladimir Putin announced that he would stand for re-election. One group member stated: 'At that point we realized that this country needs a militant, punk-feminist, street band that will rip through Moscow's streets and squares, mobilize public energy against the evil crooks of the Putinist junta and enrich the Russian cultural and political opposition with themes that are important to us: gender and LGBT rights, problems of masculine conformity, absence of a daring political message on the musical and art scenes, and the domination of males in all areas of public discourse.'[15] In this and other statements, Pussy Riot explicitly positioned themselves as feminist and as part of the political opposition in Russia. Their performances in colourful dresses and balaclavas was inspired by feminist and queer theory, performance art, the feminist punk 'Riot grrrl' movement and a range of other transnational intellectual and political movements. Although there were unauthorized feminist protests in West German churches in the early 1970s, these did not spark the same attention and controversy as Pussy Riot's 'punk prayer' in the Cathedral of Christ the Saviour in Moscow.

The performance met with shock and anger in Russian-Orthodox communities and resulted in court proceedings against some of the actors involved. Similar to some of the protest actions discussed in this study, the punk prayer met with mixed responses from feminist activists. Some feminists in Russia criticized Pussy Riot, as Valerie Sperling shows, for writing lyrics that promoted violence, rather than 'a specifically nonviolent feminist agenda'.[16] Yet there was also support and admiration for the group.[17] The trial against Yekaterina Samutsevich, Nadezhda Tolokonnikova and Maria Alyokhina in 2012 made headlines across the world. When the three women were convicted under article 213 of the Criminal Code of the Russian Federation for hooliganism and were sentenced to two years in a penal colony, many observers criticized the judgment as disproportionate. Artists, feminists, political activists and human rights groups from Russia and many other countries campaigned for the release of Pussy Riot, but they remained in prison for several months. The harsh sentence against Samutsevich, Tolokonnikova and Alyokhina did not deter the band and its supporters from staging further guerrilla performances to pursue their political goals. Although the continuum of feminist militancy has evolved as a result of discussions within feminist groups, and in response to broader social and political developments, expressions of feminist militancy continue to provoke authorities and to spark critical debates about the objectives and ethics of political protest.

Notes

1. Melzer, *Death in the Shape of a Young Girl*, 19.
2. Ibid., 13.
3. Ibid., 243.
4. Ibid., 11–12.
5. U. Meinhof (1970), '"Natürlich Kann Geschossen Werden"', *Der Spiegel*, 15 June 1970, 74–75, 74.
6. Interview with Monika Berberich on 2 May 2011.
7. Proll, *Hans und Grete*, 11.
8. J. Dean (1996), *Solidarity of Strangers: Feminism after Identity Politics*, Berkeley: University of California Press, 29.
9. Ibid.
10. J. Dean (1998), 'Feminist Solidarity, Reflective Solidarity', *Women and Politics* 18, 1–26, 15.
11. 'Proactive'. Retrieved 10 September 2015 from http://oxforddictionaries.com/definition/english/proactive?q=proactivity#proactive__6.
12. Focus group with three former members of the Red Zora on 17 August 2012.
13. 'praktische Solidarität mit dem Widerstand der Frauen in Kurdistan und der kurdischen Migrantinnen hier', Die Rote Zora. 1995. 'Ihr habt die Macht, uns gehört die Nacht', *radikal*, no. 153. Retrieved 30 June 2016 from http://www.freilassung.de/div/texte/rz/radi153_1195.htm.
14. 'Frauen in Kurdistan', *radikal*, no. 154, June 1996. Retrieved 1 July 2016 from http://www.freilassung.de/div/texte/rz/radi154b.htm.
15. H. Langston (2012), 'Meeting Pussy Riot'. Retrieved 13 December 2015 from http://www.vice.com/read/A-Russian-Pussy-Riot.
16. V. Sperling (2014), 'Russian feminist perspectives on Pussy Riot', *Nationalities Papers*, 42:4, 591–603, 592.
17. Ibid.

Bibliography

Manuscript Sources

Federal Archives, Koblenz (BAK)

BAK, B 131/173 M-157.018, arrest warrant, 14 May 1970.
BAK, 'Linksradikale Bestrebungen in den Jahren 1969 und 1970 (Fassung des DMI)', 1.
BAK B362/6827, 'Vermerk', 2 February 1978.
BAK, B 362/7379.
BAK, B 362/7379, letter from the state criminal police Baden-Wuerttemberg from 29 April 1975.
BAK, B 362/7383, 'telefax des bka, abt. sg., bonn bad godesberg', 18 November 1973.
BAK, B 106/106662, 'Auslobung', 5 March 1975.
BAK, B362/6827, 'Fernschreiben des Polizeipräsidiums Koblenz an das BKA', 15 February 1978.

Frauenmediaturm, Cologne (FMT)

FMT, PD-FB 01, 1968.
FMT, FB.05.175, 'Protestaktion gegen die Wahl der "Miß-Teenager-Beine" in Frankfurt'.
FMT, PD-FB 01, 1972, 'Protokoll zum Plenum des Bundesfrauenkongresses am 12. März 1972 in Frankfurt/M'.
FMT, Z-Ü101.
FMT, PD-SE.11.15, 'Erklärung der REVOLUTIONÄREN ZELLE zu ihrem Anschlag auf das Bundesverfassungsgericht', in *Frauenzeitung*, no. 5.
FMT, PD-SE.11.15, *WIR WOLLEN ALLES*, no. 26, March 1975.
Die Rote Zora. 1977. 'Frauen erhebt euch und die Welt erlebt euch!', FMT, FB.07.102.
FMT, PD-FB 01, 1974. 'Daß Du untergehst, wenn Du Dich nicht wehrst, wirst Du doch einsehen!'
FMT PD-G8, 'Wir kriegen Euch', *Fruezitig*, no. 33, 1990.
FMT Z149: 1977 – 16. 'Zur Diskussion gestellt: Walpurgisnacht', *protokolle: informationsdienst für frauen*, no. 16, 1977, 30–31.
FMT Z129: 1977 – 2.'Walpurgisnacht', II. *Heidelberger Frauenzeitung*, June 1977.

FMT Z125: 1978 – 25. 'Walpurgisnacht in Frankfurt und ihre Konsequenzen', in *Frauenzeitung Frauenzentrum Hamburg*, no. 25, 1978, 11.
FMT PD-G8. 'Zoff in Berlin', *Emma*, July 1986.
FMT PD-G8. Frauenzentrum Hannover: 'Solange es Männergewalt an Frauen gibt, wird es unseren Widerstand geben'.
FMT PD-G8, 'Rabiate Frauenschar fiel über Mann her', *Bremer Fraueninfo*, no. 2, 3 December 1982.
FMT PD-G8, 'Beim STERN zu Besuch – Bericht über eine kleine Aktion', Else Wohin, No. 6, 1990.

Frauenforschungs-, -bildungs- und -informationszentrum, Berlin (FFBIZ)

FFBIZ, A Rep 400, Berlin 20 Aktionsrat, 'Resolution für die 23. O. DK des SDS. Vorgelegt vom Aktionsrat zur Befreiung der Frauen Berlin'.
FFBIZ, A Rep 400, Berlin 20 Aktionsrat, Handapparat Tröger, Rundbrief vom 22. Juni 1968.
FFBIZ, A Rep 400, Berlin 20 Aktionsrat, 'Kurze Selbstdarstellung über die Entwicklung des Aktionsrats der Frauen'.
FFBIZ, A Rep. 400, Berlin, 20 FZ public letter from 28 March 1973 (1–3).
FFBIZ, F Rep. 10 BRD 19.5.1 a (1099), 'Aufruf Erster Gemeinsamer Frauenkongress'.

Material from Other Archives

H.D. Nagel. 1970. 'Schwurgerichtsanklage', RAF collection at the IISH. Retrieved 1 July 2015 from labourhistory.net.
IISH, 'Knastarchiv', Box 23, folder 104, envelope 444, 3.
H.J. Schneider. 1970. 'So fing es an . . .', unpublished report from the archive at the Institute for Social Issues, Berlin.
Hamburg Institute for Social Research, Me, U/008,003.
Stasi Archiv Berlin, MfS HA XXII 5216/8, 288–89.

Published Sources

'§218: "Mit sozialer Notlage ist nichts drin"', *Der Spiegel*, no. 49, 29 November 1976, 68–75.
'1st World Conference on Women, Mexico 1975'. Retrieved 27 October 2015 from http://www.choike.org/nuevo_eng/informes/1453.html.
'1974', *Chronik der Neuen Frauenbewegung*. Retrieved 25 October 2015 from http://www.frauenmediaturm.de/themen-portraets/chronik-der-neuen-frauenbewegung/1974/.
'1977', *Chronik der Neuen Frauenbewegung*. Retrieved 20 December from http://www.frauenmediaturm.de/themen-portraets/chronik-der-neuen-frauenbewegung/1977/.
'Abtreibung: Massenmord oder Privatsache?' *Der Spiegel*, 21 May 1973, 38–58.
'Adler- Anschlag per Feuerzeug', *die tageszeitung*, 24 September 1987.
Adler Modemärkte AG. 2012. 'Bericht über das erste Halbjahr 2012'. Retrieved 30 January 2013 from http://www.adlermode-unternehmen.com/fileadmin/2012/IR/q2-2012/bericht/de/Adler_Bericht_2_Quartal_2012_deutsch.pdf.
'Aktion Stoppt Frauenhass', *Emma*, no. 10, 1992, 36–41.

Alihusain, C. 2105. 'International Congress of Women of 1915'. Retrieved 20 October 2015 from http://soz-kult.hs-duesseldorf.de/.
Alison, M. 2009. *Women and Political Violence: Female Combatants in Ethno-National Conflict*. London and New York: Routledge.
Altbach, E.H. 1984. 'The New German Women's Movement', *Signs* 9, 454–69.
Anders, F. and A. Sedlmaier. 2013. '"Unternehmen Entebbe" 1976: Quellenkritische Perspektiven auf eine Flugzeugentführung', *Jahrbuch für Antisemitismusforschung* 22, 267–89.
———. 2013. 'The Limits of the Legitimate: The Quarrel over "Violence" between Autonomist Groups and the German Authorities', in W. Steinmetz, H.G. Haupt and I. Gilcher-Holtey (eds), *Writing Political History Today*. Frankfurt: Campus, 291–316.
Anders, F. 2006. 'Die Zeitschrift radikal und das Strafrecht', in F. Anders and I. Gilcher-Holtey (eds), *Herausforderungen des staatlichen Gewaltmonopols. Recht und politisch motivierte Gewalt am Ende des 20. Jahrhunderts*. Frankfurt: Campus, 221–59.
'Anschlag in Karlsruhe noch ungeklärt', *Frankfurter Rundschau*, 6 March 1975.
Antiquariat Schwarzer Stern (ed.). 1982. *Der Blues gesammelte Texte der Bewegung 2. Juni*. Dortmund.
'Antwort auf eine Vergewaltigung', in Jahrbuchgruppe des Münchner Frauenzentrums (ed), *Frauenjahrbuch '76*. Munich: Frauenoffensive, 1976, 202–16.
'Aufruf an alle Frauen zur Erfindung des Glücks', *Courage: Berliner Frauenzeitung*, 1977, 10.
'Aufruf des ersten bundesweiten Kongresses ausländischer und deutscher Frauen und Mädchen!', in Arbeitsgruppe Frauenkongreß (ed.), *Sind wir uns so fremd? Dokumentation des 1. Gemeinsamen Kongresses ausländischer und deutscher Frauen 23. – 25. März 1984*. Frankfurt, 202–8.
Augstein, R. 1978. 'Die Frauen schlagen zurück', *Der Spiegel*, no. 27, 76
'Auseinandersetzungen nach der Walpurgisnacht', *Analyse & Kritik*, no. 107, June 1977.
Ayim, M. 1995. 'grenzlos und unverschämt. Ein gedicht gegen die deutsche sch-einheit', in *Blues in schwarz-weiß*. Berlin. Orlanda Frauenverlag.
Bade, K.J., and J. Oltmer. 2005. 'Migration, Ausländerbeschäftigung und Asylpolitik in der DDR'. Retrieved 4 November 2015 from http://www.bpb.de/gesellschaft/migration/dossier-migration/56368/migrationspolitik-in-der-ddr?p=all.
Balz, H. 2008. *Von Terroristen, Sympathisanten und dem starken Staat: Die öffentliche Debatte über die RAF in den 70er Jahren*. Frankfurt and New York: Campus.
Bandhauer-Schöffmann, I. 2009. '"Emanzipation mit Bomben und Pistolen?" Feministinnen und Terroristinnen in deutschsprachigen Sicherheitsdiskursen der 1970er Jahre', *L'Homme*, 20, 65–84.
'Bärendienst für wen?' *die tageszeitung*, 8 October 1987.
Baumann, M. 1980. *Wie alles anfing*. Munich: Trikont.
Becker, J. 1977. *Hitler's Children: The Story of the Baader-Meinhof Terrorist Gang*. Philadelphia, PA: Lippincott.
Bender, C. (ed.). 1973. *Die Frauengruppe im Revolutionärer Kampf*. Frankfurt.
Bielby, C. 2012. *Violent Women in Print: Representations in the West German Print Media of the 1960s and 1970s*. Rochester, NY: Camden House.

Binder, S. 1968. 'Barbusig vor der Barriere', *Die Zeit*, 20 December.
———. 1969. 'Erst das Kind und dann die Politik', *Die Zeit*, 24 January.
'Blinder Hass', *Frankfurter Rundschau*, 6 March 1975.
'Blockade für Südkoreanerinnen', *die tageszeitung Bremen*, 22 July 1987.
Boeden, G. 1989. 'Die Herausforderung unseres demokratischen Rechtsstaates durch den linksextremistischen Terrorismus', in Bundesminister des Innern (ed.), *Extremismus und Terrorismus*. Bonn: Bundesminister des Innern, 63–79.
Boettcher, I. 1978. *Frauen gegen Männergewalt: Berliner Frauenhaus für Mißhandelte Frauen*. Berlin: Frauenselbstverlag.
Boschmann, N. 1988. 'Aufbruchstimmung Bei "Flair Fashion"', *die tageszeitung*, 11 January.
'Böse Schlieren', *Der Spiegel*, no. 2, 11 January 1988, 116–17.
Bressan, S., and M. Jander. 2006. 'Gudrun Ensslin', in W. Kraushaar (ed.), *Die RAF und der linke Terrorismus*. Hamburg: Hamburger Edition, 398–429.
'Briefe', *konkret*, no. 5, 1977, 5–6.
Brown, T.S. 2015. *West Germany and the Global Sixties: The Antiauthoritarian Revolt, 1962–1978*. Cambridge: Cambridge University Press.
Bührmann, T. 1978. 'Kongress in Frankfurt: die Arbeitsgruppen; was heißt hier "politisch"?' *Courage: Berliner Frauenzeitung* 4, 5.
Bundesministerium für Familie, Senioren, Frauen und Jugend (ed.). 2012. 'Lebenssituation, Sicherheit und Gesundheit von Frauen in Deutschland', Rostock. Retrieved 21 November 2015 from http://www.bmfsfj.de/BMFSFJ/Service/Publikationen/publikationen,did=20560.html.
Burns, R., and W. van der Will. 1988. *Protest and Democracy in West Germany: Extra-Parliamentary Opposition and the Democratic Agenda*. Basingstoke: Macmillan Press.
Claessens, D., and K. de Ahna. 1982. 'Das Milieu der Westberliner "Scene" und die "Bewegung 2. Juni"', in W. von Baeyer-Katte (ed.), *Gruppenprozesse*. Opladen: Westdeutscher Verlag, 20–181.
Colvin, S. 2009. *Ulrike Meinhof and West German Terrorism: Language, Violence and Identity*. Rochester, NY: Camden House.
Davenport, C. 2007. 'State Repression and Political Order', *Annual Review of Political Science* 10, 1–23.
Davis, B. 2005. '"Women's Strength Against Crazy Male Power": Gendered Language in the West German Peace Movement of the 1980s', in J.A. Davy, K. Hagemann and U. Kätzel (eds), *Frieden – Gewalt – Geschlecht Friedens- und Konfliktforschung als Geschlechterforschung*. Essen: Klartext Verlag, 244–65.
Davy, J.A. 2005. '"Manly" and "Feminine" Antimilitarism', in J.A. Davy, K. Hagemann and U. Kätzel (eds), *Frieden – Gewalt – Geschlecht. Friedens- und Konfliktforschung als Geschlechterforschung*, Essen: Klartext Verlag, 144–63.
Dean, J. 1996. *Solidarity of Strangers: Feminism after Identity Politics*. Berkeley: University of California Press.
———. 1998. 'Feminist Solidarity, Reflective Solidarity', *Women and Politics* 18, 1–26.
Deckwerth, S. 2007. 'Geständnis nach 20 Jahren', *Berliner Zeitung*, 12 April.
Dehnavi, M. 2013. *Das politisierte Geschlecht : biographische Wege zum Studentinnenprotest von '1968' und zur Neuen Frauenbewegung*. Bielefeld: transcript.

Della Porta, D. 1995. *Social Movements, Political Violence, and the State: A Comparative Analysis of Italy and Germany*. Cambridge: Cambridge University Press.
'Der Aufstand der Frauen', *Emma*, no. 6, 1991, 16–21.
Der Baader-Meinhof-Report. Dokumente, Analysen, Zusammenhänge. 1972. Mainz: Hase und Koehler.
Der Spiegel, no. 22, 23 May 1977.
Deutsche Welle, KalenderBlatt, '25.2.1975: Urteil zum "Abtreibungsparagrafen" 218'. Retrieved 15 June 2015 from http://www.kalenderblatt.de/index.php?what=thmanu&lang=de&manu_id=123&sdt=20120225&maca=de-podcast_kalenderblatt-1086-xml-mrss.
Die Amazonen. 1988. 'Gewisses Risiko', *konkret*, no. 2.
Die Bewegung 2. Juni. 1980. 'Auflösungspapier Bewegung 2. Juni'. Retrieved 16 February 2014 from http://bewegung.nostate.net/mate_aufloesung.html.
'Die Frauenbewegung zu Gast bei Rechtsanwalt Becker', *die tageszeitung*, 15 June 1979.
Die Rote Zora. 1977. 'Frauen erhebt euch und die Welt erlebt euch!' FMT, FB.07.102.
———. 1993. 'Mili's Tanz auf dem Eis. Von Pirouetten, Schleifen, Einbrüchen, doppelten Saltos und dem Versuch, Boden unter die Füße zu kriegen'. Retrieved 3 December 2015 from http://www.freilassung.de/div/texte/rz/milis/milis1.htm.
———. 1995. 'Ihr habt die Macht, uns gehört die Nacht', *radikal*, no. 153. Retrieved 30 June 2016 from http://www.freilassung.de/div/texte/rz/radi153_1195.htm.
Diewald-Kerkmann, G. 2007. 'Frauen in Der RAF', in *'Wer wenn nicht wir'*. Retrieved 12 January 2013 from http://www.bpb.de/gesellschaft/kultur/filmbildung/43364/frauen-in-der-raf?p=all.
———. 2009. *Frauen, Terrorismus und Justiz: Prozesse gegen weibliche Mitglieder der RAF und der Bewegung 2. Juni*. Düsseldorf: Droste.
Dischereit, E. 1988. 'Absolution vom Mainzer Bischof', *vorwärts*, 2 January 1988.
Ditfurth, J. 2007. *Ulrike Meinhof: Die Biografie*. Berlin: Ullstein
Doderer, Y.P. 1999. *Never Give Up! Zur Neuen Frauenbewegung*. Munich: Kunstverein.
Duggan, L., and N.D. Hunter. 2006. *Sex Wars: Sexual Dissent and Political Culture*. New York: Routledge.
Edschmid, U. 2001. *Frau mit Waffe: Zwei Geschichten aus terroristischen Zeiten*, 1st edn. Frankfurt: Suhrkamp.
'Eier von links', *Der Spiegel*, 14 February 1966.
'Ein Bauwerk mit Anspruch auf Qualität', *Badische Neueste Nachrichten*, 6 May 1969.
Elendt, G. 'Das hält die Polizei für möglich: Frauentrupps räumen Kölner Sex Shops aus', *Express*, 4 February 1978.
Ensslin, G., C. Ensslin and G. Ensslin. 2005. *"Zieht den Trennungsstrich, jede Minute": Briefe an ihre Schwester Christiane und ihren Bruder Gottfried aus dem Gefängnis 1972–1973*. Hamburg: Konkret Literatur Verlag.
'Erklärung von Rechtsanwalt Becker', *die tageszeitung*, 18 June 1979.
'Ermittlungen gegen die Rote Zora', *Frankfurter Rundschau*, 24 October 1986.
'Es reicht', *Emma*, no. 4, 1990, 11.
Fahlenbrach, K. 2002. *Protest-Inszenierungen: Visuelle Kommunikation und kollektive Identitäten in Protestbewegungen*. Wiesbaden: Westdeutscher Verlag.
Falck, U. 1998. *VEB Bordell*. Berlin: Ch. Links.
Fichter, T., and S. Lönnedonker. 1976. *Kleine Geschichte des SDS*. Berlin: Rotbuch Verlag.

Fiddler, A. 2004. 'Subjectivity and women's writing of the 1970s and early 1980s', in G. Bartram (ed.), *The Cambridge Companion to the Modern German Novel*, 1st ed. Cambridge: Cambridge University Press, 249–65. Retrieved 24 July 2015 from http://dx.doi.org/10.1017/CCOL0521482534.

Fischer, E., B. Lehmann and K. Stoffl. 1977. *Gewalt gegen Frauen*. Cologne: Kiepenheuer & Witsch.

'Flambieren, demolieren', *Der Spiegel*, 24 August 1987.

'Flammende Grüße bei Adler', *die tageszeitung*, 18 August 1987.

Franke, Y., et al. (eds). 2014. *Feminismen heute: Positionen in Theorie und Praxis*. Bielefeld: transcript.

'Frauenaktion bei Rechtsanwalt Becker', *Courage: Berliner Frauenzeitung* 4, no. 8, 1979, 42–43.

'Frauen bekennen: Wir legten die Bombe', *Die Welt*, 6 March 1975.

'Frauen im Untergrund – "Etwas Irrationales"', *Der Spiegel*, 8 August 1977, 22–33.

'Frauen in Kurdistan', *radikal*, no. 154, June 1996. Retrieved on 1 July 2016 from http://www.freilassung.de/div/texte/rz/radi154b.htm.

'Frauen klagen gegen den Stern', *Emma*, no. 8, 1978, 6–15.

Frauenhauskoordinierung e.V. (ed.), 'FrauenHäuser in Deutschland'. Retrieved 15 December 2015 from http://www.frauenhauskoordinierung.de/fileadmin/ redakteure/pdfs/Medienpaket/RZ_frauenhaus_broschuere_ANSICHTS.pdf.

'Frauen klagen gegen den Stern', *Emma*, no. 8, 1978, 6–15.

'Frauenoffensive', *Chronik der Neuen Frauenbewegung*. Retrieved 20 December 2015 from http://www.frauenmediaturm.de/themen-portraets/ chronik-der-neuen-frauenbewegung/1975/frauenoffensive-presseinformation/.

Frauenzentrum (ed.). 1976. *Gewalt gegen Frauen in Ehe, Psychiatrie, Gynäkologie, Vergewaltigung, Beruf, Film und was Frauen dagegen tun: Beiträge zum Internationalen Tribunal über Gewalt gegen Frauen, Brüssel März 1976*. Berlin: Agit Druck.

Frevert, U. 1986. *Frauen-Geschichte: Zwischen bürgerlicher Verbesserung und neuer Weiblichkeit*. Frankfurt: Suhrkamp.

———. 1997. *Women in German History: From Bourgeois Emancipation to Sexual Liberation*, translated by Stuart McKinnon-Evans. Oxford and New York: Berg.

Fritzsch, R., and R. Reinders. 1995. *Die Bewegung 2. Juni: Gespräche über Haschrebellen, Lorenzentführung, Knast*. Berlin: Edition ID-Archiv.

'Gebäude'. Retrieved 20 December 2015 from http://www.bundesverfassungsgericht. de/DE/Gebaeude/gebaeude_node.html.

Gebhardt, M. 2012. *Alice im Niemandsland – Wie die deutsche Frauenbewegung die Frauen verlor*. Munich: DVA.

Gerhard, U. 2002. 'The Women's Movement in West Germany', in G. Griffin and R. Braidotti (eds), *Thinking Differently*. London: Zed Books, 321–31.

———. 2008. 'Frauenbewegung', in R. Roth and D. Rucht (eds), *Die Sozialen Bewegungen in Deutschland seit 1945*. Frankfurt and New York: Campus, 188–217.

Geronimo. 1990. *Feuer und Flamme*. Berlin: Edition ID-Archiv.

'Geschlechterkampf im Untergrund', *die tageszeitung*, 21 July 1987.

Geulen, R., and O. Schily, 'Seht ihr denn keinen Unterschied zwischen 'Verteidigung von Vergewaltigung' und Verteidigung eines Angeklagten, der verdächtigt wird, eine Vergewaltigung begangen zu haben?' *die tageszeitung*, 21 June 1979.

Gilcher-Holtey, I. 2008. 'Kritische Theorie und Neue Linke', in I. Gilcher-Holtey (ed.), *1968 – Vom Ereignis zum Mythos*. Frankfurt: Suhrkamp, 223–47.
Glick Schiller, N., and P. Levitt. 2006. 'Haven't We Heard This Somewhere Before? A Substantive View of Transnational Migration Studies by Way of a Reply to Waldinger and Fitzgerald', the Center for Migration and Development – Working Paper Series 2008. Retrieved 25 October 2015 from http://www.princeton.edu/cmd/working-papers/papers/wp0601.pdf.
Grisard, D. 2011. *Gendering Terror: Eine Geschlechtergeschichte des Linksterrorismus in der Schweiz*. Frankfurt: Campus.
Groebel, J., and H. Feger. 1982. 'Analyse von Strukturen terroristischer Gruppierungen', in W. von Baeyer-Katte (ed.), *Gruppenprozesse, Analysen zum Terrorismus 3*. Opladen: Westdeutscher Verlag, 393–431.
Haffner, S. 1977. 'Die Angst ist unser schlimmster Feind', *Courage: Berliner Frauenzeitung*, no. 4, 5.
Halperin, D.M. 1997. *Saint Foucault: Towards a Gay Hagiography*. New York: Oxford University Press.
Hanshew, K. 2012. *Terror and Democracy in West Germany*. New York: Cambridge University Press.
Haug, F. 1986. 'The Women's Movement in West Germany', *New Left Review*, 50–74.
Haunss, S. 2004. *Identität in Bewegung: Prozesse kollektiver Identität bei den Autonomen und in der Schwulenbewegung*. Wiesbaden: VS Verlag für Sozialwissenschaften.
Hauser, D. 2006. 'Deutschland, Italien, Japan. Die ehemaligen Achsenmächte und der Terrorismus der 1970er Jahre', in W. Kraushaar (ed.), *Die RAF und der linke Terrorismus*. Hamburg: Hamburger Edition, 1272–98.
Hayes, P., and J. Campbell. 2005. *Bloody Sunday: Trauma, Pain and Politics*. London: Pluto Press.
Heinemann, E. 2010. 'Jörg Schröter, linkes Verlagswesen und Pornografie', in S. Reichardt and D. Siegfried (eds), *Das Alternative Milieu: antibürgerlicher Lebensstil und linke Politik in der Bundesrepublik Deutschland und Europa 1968–1983*. Göttingen: Wallstein, 290–312.
Heinrich-Böll-Stiftung and Feministisches Institut (eds). 1999. *Wie weit flog die Tomate?: Eine 68erinnen-Gala der Reflexion*. Berlin: Heinrich-Böll-Stiftung.
Helwerth, U. 1988. 'Von der Panthertante zur Quotilde', interview with Sigrid Damm-Rüger, Margit Eschenbach and Ingrid Schmidt-Harzbach, *die tageszeitung*, 13 September.
Helwig, G. 1997. 'Frau und Gesellschaft', in Bundeszentrale für politische Bildung (ed.), *Frauen in Deutschland – Informationen zur politischen Bildung*. Retrieved 10 October 2015 from http://www.bpb.de/publikationen/D6SSWQ,0,0,Frau_und_Gesellschaft.html#art0.
Henry, A. 2004. *Not My Mother's Sister: Generational Conflict and Third-Wave Feminism*. Bloomington: Indiana University Press.
Hertrampf, S. 2008. 'Ein Tomatenwurf und seine Folgen. Eine neue Welle des Frauenprotests in der BRD', in *bpb dossier*. Retrieved 1 March 2015 from http://www.bpb.de/gesellschaft/gender/frauenbewegung/35287/neue-welle-im-westen?p=0.
Hewitt, N.A. 1985. 'Beyond the Search for Sisterhood: American Women's History in the 1980s', *Social History* 10, 299–321.

'Hiermit erkläre ich . . .', *Der Spiegel*, 11 March 1974.
Hoffmann, M. (ed.). 1997. *Rote Armee Fraktion: Texte und Materialien zur Geschichte der RAF*. Berlin: ID Verlag.
Hooks, B. 2000. *Feminist Theory: From Margin to Center*. Cambridge, MA: South End Press.
Horst, L. 1970. 'Die Rote Ulrike ist mit der Gewalt verheiratet', *Bild*, 16 May.
Hüttner, B. 2001. 'Die Autonomen zwischen Subkultur und sozialer Bewegung'. Retrieved 14 October 2015 from http://www.archivbremen.de/cgeschic/schwarzm.htm.
ID Verlag (ed.). 1993. *Die Früchte des Zorns*. Amsterdam: ID Verlag.
'In eigener Sache'. 1983. *Courage: Berliner Frauenzeitung*, no. 9, September.
Jander, M. 2006. 'Horst Mahler', in W. Kraushaar (ed.), *Die RAF und der linke Terrorismus*. Hamburg: Hamburger Edition, 372–397.
Janz, O., and D. Schönpflug (eds). 2014. *Gender History in a Transnational Perspective: Networks, Biographies, Gender Orders*. New York: Berghahn Books.
Joannou, M., and J. Purvis. 1998. *The Women's Suffrage Movement: New Feminist Perspectives*. Manchester: Manchester University Press.
Karcher, K. 2013. 'Sisters in Arms? Female Participation in Leftist Political Violence in the Federal Republic of Germany Since 1970', unpublished PhD thesis, Department of German Studies, University of Warwick.
———. 2016. 'How (not) to "Hollaback": Towards a transnational debate on the "Red Zora" and militant tactics in the feminist struggle against gender-based violence', *Feminist Media Studies* 16 (1), 70–85, DOI:10.1080/14680777.2015.1093099.
Kämper, H., and E. Link. 2013. *Wörterbuch zum Demokratiediskurs 1967/68*. Berlin: Akademie Verlag. Retrieved 4 November 2015 from http://alltitles.ebrary.com/Doc?id=10861362.
'Kampf um Emma', *Der Spiegel*, 29 November 1976, 219–21.
Kästli, E., M. Brenner and A. Ernst. 1982. 'Asiatinnen: Import -Export', *Emma*, no. 6, 28–31.
Katsiaficas, G. 1997. *The Subversion of Politics: European Autonomous Social Movements and the Decolonialization of Everyday Life*. Atlantic Highlands, NJ: Humanities Press.
Kätzel, U. 2002. *Die 68erinnen: Porträt einer rebellischen Frauengeneration*. Berlin: Rowohlt.
———. 2005. 'Geschlecht, Gewalt und Pazifismus. 1968 und die Anti-Vietnamkriegsbewegung in der Bundesrepublik Deutschland', in J.A. Davy, K. Hagemann and U. Kätzel (eds), *Frieden – Gewalt – Geschlecht. Friedens- und Konfliktforschung als Geschlechterforschung*. Essen: Klartext Verlag, 222–43.
Kawaters, C. 1984. *Zora Zobel findet die Leiche: Roman*. Frankfurt: Zweitausendeins.
———. 1987. 'Ein lila Auto ist sehr verdächtig', *die tageszeitung*, 9 February.
Kempton, R. 2007. *Provo: Amsterdam's Anarchist Revolt*. Brooklyn, NY: Autonomedia.
Kinder, K. 2006. '20 Jahre Schwarze (Frauen-) Bewegung in Deutschland'. Retrieved 4 November 2015 from https://heimatkunde.boell.de/2006/05/01/20-jahre-schwarze-frauen-bewegung-deutschland.
Kirchhoff, B. 1982. 'Nach Abzug der Scham', *Kursbuch*, no. 68, 119–25.
Klimke, M., and J. Scharloth. 2008. *1968 in Europe: A History of Protest and Activism, 1956–1977*. Basingstoke: Palgrave Macmillan.

Koenen, G. 2009. *Vesper, Enslin, Baader: Urszenen des deutschen Terrorismus*, 3rd edn. Frankfurt: Fischer Taschenbuch Verlag.
König, K. 2006. 'Zwei Ikonen des bewaffneten Kampfes', in W. Kraushaar (ed.), *Die RAF und der linke Terrorismus*. Hamburg: Hamburger Edition, 430–71.
'konkret intern', *konkret*, no. 5, 1977, 4.
Kosczy, U., C. Stolle, and J.S. Pak. 1988. 'Die Bescheidenheit ist vorbei. Koreanische Frauen wehren sich gegen Ausbeutung und ungerechte Weltwirtschaftsstrukturen. Das Beispiel Flair Fashion/Adler'. Frankfurt: Entwicklungspolitischer Informationsdienst des Evangelischen Pressedienstes.
Kramm, J. 2001. 'Sie war eine der Frauen, die vor 30 Jahren bekannten: "Wir haben abgetrieben!" Heute, in der Gendebatte, fällt Nori Möding das Argumentieren schwerer Zwei Leben', *Berliner Zeitung*, 6 June.
Kraushaar, W. 2005. *Die Bombe im Jüdischen Gemeindehaus*. Hamburg: Hamburger Edition.
———. 2006. 'Die Tupamaros West-Berlin', in W. Kraushaar (ed.), *Die RAF und der linke Terrorismus*. Hamburg: Hamburger Edition, 512–30.
———. 2006. 'Im Schatten der RAF. Zur Entstehung der Revolutionären Zellen', in W. Kraushaar (ed.), *Die RAF und der linke Terrorismus*. Hamburg: Hamburger Edition, 583–601.
Krebs, M. 1988. *Ulrike Meinhof: Ein Leben im Widerspruch*. Reinbek: Rowohlt.
Kühnert, H. 1975. 'Vogel: Anschlag auf Rechtsstaatlichkeit', *Süddeutsche Zeitung*, 6 March.
Lamprecht, R. 2011. *Das Bundesverfassungsgericht: Geschichte und Entwicklung*. Bonn: Bundeszentrale für Politische Bildung.
Langguth, G. 1983. *Protestbewegung: Entwicklung, Niedergang, Renaissance: Die Neue Linke seit 1968*. Cologne: Verlag Wissenschaft und Politik.
H. Langston. 2012. 'Meeting Pussy Riot'. Retrieved 13 December 2015 from http://www.vice.com/read/A-Russian-Pussy-Riot.
Leach, D.K. 2009. 'An Elusive "We": Antidogmatism, Democratic Practice, and the Contradictory Identity of the German Autonomen', *American Behavioral Scientist* 52, 1042–68.
Lee, M. 2014. 'Political Pornography in the West German Underground Press', *History Workshop Journal* (1) 78, 186–203.
Lehmann, I. 1999. 'Auf der Hut vor Nebenwidersprüchen', in Heinrich-Böll-Stiftung and Feministisches Institut (eds), *Wie weit flog die Tomate? Eine 68erinnen-Gala der Reflexion*. Berlin: Heinrich-Böll-Stiftung, 57–64.
Leidinger, C. 2010. '11 Jahre Widerstand Frauenwiderstandscamps in Reckershausen im Hunsrück von 1983 bis 1993', in *Wissenschaft & Frieden* 2010–2, 47–50. Retrieved 11 November 2015 from http://www.wissenschaft-und-frieden.de/seite.php?artikelID=1620.
Lenz, I. 2010. *Die Neue Frauenbewegung in Deutschland: Abschied vom kleinen Unterschied: Eine Quellensammlung*, 2nd rev. edn. Wiesbaden: VS-Verlag.
Lindenberger, T., and A. Lüdtke (eds). 1995. *Physische Gewalt: Studien zur Geschichte der Neuzeit*, 2nd edn. Frankfurt: Suhrkamp.
Lindner, W. 1996. *Jugendprotest seit den fünfziger Jahren: Dissens und kultureller Eigensinn*. Opladen: Leske und Budrich.

Lord, C., and R.N. Watkins. 1973. *Storefront Day Care Centers: The Radical Berlin Experiment*. Boston: Beacon Press.
'Löwe Los', *Der Spiegel*, 22 February 1971, 26–34.
'Magazin', *Emma*, no. 9, 1987, 7.
'Männer – Frauen – Männer', *die tageszeitung*, 22 June 1979.
Malhotra, S., and A. Carrillo Rowe. 2013. *Silence, Feminism, Power: Reflections at the Edges of Sound*. New York: Palgrave Macmillan.
Markovits, A.S., and P.S. Gorski. 1993. *The German Left: Red, Green and Beyond*. Cambridge: Polity Press.
Marx Ferree, M. 2012. *Varieties of Feminism: German Gender Politics in Global Perspective*. Stanford, CA: Stanford University Press.
Mayhall, L.N. 2000. 'Defining Militancy: Radical Protest, the Constitutional Idiom, and Women's Suffrage in Britain, 1908–1909', *Journal of British Studies* 39, 340–71.
———. 2003. *The Militant Suffrage Movement: Citizenship and Resistance in Britain, 1860–1930*. Oxford: Oxford University Press.
Meinhof, U. 1968. 'Frauen im SDS oder in eigener Sache', *konkret*, 7 October.
———. 1970. '"Natürlich Kann Geschossen Werden"', *Der Spiegel*, 15 June.
Melzer, P. 2012. '"Frauen gegen Imperialismus und Patriarchat zerschlagen den Herrschaftsapparat": autonome Frauen, linksradikaler feministischer Protest und Gewalt in Westdeutschland', in H. Balz and J.H. Friedrichs (eds), *'All we ever wanted . . .' eine Kulturgeschichte europäischer Protestbewegungen der 1980er Jahre*. Berlin: Dietz, 157–177.
———. 2015. *Death in the Shape of a Young Girl: Women's Political Violence in the Red Army Faction*. New York: New York University Press.
Merkel, I. 2010. 'Ohne Frauen ist kein Staat zu machen', in I. Lenz (ed), *Die Neue Frauenbewegung in Deutschland*, 878–84.
Messner, D. 'Deutscher Multi fährt einen brutalen Kurs', *die tageszeitung*, 11 April 1987.
Meyer, T. 2008. *Staatsfeind Erinnerungen*. Berlin: Rotbuch.
Mika, B. 1998. *Alice Schwarzer. Eine kritische Biographie*. Reinbek: Rowohlt.
'militant'. Retrieved 21 November 2015 from http://www.duden.de/rechtschreibung/militant.
'militant'. Retrieved 21 November 2015 from http://www.oxforddictionaries.com/definition/english/militant.
Mohanty, C.T. 2003. *Feminism without Borders: Decolonizing Theory, Practicing Solidarity*. Durham, NC, and London: Duke University Press.
Morgan, R. 1985. *Sisterhood is Global: The International Women's Movement Anthology*. Harmondsworth: Penguin.
Münzing, I. 1975. 'Ärzte-Anzeige gegen Münchner Frauenzentrum', *Abendzeitung München*, 15 July.
Narr, W.D. 2008. 'Der CDU- Staat (1949–1966)', in R. Roth and D. Rucht (eds), *Die Sozialen Bewegungen in Deutschland Seit 1945: Ein Handbuch*. Frankfurt and New York: Campus, 51–70.
Neidhardt, F. 1982. 'Linker und rechter Terrorismus. Erscheinungsformen und Handlungspotentiale im Gruppenvergleich', in W. von Baeyer-Katte (ed.) *Gruppenprozesse, Analysen zum Terrorismus 3*. Opladen: Westdeutscher Verlag, 433–76.

'Neuer Anschlag auf eine Filiale von Adler in Berlin', *Neue Züricher Zeitung*, 14 September 1987.
Notruf und Beratung für vergewaltigte Frauen (ed.). 1979. *Gewalt gegen Frauen und was Frauen dagegen tun*. Berlin: Wagenbach.
Notz, G. 2004. 'Die autonomen Frauenbewegungen der Siebzigerjahre: Entstehungsgeschichte, Organisationsformen, politische Konzepte', *Archiv für Zeitgeschichte*, 123–48.
———. 2006. *Warum flog die Tomate?: Die autonomen Frauenbewegungen der Siebzigerjahre: Entstehungsgeschichte, Organisationsformen, politische Konzepte*. Neu-Ulm: AG-SPAK-Bücher.
———. 2014. '(Kein) Abschied von der Idee der Schwesterlichkeit? Herausforderungen für feministische Solidarität', in Y. Franke et al. (eds), *Feminismen heute. Positionen in Theorie und Praxis*. Bielefeld: transcript-Verlag. Retrieved 1 November 2015 from http://www.degruyter.com/view/product/430299.
Oguntoye, K. 1989. 'Die Schwarze deutsche Bewegung und die Frauenbewegung in Deutschland', *Afrekete. Zeitung für afro-deutsche und schwarze Frauen*, 4, 3–5.
O'keefe, T. 2014. 'My Body is My Manifesto! SlutWalk, FEMEN and Femmenist Protest', *Feminist Review* 107, 1–19.
Perincioli, C. 1999. 'Anarchismus -> Lesbianismus -> Frauenzentrum. Warum musste die Tomate so weit fliegen?' Heinrich-Böll-Stiftung and Feministisches Institut (eds), *Wie weit flog die Tomate?* Berlin: Heinrich-Böll-Stiftung, 98–117.
———. 2015. *Berlin wird feministisch. Das Beste, was von der 68er Bewegung blieb*. Berlin: Querverlag.
Peters, B. 1991. *RAF: Terrorismus in Deutschland*. Stuttgart: Deutsche Verlags-Anstalt.
Piesche, P., 'Schwarz und deutsch? Eine ostdeutsche Jugend vor 1989 – Retrospektive auf ein ‚nichtexistentes' Thema in der DDR'. Retrieved 22 December 2015 from https://heimatkunde.boell.de/2006/05/01/schwarz-und-deutsch-eine-ostdeutsche-jugend-vor-1989-retrospektive-auf-ein.
Plogstedt, S. 1978. 'Rückzug der Frauenbewegung?' *Courage: Berliner Frauenzeitung*, no. 4, 7.
———. 1978. '2000 mussten nach Korea zurück', *Courage: Berliner Frauenzeitung*, no. 4, 27–28.
———. 1978. 'Die Gewalt in unseren Köpfen: Kölner Kongreß', *Courage: Berliner Frauenzeitung*, no. 67–8.
———. 1979. 'Wir haben gegründet und sind von Herzen froh darüber: Frauenpartei', *Courage: Berliner Frauenzeitung* no.12, 4–5.
Prinz. A. 2003. *Lieber wütend als traurig: Die Lebensgeschichte der Ulrike Marie Meinhof*. Weinheim: Beltz und Gelberg.
'Proactive'. Retrieved 10 September 2015 from http://oxforddictionaries.com/definition/english/proactive?q=proactivity#proactive__6.
Proll, A. 2004. *Hans und Grete: Bilder der RAF 1967–1977*. Berlin: Aufbau-Verlag.
Purvis, J. 2013. 'Gendering the Historiography of the Suffragette Movement in Edwardian Britain: Some Reflections', *Women's History Review* 4(22), 576–90.
Raab, H. 2014. 'Dis/Ability, Feminismus und Geschlecht', in Y. Franke et al. (eds), *Feminismen heute. Positionen in Theorie und Praxis*. Bielefeld: transcript, 101–14.
'Rauchzeichen: Ein Rückblick auf 20 Jahre RZ'. 2001. Retrieved 2 February 2015 from http://www.freilassung.de/div/texte/rz/rauchz/rauchz.htm.

Raymond, J. 1988. 'S & M', *Emma*, no. 9, 23–25.
Reichardt, S. 2008. 'Große und Sozialliberale Koalition (1966–1974)', in R. Roth and D. Rucht (eds), *Die Sozialen Bewegungen in Deutschland seit 1945: Ein Handbuch*. Frankfurt and New York: Campus, 71–91.
Richter, P. 1998. 'Die Außerparlamentarische Opposition in der Bundesrepublik Deutschland 1966 bis 1968', in I. Gilcher-Holtey (ed.), *1968, Vom Ereignis zum Gegenstand der Geschichtswissenschaft*. Göttingen: Vandenhoeck und Ruprecht, 35–55.
Rinner, S. 2013. *The German Student Movement and the Literary Imagination: Transnational Memories of Protest and Dissent*. New York and Oxford: Berghahn Books.
'Riot statt Rosen'. 2016. Retrieved 18 June 2016 from http://frauenkampftag2015.de/.
Rollnik, G., and D. Dubbe. 2004. *Keine Angst vor Niemand: Über die Siebziger, die Bewegung 2. Juni und die RAF*. Hamburg: Edition Nautilus.
Rosenbladt, S. 1978. 'Walpurgisnacht', *Emma*, no. 6, 16–17.
'Rote Armee Fraktion: Leninisten mit Knarren', *Agit 883*, 6 December 1971, 8–9.
'Rote Zora: Anschläge bei Adler verübt', *Süddeutsche Zeitung*, 18 August 1987.
'"Rote Zora" bekennt sich zu Brandanschlägen', *Rheinische Post*, 18 August 1987.
Rubin, G. 1993. 'Misguided, Dangerous and Wrong: an Analysis of Anti-Pornography Politics', in A. Assiter and A. Carol (eds), *Bad Girls & Dirty Pictures*. London: Pluto Press, 18–40.
Rucht, D. 1991. 'Soziale Bewegungen, Gegenbewegungen und Staat: Der Abtreibungskonflikt in den USA, Frankreich und der Bundesrepublik Deutschland', *Forschungsjournal Neue Soziale Bewegungen* 2.
'Ruf nach mehr Härte in Berlin', *Süddeutsche Zeitung*, 16 May 1970.
Rupp, L.J. 1997. *Worlds of Women: The Making of an International Women's Movement*. Princeton, NJ: Princeton University Press.
Russell, D.E.H., and N. van de Ven. 1990. 'Crimes Against Women: Proceedings of the International Tribunal', 3rd edn. Retrieved 21 December 2015 from http://www.dianarussell.com/f/Crimes_Against_Women_Tribunal.pdf.
Sander, H. 1999. 'Rede des Aktionsrates zur Befreiung der Frauen', in A. Conrad and K. Michalik (eds), *Quellen zur Geschichte der Frauen*. Stuttgart: Reclam, 358–68.
———. 1999. 'Der Seele ist das Gemeinsame eigen, das sich mehrt', in Heinrich-Böll-Stiftung and Feministisches Institut (eds), *Wie weit flog die Tomate? Eine 68erinnen-Gala der Reflexion*. Berlin: Heinrich-Böll-Stiftung, 43–56.
Schäfer, C., and C. Wilke. 2000. *Die Neue Frauenbewegung in München 1968–1985. Eine Dokumentation*. Munich: Buchendorfer Verlag.
Scharlau, W. 1984. 'Die Freier sind das Problem, nicht die Mädchen', *Die Zeit*, 11 May.
Scheunemann, R., and K. Scheunemann. 1971. 'Die Kampagne der "Frauenaktion 70" gegen den § 218. Ein Versuch zur Emanzipation durch Selbsttätigkeit', in H. Grossmann (ed.), *Bürgerinitiativen: Schritte zur Veränderung?* Frankfurt: Fischer, 71–84.
Schiller, K., and C. Young. 2010. *The 1972 Munich Olympics and the Making of Modern Germany*. Berkeley: University of California Press.
Schiller, M. 2001. *Es war ein harter Kampf um meine Erinnerung: Ein Lebensbericht aus der RAF*. Munich: Piper.

Schlaeger, H., and N. Vedder-Shults. 1978. 'The West German Women's Movement', *New German Critique*, 59–68.
Schmid, M. 1977. 'Zwischen Angst und Unsicherheit: ausländische Frauen', *Courage: Berliner Frauenzeitung*, no. 11, 25–27.
Schmidtchen, G. 1981. 'Terroristische Karrieren. Soziologische Analyse anhand von Fahndungsunterlagen und Prozessakten', in H. Jäger, G. Schmidtchen and L. Süllwold (eds), *Lebenslaufanalysen*. Opladen: Westdeutscher Verlag, 14–77.
Schneider, C. 2006. 'Omnipotente Opfer. Die Geburt der Gewalt aus dem Geist des Widerstands', in W. Kraushaar (ed.), *Die RAF und der linke Terrorismus*. Hamburg: Hamburger Edition, 1328–42.
Schruff, S. 1977. 'Die Hexen sind los', *Emma*, no. 6, 58.
Schultz, D. 1981. 'Dem Rassismus in sich begegnen', *Courage: Berliner Frauenzeitung*, No. 10, 17–21.
———. 1984. 'Ausländische und deutsche . . .', *Courage: Berliner Frauenzeitung* 9, no. 15, 7.
Schultz, H.E. 1971. 'Justizbeamte sollten Baader ohne Waffen ausführen. Angeklagte von Institutsangestellten "mit 99 prozentiger Sicherheit" erkannt', *Der Abend*, 19 March.
Schulz, K. 2002. *Der Lange Atem der Provokation: Die Frauenbewegung in der Bundesrepublik und in Frankreich, 1968–1976*. Frankfurt and New York: Campus.
———. 2004. 'Echoes of Provocation: 1968 and the Women's Movements in France and Germany', in G.R. Horn and P. Kenney (eds), *Transnational Moments of Change: Europe 1945, 1968, 1989*. Lanham: Rowman and Littlefield, 137–54.
———. 2008. 'Ohne Frauen keine Revolution. 68er und Neue Frauenbewegung'. Retrieved 16 February 2015 from http://www.bpb.de/geschichte/deutsche-geschichte/68er-bewegung/51859/frauen-und-68?p=all.
Schwall, E. 1986. 'Gespräch Mit Enno. Schwall'. Retrieved 3 November 2014 from http://www.freilassung.de/prozess/ticker/history/rz/hinter/enno1.htm.
Schwarz, B. 1987. 'Adler in Südkorea. Ausbeutung und sexuelle Nötigung, "Die Zwänge der Marktwirtschaft"', *klenkes*, 16–17.
Schwarzer, A. 1978. 'Antwort an Nannen & Co', *Emma*, no. 8, 5.
———. 1981. *So fing es an! 10 Jahre Frauenbewegung*. Cologne: Emma-Frauenverlag.
Scribner, C. 2015. *After the Red Army Faction: Gender, Culture, and Militancy*. New York: Columbia University Press.
Seguino, S. 1997. 'Gender Wage Inequality and Export-led Growth in South Korea', *Journal of Development Studies* 34, 102–32.
Seifert, J. 2006. 'Ulrike Meinhof', in W. Kraushaar (ed.), *Die RAF und der linke Terrorismus*. Hamburg: Hamburger Edition, 350–71.
'Selbstherrlich und zynisch', *Der Spiegel*, 17 February 1975.
'Sex-Professor erhängte sich', *Bild*, 31 October 1986.
'Sie schlug mich, ohne mich anzusehen', *Der Spiegel*, no. 27, 3 July 1978.
Silies, E.M. 2011. 'Ein, zwei, viele Bewegungen?' in C. Baumann, S. Gehrig and N. Büchse (eds), *Linksalternatives Milieu und Neue Soziale Bewegungen in den 1970er Jahren*. Heidelberg: Universitätsverlag Winter, 87–106.
Siemens, A.M. 2006. 'Durch die Institutionen oder in den Terrorismus: Die Wege von Joschka Fischer, Daniel Cohn-Bendit, Hans-Joachim Klein und Johannes Weinrich', PhD thesis, Ludwig-Maximilians-University-Munich.

Slobodian, Q. 2012. *Foreign Front: Third World Politics in Sixties West Germany*. Durham, NC: Duke University Press.
Sontheimer, M. 2010. *Natürlich kann geschossen werden. Eine kurze Geschichte der Roten Armee Fraktion*. Munich: Deutsche Verlags-Anstalt.
'Spuren zum BVG-Anschlag', *Badische Neueste Nachrichten*, 7 March 1975.
Sperling, V. 2014. 'Russian feminist perspectives on Pussy Riot', *Nationalities Papers* 42:4, 591–603.
Steffen, M. 1984. 'Dekonstruktion feministischer Legendenbildung. Weiberräte contra Feminismus – Anfänge der autonomen Frauenbewegung', *die tageszeitung*, 17 October.
———. 1998. 'SDS, Weiberräte, Feminismus?' in W. Kraushaar (ed.), *Frankfurter Schule und Studentenbewegung: Von der Flaschenpost zum Molotowcocktail 1946–1995*, vol. 3. Frankfurt: Rogner & Bernhard bei Zweitausendeins, 126–40.
Stelzer, T. 2003. 'Die Zumutung des Fleisches', *Der Tagesspiegel*, 7 December.
———. 2007. 'Die Waffen der Frauen', *Die Zeit*, 27 September.
Stolle, C. 1986. 'Freiwild in der Freihandelszone', *die tageszeitung*, 22 December.
Strobl, I. 1982. 'Laß jucken, Genosse', *Emma Sonderband*, no. 3, 53–55.
Strobel, R. 2004. 'Die Neue Frauenbewegung', in W. Faulstich (ed.), *Die Kultur der 70er Jahre*. Munich: Wilhem Fink, 259–72.
Süllwold, L. 1981. 'Stationen in der Entwicklung von Terroristen. Psychologische Aspekte biographischer Daten', in H. Jäger, G. Schmidtchen and L. Süllwold (eds), *Lebenslaufanalysen*. Opladen: Westdeutscher Verlag, 80–116.
Sung, S. 2003. 'Women Reconciling Paid and Unpaid Work in a Confucian Welfare State: The Case of South Korea', *Social Policy & Administration* 37, 342–60.
Terre des Femmes, 'English Site'. Retrieved 30 August 2015 from http://www.terre-des-femmes.de/.
Tolmein, O., and I. Möller. 2005. *'RAF – Das war für uns Befreiung': Ein Gespräch mit Irmgard Möller über bewaffneten Kampf, Knast und die Linke*. Hamburg: Konkret Literatur Verlag.
'Top 25 Deutschland 1975'. Retrieved 18 October 2015 from http://www.insidekino.com/DJahr/D1975.htm.
'. . . Und keiner beschmutze das eigene Nest . . .', *die tageszeitung*, 21 June 1979.
'Unter Adlern', *Schwäbisches Tageblatt*, 18 April 1987.
'Urteil im Zwielicht', *Der Spiegel*, 27 November 1967, 74.
Usborne, C. 2007. *Cultures of Abortion in Weimar Germany*. New York: Berghahn Books.
Varon, J. 2004. *Bringing the War Home: The Weather Underground, the Red Army Faction, and Revolutionary Violence in the Sixties and Seventies*. Berkeley: University of California Press.
Vertovec, S. 2009. *Transnationalism*. London and New York: Routledge.
Viehmann, K., R. Fritzsch and R. Reinders. 1980. 'Zu der angeblichen Auflösung der Bewegung 2. Juni'. Retrieved 16 February 2015 from http://bewegung.nostate.net/mate_nichtaufloesung.html.
Viett, I. 1997. *Nie war ich furchtloser*. Hamburg: Edition Nautilus.
Volk, S. 2015. 'Mit Hundehalsband, ohne Höschen', *Spiegel Online*. Retrieved 17 October 2015 from http://www.spiegel.de/einestages/sadomaso-film-die-geschichte-der-o-mit-hundehalsband-ohne-hoeschen-a-1017550.html.

von Dirke, S. 1997. *All Power to the Imagination! The West German Counterculture from the Student Movement to the Greens*. Lincoln: University of Nebraska Press.
'Von hinten gegriffen', *Der Spiegel*, 24 February 1975.
von Paczensky, S. (ed.). 1978. *Frauen und Terror: Versuche, die Beteiligung von Frauen an Gewalttaten zu erklären*. Reinbek: Rowohlt.
Vukadinović, S.V. 2004. 'Der unbegründete Feminismusverdacht. Die RAF und die Frage der Frauenemanzipation', in K. Hentschel and T. Hensch (eds), *Terroristinnen – Bagdad '77*. Berlin: Edition Der Freitag, 85–106.
———. 2010. 'Feminismus im Visier. Zur Verknüpfung von Linksterrorismus und Feminismus in der BRD', *Ariadne*, 54–59.
———. 2013. 'Spätreflex. Eine Fallstudie zu den Revolutionären Zellen, der Roten Zora und zur verlängerten Feminismus-Obsession bundesdeutscher Terrorismusfahnder', in I. Bandhauer-Schöffmann and D. van der Laak (eds), *Der Linksterrorismus der 1970er-Jahre und die Ordnung der Geschlechter*. Trier: Wissenschaftlicher Verlag, 140–61.
'"Walpurgisnacht" gegen "Männergewalt"', *Analyse & Kritik*, no. 104, May 1977.
Walsh, D. 2000. *Bloody Sunday and the Rule of Law in Northern Ireland*. Basingstoke: Palgrave Macmillan. Retrieved 12 January 2013 from Palgrave Connect.
Weber, M., et al. 2004. *The Vocation Lectures*. Indianapolis, IN: Hackett Pub.
Weber-Nau, M. 1982. 'Einige "Hexen" zogen sogar in ein Eros-Center', *Frankfurter Rundschau*, 3 May.
Weinhauer, K., J. Requate and H.G. Haupt. 2006. *Terrorismus in der Bundesrepublik: Medien, Staat und Subkulturen in den 1970er Jahren*. Frankfurt and New York: Campus.
Weiss, V. 2005. '"Volksklassenkampf" – Die Antizionistische Rezeption des Nahostkonflikts in der militanten Linken der BRD', *Tel Aviver Jahrbuch für deutsche Geschichte*, 214–38.
Wichterich, C. 1987. 'Südkoreanerinnen protestieren gegen deutsche Ausbeutung', *Frankfurter Rundschau*, 20 May.
———. 1987. 'Einen Bärendienst erwiesen', *die tageszeitung*, 21 September.
———. 1987. 'Adler', *die tageszeitung*, 15 October.
'Widersprüchliche Informationen', *Frankfurter Rundschau*, 10 September 1987.
'Wie Vieh', *Der Spiegel*, no. 38, 19 September 1983, 77–79.
Wieland, K. 2005. 'A.', in W. Kraushaar, K. Wieland and J.P. Reemtsma (eds), *Rudi Dutschke, Andreas Baader und die RAF*. Hamburg: Hamburger Edition, 51–99.
Winkler, W. 2007. *Die Geschichte der RAF*. Berlin: Rowohlt.
Wippermann, C. 2012. '25 Jahre Bundesfrauenministerium. Von der Frauenpolitik zu einer nachhaltigen Politik der fairen Chancen für Frauen und Männer'. Berlin: Bundesministerium für Familie, Senioren, Frauen und Jugend. Retrieved 20 December 2015 from http://www.bmfsfj.de/RedaktionBMFSFJ/Broschuerenstelle/Pdf-Anlagen/25-Jahre-Bundesfrauenministerium,property=pdf,bereich=bmfsfj,sprache=de,rwb=true.pdf.
'Wir fordern die Enteignung Axel Springers', *Der Spiegel*, 10 July 1967, 29–33.
'Wir haben abgetrieben', *Stern*, no. 24, 6 June 1971, 16–23.
Wittig, M., and S. Zweig. 1979. *Lesbian Peoples: Material for a Dictionary*. New York: Avon.

Wunschik, T. 2006. 'Die Bewegung 2. Juni', in W. Kraushaar (ed.), *Die RAF und der linke Terrorismus*. Hamburg: Hamburger Edition, 531–61.
Young, B. 1999. *Triumph of the Fatherland: German Unification and the Marginalization of Women*. Ann Arbor: University of Michigan Press.
Zellmer, E. 2011. *Töchter der Revolte? Frauenbewegung und Feminismus in den 1970er Jahren in München*. Munich: Oldenbourg Verlag.
Ziarek, E.P. 2008. 'Right to Vote or Right to Revolt? Arendt and the British Suffrage Militancy', *differences* 3(19), 1–27.
Zimmer, D.E. 1975. 'Denunzieren wider Willen', *Die Zeit*, 7 March.
'Zora', *die tageszeitung*, 30 September 1987.
'Zum "Vorfall" Frauenbewegung zu Gast bei RA Becker', *die tageszeitung*, 25 June 1979.
'Zuviel der Ehre', *konkret*, no. 5, 1977, 5.

INDEX

A

Abortion, 1, 14, 26, 27, 29, 30, 37, 58, 63, 71–89, 96, 115, 119. See also *Indikationsmodell*; *Fristenlösung*
Adenauer, Konrad, 3
Adler, 15, 123–130, 139–140
African Student League, 4
AKTION 218, 74
Aktionsrat zur Befreiung der Frauen, 6, 21, 22, 23, 25–27, 29, 50, 68n96
Allen, Pamela, 28
Alyokhina, Maria, 141
Amazons, 128–29
Anders, Freia, 7
anti-fascism, 3, 50–51, 62
antimilitarism, 9, 34–35. See also peace movement
anti-nuclear movement, 4, 7, 13, 34–35, 58, 59
anti-Semitism, 50, 119
anti-Zionism, 49–51
arson, 11, 13, 15, 39, 45–46, 48, 63, 77, 122, 126–30, 136, 139
Autonome Frauenbewegung, 2
Autonomen movement, 7–8, 13, 36–37, 103, 112n52
Ayim, May, 119

B

Baader, Andreas, 13, 45–48, 52, 64n10, 65n28, 138
Balz, Hanno, 48
Bash Back, 38
Becker, Jilian, 51
Becker, Nicolas, 99–103, 122
Becker, Verena, 50
Begrenzte Regelverletzung, 5, 75
Berberich, Monika, 55–56, 138

Berger, Senta, 72
Berlin, 34, 37, 122. See also West Berlin
Berlin Action Council. See *Aktionsrat zur Befreiung der Frauen*
Berlin Underground, 6, 18n46, 49
Bielby, Clare, 48
Bloody Sunday, 53, 67n73
bombings, 11, 13, 14, 15, 39, 50, 53, 60, 63, 76–85, 87n52, 121, 122, 126–27, 136, 140
Brecht, Berthold, 28, 91
Brot und Rosen, 26, 74
Brown, Timothy Scott, 4, 114
Brühne, Vera, 48
Brussels, 31, 93, 115
Bundesfrauenkongress, 30, 31
Busenattentat, 28
Butler, Judith, 2, 38

C

childcare, 21, 25–26. See also *Kinderlädenbewegung*; *Kinderschule*
Christian Democratic Union (CDU), 4, 74
'clandestine joy', 107
Cold War, 3, 25, 38, 39
Cologne, 14, 32, 77, 81, 93, 97–98, 104, 107, 122
Colvin, Sarah, 51, 88n59
commune movement, 65n47
Communist party, 3, 10, 52
counter-violence, 6, 8, 13, 45, 57, 62–63, 85, 94–97, 101
Courage: Berliner Frauenzeitung, 31, 33, 94, 97, 102, 119

D

Damm-Rüger, Sigrid, 22, 27. See also Rüger, Sigrid

Davis, Belinda, 34–35
Dean, Jodi, 139–40
Dehnavi, Morvarid, 23
Della Porta, Donatella, 3, 5, 52, 58
Deutscher Frauenrat. *See* German Women's Council
Diewald-Kerkmann, Gisela, 48, 53
direct action, 75, 96
disability activism, 35–36, 38
Doderer, Yvonne P., 60
Dutschke, Rudi, 4–6, 9, 62
Dworkin, Andrea, 109

E

Easter March campaign, 4
emergency laws, 4, 16–17n22
EMMA, 31, 89n68, 95, 96, 107, 108, 110, 112n78, 120
Ensslin, Gudrun, 45–46, 48, 55, 56
Erster Gemeinsamer Kongress gegen die besondere Unterdrückung von ausländischen Frauen und Mädchen, 36, 118
Eschenbach, Margit, 27

F

Fabricius-Brandt, Margarete, 54
Fanon, Frantz, 4
fascism, 3, 4, 50–51, 78, 101, 102, 115
Federal Court of Justice, 13–14, 46, 58, 59, 60, 74–81, 83, 85, 87n33, 87–88n52
FEMEN, 28, 41n44
femininity, 53, 54
  and peacableness, 8
  and deviance 48
feminism, 2, 8, 38, 55
  Afro-German, 2, 38
  and identity politics, 54
  definition of, 11, 55
  in the Autonomen movement, 7–8
  in the nineteenth and early twentieth century, 2, 9, 114–15
  in the Red Army Faction and Movement of June 2nd, 55–57
  in the Revolutionary Cells, 57–61
  in the Red Zora, 61–63
  Islamic, 38
  liberal, 1, 32, 55, 60, 67n93, 86, 116, 130
  post-colonial, 38, 116
  queer, 38, 55
  radical, 1, 16, 26, 29, 31, 32, 60, 61, 91, 93, 94, 95–96, 101, 102, 115–16, 130
  second wave, 2, 30

  socialist, 2, 23, 25, 26, 29, 31, 31, 39, 86n16, 114
feminist practices, 54
First World War, 114
Fischer, Joschka, 41n48
Flair Fashion, 123–130
Flying Lesbians, 83, 89n70
Frankfurt, 6, 12, 21–23, 27–30, 31, 32, 33, 45–46, 57, 72, 74, 75, 79, 91–92, 93, 96–99, 115, 118, 126
Frankfurt School, 4
Frauen- und Geschlechterforschung, 33
Frauenaktion 70, 73–74, 86n16
Frauenbefreiungsfront, 49–50
Frauen für den Frieden, 34
Frauen gegen Imperialistischen Krieg, 8
Frauenhandbuch, 26
Frauenhäuser. *See* women's shelter movement
Frauenjahrbuch, 28, 31, 32, 99
Frauenliteratur, 31
Frauenoffensive, 31
Frauenwiderstandscamp, 35
Frauenzeitung, 31, 80
Frevert, Ute, 1
Fristenlösung, 74
Fritzsch, Ronald, 56

G

Gastarbeiter, 117–119
Geißler, Sina-Aline, 110
gender norms, 54, 56, 85, 95, 98, 124, 137
Gerhard, Ute, 2, 9
German Autumn, 9, 34, 95, 99, 137
German Bishop's Conference, 72, 74
German Democratic Republic (GDR), 25, 34, 37–38, 93, 119
German Medical Association, 14, 29, 74, 75, 81, 83
German Women's Council, 108
Gestapo, 101
Gewalt, 5, 7, 18n51. *See also Gewalt gegen Menschen/Gewalt gegen Sachen*; violence
Gewalt gegen Menschen/Gewalt gegen Sachen, 5, 50–52, 62–63, 87–88n52. *See also* property damage; terrorism
Goergens, Irene, 46, 64n19
go-in, 29, 73, 74, 75, 81, 83
Goldman, Emma, 49
Grand Coalition, 4, 16–17n22
Grisard, Dominique, 49
guerrilla, 36, 46, 50, 56, 57, 58, 62, 79, 128, 138, 141

H
Hamburg, 8, 75, 98, 102, 103, 104, 108, 110, 122, 123, 126, 133n78, 140
Hanshew, Karrin, 10
Haug, Frigga, 26, 30
Heidelberg, 77, 97, 98
Herzog, Marianne, 26
Homosexuelle Aktion Westberlin, 31
hooks, bell, 11, 55, 67n93, 116
Horn, Klaus, 26
Huzol, Anna, 41n44

I
imperialism, 4, 55, 116, 121
Independent Women's League, 37
Indikationsmodell, 75, 89n75
International Women's Day, 39, 115, 122
internationalism, 4, 110, 114–115, 116
intersectionality, 117, 131n20

J
Jahn, Gerhard, 74
Joseph, Gloria, 119

K
Karlsruhe, 75, 76, 77, 79, 80, 81, 84, 87–88n52
Katsiaficas, George, 36
Kawaters, Corinna, 103–4
Khaled, Leila, 49
Kinderlädenbewegung, 21, 25–27
Kinderschule, 27
Kirchhoff, Bodo, 120
Klimke, Martin, 3, 5, 41
Korean Women's Group in Germany, 15, 118, 123–25, 128, 130
Kosczy, Ute, 130
Krahl, Hans-Jürgen, 4
Kuhlmann, Brigitte, 57, 59–60
Kunzelmann, Dieter, 50
Kurdistan, 140

L
left-wing terrorism. *See* Red Army Faction; Movement of June 2nd; Revolutionary Cells; Red Zora
Lehmann, Ines, 22
Leidinger, Christine, 35
Lenz, Ilse, 2, 33, 111n11
Lesbenring, 36. *See also* lesbian movement
lesbian movement, 2, 8, 19n59, 25, 35, 36, 83, 109
Leutheusser-Schnarrenberger, Sabine, 34

Lorde, Audre, 119
Luther, Angela, 50
Luxemburg, Rosa, 27

M
Mackermilitanz, 7, 8, 63
MacKinnon, Catherine, 109
Mahler, Horst, 6, 45, 46, 64n10, 64n19
Marxism, 3, 4, 7, 26, 29, 38, 55, 62
masculinity, 9, 12, 35, 48, 54, 128, 141
Mayhall, Laura, 9, 11
Meinhof, Ulrike, 13, 22, 25, 26, 30, 46–49, 51, 53, 55, 59, 64n5, 68n96, 80, 88n59
Melzer, Patricia, 8, 11, 12, 37, 54, 56–57, 137–38
Merkel, Ina, 37
Meyer, Till, 56
Middle East, 51, 133n78
migrant women, 117–9
militancy, 6, 7–12, 13, 15, 54, 55, 99
  and the Red Zora, 8
  definition of, 10
  feminist, 15, 21, 26, 27, 28, 29, 33, 36, 37, 39, 55, 59, 73, 75, 76, 137–41
  in the Autonomen movement, 7–8, 18n52, 37
  in the suffrage movement, 9, 19n62
militant democracy, 10
Militante Panthertanten, 104
Mohanty, Chandra Talpade, 116, 140
Morgan, Robin, 26, 91, 111n6
Morgner, Irmtraud, 25m, 40n21
Moscow, 141
Movement of June 2nd (MJ2), 5, 13, 50, 51, 52–53, 56–57, 58, 59, 78
Munich, 31, 51, 65n47, 66n56, 96, 111n17

N
National Socialism, 3, 98. *See also* fascism
Nebenwiderspruch, 29, 91
Neill, Alexander Sutherland, 26
New Left, 3–6, 9, 21, 23, 32, 51, 62, 110, 120
New Women's Movement, 7, 8, 9, 12, 13, 14, 72, 73, 79–83, 117, 119, 122, 136–40
  and terrorism, 45, 49, 55, 57–60, 62, 63
  and transnationalism, 114–15
  and violence against women, 90–99, 101, 110
  definition of, 3
  history of, 21–39
  militancy in, 10–11
  origins of, 6

Nollau, Günther, 48
nonviolence, 5, 9, 11, 12, 14, 15, 57, 60, 73, 75, 83, 107, 127, 128, 130, 137, 140, 141
North Atlantic Treaty Organization (NATO), 34, 35
Notz, Gisela, 1, 40n25

O
objectification, 14, 34, 91, 104, 106, 107, 122
Oguntoye, Katharina, 119
Ohnesorg, Benno, 5, 6, 9, 17n41, 52, 62

P
Pak, Jai Sin, 130
'Palestine Faction', 50
Paragraph 218, 30, 61, 71–75, 78, 81–85
peace movement, 4, 7, 9, 34–35, 114
'penis flyer', 23, 28
Perincioli, Cristina
Peschel-Gutzeit, Maria, 34
Piesche, Peggy, 119
Pizzey, Erin, 93
Popular Front for the Liberation of Palestine (PFLP), 50, 51
PorNO, 110
pornography, 34, 91, 107, 109–110, 115
Proll, Astrid, 45, 46, 47, 138
Proll, Thorwald, 45, 46
property damage, 5, 9, 11, 14, 39, 50, 52, 63, 75, 77, 87–88n52, 97, 122, 126, 136, 139
prostitution, 119–123
Provo movement, 23, 26, 40n14
Pussy Riot, 141

R
racism, 34, 39, 55, 56, 110, 116, 117–19
Rainer, Yvonne, 57
rape, 14, 30, 32, 83, 90, 91, 92–95, 99–103, 110, 112n52, 120
Reclaim the night marches, 83, 95, 98. *See also* Walpurgisnight marches
Red Army Faction (RAF), 13, 26, 32, 36, 45, 48–49, 50, 51–57, 58, 59, 62, 80, 88n59, 129, 137, 138, 139
Red Star, 27, 57
Red Zora (RZ), 8, 61–63, 83–85, 89n68, 107, 121–122, 126–130, 139–40
Reinders, Ralf, 56
repression, 25, 32, 34, 35, 37, 45, 55, 96
Republican Club, 25

reunification, 37, 75, 109, 119
revolution, 30, 52, 56, 58
    of 1948, 9
    peaceful revolution in the GDR, 37
    sexual revolution, 91
    student revolution, 23
Revolutionärer Kampf (RK), 28
Revolutionärer Zorn, 58, 79
Revolutionary Cells (RC) 13, 51, 57–60, 61, 62, 77, 79, 80, 85, 87–88n52, 127, 138
Riot Grrrl, 141
Rollnik, Gabriele, 56
Rosenbladt, Sabine, 98, 99
Rubin, Gayle, 109
Rüger, Sigrid, 6, 22. *See also* Damm-Rüger
Rupp, Leila J., 114, 116

S
sadomasochism, 109
Samutsevich, Yekaterina, 141
Sander, Helke, 6, 21–22, 25, 26
Scharloth, Joachim, 3
Schlacht am Tegeler Weg, 6
Schmidt, Helmut, 33
Schmidt, Vera Fedorowna, 26
Schmidt, Walfriede, 37
Schmidtchen, Gerhardt, 52–53
Schmidt-Harzbach, Ingrid, 26–27
Schmidtke, Susanne, 95
Schneider, Romy, 72
Schubert, Ingrid, 46–47, 64n19
Schultz, Dagmar, 119
Schulz, Kristina, 30, 73
Schwall, Enno, 58
Schwarzer, Alice, 10, 11, 29, 30, 31, 34, 60, 72–73, 107–10, 115
Scott, Joan, 2
Scribner, Charity, 10, 54, 56, 57
Second World War (WWII), 1, 9, 47, 71, 115
Seifert, Monika, 27, 41n41
Selbstjustiz, 94, 96, 102, 103
self-defence, 14, 93, 94–95
Seppel, Ursula, 28
sex shops, 1, 14, 85, 91, 92, 96–97, 99, 106–7, 109, 110, 121, 132n52
sex tourism, 119–122
sex wars, 107, 109, 113n68
sexism, 11, 12, 15, 22, 23, 28, 39, 44n107, 54, 55, 56, 59, 60, 63, 75, 85, 95, 96, 99, 102, 104–10, 116, 118, 120–22, 126–67, 137–38

sexuality, 2, 48, 60, 78, 91, 92, 109
Siepmann, Ina, 50
silence, 5, 10, 22, 80–81
Social Democratic Party (SPD) 3–4, 74
Socialist German Student League (SDS), 4–5, 6, 12, 17n26, 22–25, 27, 28, 29, 136
Solanas, Valerie, 49
solidarity, 11, 13, 22, 30, 36, 62, 72–73, 77, 78, 85, 95, 96, 102, 107, 110
  proactive, 140
  reflective, 139
  transnational, 14–15, 30, 50–51, 77, 114–30, 139
South Korea, 14–15, 118, 123–30, 139–40
Sponti movement, 28, 58, 79, 88n57
Springer, Axel, 6, 91, 120–21
Stefan, Verena, 31
Steffen, Monika, 29
Stern, 30, 34, 71–73, 74, 75, 108, 110, 111n10
Stolle, Christa, 130
Story of O, 91
Strobl, Ingrid, 120
Strobel, Käte, 74
student movement, 4–6, 9, 28, 29, 39, 49, 62, 91
suffragettes, 9, 19n62

T
Terre des Femmes (TdF), 124, 126, 128–30, 133n78
terrorism, 10, 11, 12, 39, 45–63, 104, 128, 130
Third World, 4, 5, 17n34, 50, 62, 77, 109, 110, 115, 116, 121, 124–26, 129, 130
Tolokonnikova, Nadezhda, 141
tomato throwing, 5, 6, 12, 13, 21–23, 27, 29, 136
trade unions, 4, 15, 30, 123, 124
trafficking, 63, 119–123
transnationalism, 13, 14, 33, 36, 38, 39, 73, 83, 110, 114–17, 118, 123, 130, 139, 141
Treff- und Informationsort für türkische Frauen, 117
tribunal, 1, 31, 74
  'crip' tribunal, 35
  International War Crimes Tribunal, 115
  Russel Tribunal on Crimes against Women, 31, 32, 93, 115

Tshombe, Moïse, 4
Tupamaros West Berlin (TW), 50, 52, 66n67

U
United Nations (UN), 35, 38, 115,
United States, 2, 3, 5, 16n6, 17n26, 38, 93, 95, 96, 109, 113n78, 114, 115, 117, 119

V
Varon, Jeremy, 17n26, 45
Vietnam War, 4, 25, 115
Viett, Inge, 56
violence, 5–10, 12, 13, 18n51, 26, 35–36, 38–39, 45, 48, 49–63, 66n67, 75, 78, 81–83, 85, 128, 129, 137, 138, 140, 141
  against women, 1, 12, 13, 14, 30–34, 38, 76, 83, 90–99, 101–5, 107, 109, 110, 111n10, 112n52, 115, 116, 120, 122, 123
  See also counter-violence; nonviolence
Vogel, Hans-Jochen, 79
Von Lehndorff, Veruschka, 72
Von Paczensky, Susanne, 54
Vormärz, 9
Vukadinović, Vojin Saša, 10, 49

W
Walpurgisnight marches, 83, 89n71, 95–99
Wander, Maxi, 25
wehrhafte Demokratie. *See* militant democracy
Weiberräte, 23, 27–31
Weimar Republic, 9, 71
Weiss, Volker, 51
West Berlin, 4–6, 7, 13, 15, 41n34, 123
  leftist violence in, 49–51, 52–53, 66n67, 87n52, 138
Wichterich, Christa, 129–30, 139
Wolf, Christa, 25
Women of the Revolutionary Cell (WoRC), 58, 61, 76–81, 84–85
women's shelter movement, 14, 30, 32, 33, 93–94, 111n17, 115, 118
Women's Social and Political Union (WSPU), 9
Wunschik, Tobias, 19n69, 56

Z
Zentralrat der umherschweifenden Haschrebellen, 4
Zetkin, Clara, 25, 27

Monographs in German History

Volume 1
Osthandel and Ostpolitik: German Foreign Trade Policies in Eastern Europe from Bismarck to Adenauer
Mark Spaulding

Volume 2
A Question of Priorities: Democratic Reform and Economic Recovery in Postwar Germany
Rebecca Boehling

Volume 3
From Recovery to Catastrophe: Municipal Stabilization and Political Crisis in Weimar Germany
Ben Lieberman

Volume 4
Nazism in Central Germany: The Brownshirts in 'Red' Saxony
Claus-Christian W. Szejnmann

Volume 5
Citizens and Aliens: Foreigners and the Law in Britain and the German States, 1789–1870
Andreas Fahrmeir

Volume 6
Poems in Steel: National Socialism and the Politics of Inventing from Weimar to Bonn
Kees Gispen

Volume 7
"Aryanisation" in Hamburg
Frank Bajohr

Volume 8
The Politics of Education: Teachers and School Reform in Weimar Germany
Marjorie Lamberti

Volume 9
The Ambivalent Alliance: Konrad Adenauer, the CDU/CSU, and the West, 1949–1966
Ronald J. Granieri

Volume 10
The Price of Exclusion: Ethnicity, National Identity, and the Decline of German Liberalism, 1898–1933
Eric Kurlander

Volume 11
Recasting West German Elites: Higher Civil Servants, Business Leaders, and Physicians in Hesse between Nazism and Democracy, 1945–1955
Michael R. Hayse

Volume 12
The Creation of the Modern German Army: General Walther Reinhardt and the Weimar Republic, 1914–1930
William Mulligan

Volume 13
The Crisis of the German Left: The PDS, Stalinism and the Global Economy
Peter Thompson

Volume 14
'Conservative Revolutionaries': Protestant and Catholic Churches in Germany After Radical Political Change in the 1990s
Barbara Thériault

Volume 15
Modernizing Bavaria: The Politics of Franz Josef Strauss and the CSU, 1949–1969
Mark Milosch

Volume 16
Sex, Thugs and Rock 'N' Roll: Teenage Rebels in Cold-War East Germany
Mark Fenemore

Volume 17
Cultures of Abortion in Weimar Germany
Cornelie Usborne

Volume 18
Selling the Economic Miracle: Economic Reconstruction and Politics in West Germany, 1949–1957
Mark E. Spicka

Volume 19
Beyond Tradition and Modernity: Aby Warburg and the Public Purposes of Art in Hamburg 1896–1918
Mark A. Russell

Volume 20
A Single Communal Faith? The German Right from Conservatism to National Socialism
Thomas Rohkrämer

Volume 21
Environmental Organizations in Modern Germany: Hardy Survivors in the Twentieth Century and Beyond
William T. Markham

Volume 22
Crime Stories: Criminalistic Fantasy and the Culture of Crisis in Weimar Germany
Todd Herzog

Volume 23
Liberal Imperialism in Germany Expansionism and Nationalism, 1848–1884
Matthew P. Fitzpatrick

Volume 24
Bringing Culture to the Masses: Control, Compromise and Participation in the GDR
Esther von Richthofen

Volume 25
Banned in Berlin: Literary Censorship in Imperial Germany, 1871–1918
Gary D. Stark

Volume 26
After the 'Socialist Spring': Collectivisation and Economic Transformation in the GDR
George Last

Volume 27
Learning Democracy: Education Reform in West Germany, 1945–1965
Brian M. Puaca

Volume 28
Weimar Radicals: Nazis and Communists between Authenticity and Performance
Timothy S. Brown

Volume 29
The Political Economy of Germany under Chancellors Kohl and Schröder: Decline of the German Model?
Jeremy Leaman

Volume 30
The Surplus Woman Unmarried in Imperial Germany, 1871–1918
Catherine L. Dollard

Volume 31
Optimizing the German Workforce: Labor Administration From Bismarck to the Economic Miracle
David Meskill

Volume 32
The Masculine Woman in Weimar Germany
Katie Sutton

Volume 33
State and Minorities in Communist East Germany
Mike Dennis and Norman LaPorte

Volume 34
Fragmented Fatherland: Immigration and Cold War Conflict in the Federal Republic of Germany, 1945–1990
Alexander Clarkson

Volume 35
Death in East Germany, 1945–1990
Felix Robin Schulz

Volume 36
Sex and Control: Venereal Disease, Colonial Physicians, and Indigenous Agency in German Colonialism, 1884–1914
Daniel J. Walther

Volume 37
From Craftsmen to Capitalists: German Artisans from the Third Reich to the Federal Republic, 1939–1953
Frederick L. McKitrick

Volume 38
Sisters in Arms: Militant Feminisms in the Federal Republic of Germany since 1968
Katharina Karcher

www.ingramcontent.com/pod-product-compliance
Lightning Source LLC
Chambersburg PA
CBHW070042120526
44589CB00035B/2263